Margret Beran

Hitting the nail on the head

3000 Redensarten
Deutsch-Englisch

Max Hueber Verlag

Das Werk und seine Teile sind urheberrechtlich geschützt.
Jede Verwertung in anderen als den gesetzlich zugelassenen
Fällen bedarf deshalb der vorherigen schriftlichen
Einwilligung des Verlages.

| 3. | Die letzten Ziffern |
| 1999 98 | bezeichnen Zahl und Jahr des Druckes. |

Alle Drucke dieser Auflage können, da unverändert,
nebeneinander benutzt werden.
1. Auflage
© 1995 Max Hueber Verlag, D-85737 Ismaning
Verlagsredaktion: Cornelia Dietz, München
Umschlaggestaltung: Zembsch' Werkstatt, München
Satz: Design-Typo-Print GmbH, Ismaning
Druck: Allgäuer Zeitungsverlag, Kempten
Printed in Germany
ISBN 3–19–002429–4

Vorwort

Die Aneignung einer fremden Sprache wird mit dem Öffnen eines Fensters zur Welt verglichen, und in der Tat erfährt derjenige, der sich sprachlich eine andere Kultur erschließt, daß mit dem Wort Erfahrungen, Bilder und Denkweisen widergespiegelt werden, die nicht unbedingt mit den eigenen übereinstimmen müssen.

So gelangt man früher oder später an den Punkt, daß man zwar den Sinn einer beabsichtigten Äußerung übermitteln kann, aber dies doch unbefriedigend bleibt, da man den „Nagel nicht auf den Kopf zu treffen" vermag.

Redensarten sind das „Salz in der Suppe" einer jeden Sprache, sind sie es doch, die aus aneinandergereihten Lauten, Gerüsten von Konjugationen, Deklinationen und Rektionen etwas Lebendiges erstehen lassen und den Ausdruck mit Farbe beleben.

Allerdings sind sie es auch, die leicht in die Irre zu führen vermögen. Ähnlich lautende Idiome und Redensarten können in der fremden Sprache mit einem anderen Sinn gefüllt, bedeutungsverschoben sein, oder sie existieren in einem völlig anderen Bild. So ist beispielsweise „auf den Busch klopfen" im Englischen keineswegs mit *to beat about the bush* wiederzugeben; tragen die Deutschen Eulen nach Athen, bedeutet dies für den Engländer *to carry coals to Newcastle*.

Auch kann es vorkommen, daß in der fremden Sprache gar kein idiomatisches Äquivalent existiert, der Gebrauch der Redensart auf eine Anwendung in einem bestimmten Kontext eingeschränkt ist oder aus mehreren Varianten die treffende auszuwählen ist.

Ferner ist zu beachten, daß die meisten Ausdrücke nicht stilistisch indifferent verwendet werden können, häufig recht salopp sind und in die Umgangssprache gehören.

Welche Verwirrungen der falsche oder unangebrachte Gebrauch der Redensarten stiften kann, mag sich jeder selbst ausmalen.

Die vorliegende Sammlung deutscher Redensarten einschließlich bildhafter Einzelworte mit ihren englischen Entsprechungen soll helfen, Mißverständnisse im Sprachgebrauch zu verhindern, indem Vorschläge für die Wiedergabe von gebräuchlichen deutschen Wendungen im Englischen gegeben werden. Dabei wird davon ausgegangen, daß der

Vorwort

Benutzer die deutsche Sprache und deren unterschiedliche stilistische Ebenen sicher beherrscht.

Als Ordnungsprinzip wurde das erste Substantiv der Wendung bzw. ein Hauptstichwort gewählt.
Die Wiedergabe deutscher Redensarten und idiomatischer Wendungen realisiert sich im britischen Englisch.
Während Sprichworte (prov) auch im Deutschen gekennzeichnet sind, werden stilistische Einschränkungen nur für das Englische angegeben.

Folgende Abkürzungen werden verwendet:
(coll) umgangssprachlich, (vulg) vulgär, (dated) veraltet, (bibl) biblischen Ursprungs, FF = false friend / faux amie, ▷ siehe

Anmerkung:
Leider stößt man immer wieder auf gebräuchliche deutsche Redewendungen, die nur mit einer direkten Übersetzung ins Englische übertragen werden könnten, aber dort keinen Sinn machen.
Hier seien nur einige wichtige genannt:
Undank ist der Welt Lohn. Mal den Teufel nicht an die Wand! Höflichkeit ist eine Zier …. Bei Nacht sind alle Katzen grau. Humor ist, wenn man trotzdem lacht. Aller guten Dinge sind drei. Man soll die Feste feiern wie sie fallen. Was sich liebt, das neckt sich. Scherben bringen Glück. Schenken und wiederholen ist gestohlen. Ein Kuckucksei ins Nest legen; eine Schnapszahl.

Ich möchte Peter Harvey, Dr. Katherine Vanovitch sowie Franziska und Rolf-Dietrich Beran für ihre Unterstützung danken.

Margret Beran

A

A • von A bis Z
from A to Z (coll), from start to finish
He will have no difficulty explaining what has happened because he knows the whole story from A to Z.

A • Wer A sagt, muß auch B sagen. (prov)
In for a penny, in for a pound. (prov)

A • das A und O
the be-all and end-all, the essence
Flexibility and politeness are the be-all and end-all of my present job.

Aal • sich winden wie ein Aal
to wriggle like an eel (coll)
The witness wriggled like an eel under cross-examination and would not give a straight answer.

aalen • sich aalen
to lounge (coll)
After working hard all the year round, he spent his holidays lounging on a Mediterranean beach.

aalglatt • aalglatt sein
to be as slippery as an eel (coll)
He can't be pinned down on any of these crimes. He is as slippery as an eel.

Aasgeier • wie ein Aasgeier
like a vulture (coll)
Ever since he heard the bad news he has been hanging around like a vulture waiting for his opportunity.

ab • von etwas ab sein
to have given sth up, to have kicked the habit (coll)
I've kicked the habit of smoking and feel much better now.

abblasen • etwas abblasen
to call off (coll), to cancel
The couple had a bitter argument and called the wedding off at the last minute.

abblitzen • jmd abblitzen lassen
to give sbd the brush-off / the cold shoulder (coll), to snub sbd
I pressed for a change of plan, but the management gave me the brush-off.

ABC • ein Abc-Schütze sein
to be doing one's ABC, to be starting school, to be learning one's letters, to be learning the "Three Rs" (hum: Reading, (W)riting, (A)rithmetic) (coll)
German children learn their letters two years later than English children.

Abfuhr • jmd eine Abfuhr erteilen ▷ abblitzen

abgebrannt • abgebrannt sein
to be (flat) broke (coll), to be skint (coll), to be stony (dated) (coll), to be stony broke (dated) (coll), not to have a bean (dated) (coll), to be cleaned out (coll)
I can't lend you anything – I'm flat broke.

abgebrüht • abgebrüht sein
to be a tough cookie (coll), to be thick-skinned (coll), to be hard-boiled (dated) (coll)
He is a very tough cookie. When I told him about his sister's death, he didn't react at all.

abgedroschen • eine abgedroschene Phrase
a hackneyed expression
"There is light at the end of the tunnel" rapidly became one of the most hackneyed of political phrases during the long dark months of the recession.

abgehoben • **(mit seinen Ideen) zu abgehoben sein** ▷ Rosinen im Kopf haben

abgestumpft • **abgestumpft sein**
to have one's feelings blunted
His feelings for his fellow men had become blunted through his constant exposure to their sufferings.

abgewickelt • **abgewickelt werden**
to be shut down, to be closed down (<u>Firmen, Unternehmen</u>), to be wound up (<u>nur GmbHs und AGs</u>), to be laid off, sacked (coll), fired (coll), made redundant
After making further heavy losses the Birmingham factory was shut down in December and hundreds of workers were laid off. The whole company was wound up shortly afterwards.

abgöttisch • **jmd abgöttisch lieben**
to cherish sbd as the apple of one's eye, to idolise sbd, to be foolish about sbd
His daughter is the apple of his eye.

abkanzeln
to give somebody a lecture, to give sbd a rocket (coll), to have sbd up on one's carpet (coll), to carpet sbd (coll), to give sbd an earful (coll), to give sbd a dressing-down (coll), to bawl sbd out (coll) (U.S.), to give sbd a bollocking (vulg)
It's the third time this week that John has been late. Our teacher gave him a proper dressing-down.

sich abkapseln
to cut oneself off, to isolate oneself, to hide oneself away
After his mother's death he went into deep mourning and cut himself off from his friends for months.

abklappern • **alles abklappern**
to do the rounds (of houses, flats, people) (coll)
I did the rounds of all my friends to ask for help but in vain.
to try (shops, etc.)
I tried all the shops but I couldn't get the book we wanted to give her for her birthday.

Abklatsch • ein Abklatsch von etwas sein
to be a re-hash (Bücher, Ideen, Theaterstücke) (coll)
The musical Miss Saigon is a re-hash of Madam Butterfly.

abkratzen
(engl. keine starke negative Bedeutung!)
to kick the bucket (coll), to snuff it (coll), to peg out (dated)
My father pegged out shortly before the War.

abnabeln • sich abnabeln
to sever the umbilical cord
He loved his mother so much that even though he worked in another town he repeatedly returned home to visit her and for years he didn't sever the umbilical cord.

abnehmen • Das nehme ich dir nicht ab!
You're (You have got to be) kidding! (coll) / Pull the other one! (coll) / It's got bells on! (coll) / You're having me on! (coll) / You're winding me up! (coll) / You can tell those tales to the Marines! (coll) (dated)

absahnen
to cash in (on sth) (coll), to rake it in (coll), to make a pretty penny (out of sth) (coll)
Car manufacturers have been able to cash in on inadequate public transport systems.

abschminken • Das kannst du dir abschminken!
to forget sth (coll), to put sth out of one's mind (coll)
You can forget that idea.
You can put that idea right out of your mind.

abschreiben • jmd / etwas abschreiben können ▷ abschminken

abservieren • jmd abservieren
to give sbd the chop (coll), to get rid of sbd (coll)
After repeated attempts he managed to get rid of his secretary.

abspeisen • jmd mit leeren Worten abspeisen
to fob sbd off
The workers wanted a substantial pay increase, but the employers fobbed them off.

abstauben • etwas abstauben
<u>bereits getragene Kleidung als Geschenk bekommmen, etwas negativ:</u> to get someone's cast-offs
I can't afford to buy my younger son new clothes all the time – he gets his elder brother's cast-offs.
<u>kostenlose Werbegeschenke:</u> freebie (coll)
At those petrol stations you can get a world cup poster as a freebie.

Abstellgleis • aufs Abstellgleis geschoben werden
to put sbd in a backwater (coll)
After his successes in America the boss put him in a backwater for fear of being overtaken by him.

Abwasch • ein Abwasch sein
in one go (coll)
I sent the children to the supermarket where they could buy all the food we needed in one go.

Achillesferse
an Achilles heel, vulnerable spot, weak spot
The Achilles heel of the Japanese economy is the lack of natural resources.

Achse • ständig auf Achse sein
to be always on the move
Ever since he got that new job he has been constantly on the move, one week in London, one week in Rome.

achtkantig • achtkantig hinauswerfen
turf sbd out (coll), to chuck sbd out (coll), to boot sbd out (coll), to throw sbd out on his ear (coll)
Instead of turfing him out, his boss promoted him, in spite of his bribes and blackmailing.

ad

ad • ad acta legen
to shelve sth (coll), to put sth to bed (coll)
Let's shelve the question since we won't be able to solve the problem anyway.

Adamskostüm • im Adamskostüm sein
to be starkers (coll), to be in the altogether (U.S.) (coll), to be in one's birthday suit (coll), to be nude, to be in the nude
He had to get out of the bath and answer the phone in his birthday suit.

Adel • Adel verpflichtet
noblesse oblige (Fr.)

Ader • eine Ader für etwas haben
to be a gifted person, to be a born …
He is a gifted musician./He is a born musician.

Adresse • an die falsche Adresse kommen
to come to the wrong house, to come to the wrong address, to mistake your man, to knock at the wrong door
He asked Simon to vote for the Radical Party, but he had come to the wrong address – Simon's very conservative.

Affäre • sich aus der Affäre ziehen
to wriggle out of sth (coll), to get out of sth, to extricate oneself from sth
The Government has been trying to wriggle out of the mess for months, but nobody believes that it was not involved.

Affe • Mich laust der Affe! ▷ Himmel- Ach, Du lieber Himmel!
Would you believe it! Fancy that! (dated), Mercy me! (dated), Bless me! (dated), Bless my soul! (dated)
I didn't even know he was in the country and all of a sudden he turned up in my office. Would you believe it?

Affe • einen Affen haben
<u>Redewendungen, die einem immer zunehmendem Maß an Betrunkenheit entsprechen:</u> to be tipsy, to have had a few (coll), to be oiled

(coll), to be lubricated (coll), to be well gone (coll), to be half-seas over (coll) (dated), to be plastered (coll), to be smashed (coll), to be pissed (vulg), to be rat-arsed (vulg), to be ratted (coll), to be legless (coll)
The football team went to the pub after the match and they all got completely smashed.

affengeil
right on (coll), safe (coll), wicked (coll), ace (coll), magic (coll), cool (coll), brill (coll), fucking brilliant (vulg), really really good
The "Blown Gasket and the Dipsticks" concert was wicked!

Affenliebe • mit einer Affenliebe an jmd hängen
to dote on, to suffocate sbd with affection
She dotes on her daughter so much, she never has a chance to make friends of her own age.

Affenschande • Das ist eine Affenschande!
<u>Pech:</u> That is a crying shame.
<u>Unverschämtheit:</u> That is a disgrace. That is monstrous. That is pretty shitty (vulg). That is shit-like (vulg).

allerhand • Das ist ja allerhand!
<u>tadelnd:</u> What cheek! (Frechheit!) / That is a bit thick! (coll) / That is a bit much! (coll)
<u>anerkennend:</u> There's a thing! (coll) / That's quite something! (coll)

allzuviel • Allzuviel ist ungesund.
You can have too much of a good thing.

Altenteil • sich aufs Altenteil setzen
to retire, to put oneself out to grass (coll)
After working for forty-five years of my life I was glad to retire.

Alter • Alter schützt vor Torheit nicht. (prov)
There's no fool like an old fool. (prov)

Amen • Das ist so sicher wie das Amen in der Kirche.
That is as sure as eggs are eggs.

Amt

Amt • in Amt und Würden sein
to hold office
He held office as chairman for three and a half years.

Amtsschimmel
red tape
We are getting buried in red tape!

anbaggern • jmd anbaggern ▷ anbändeln

anbändeln • mit jmd anbändeln
to pick up (coll), to get off with (coll) (stärker, normalerweise mit sexuellen Folgen)
He picks up a different girl every other week, but I don't know if he ever really gets off with them.

Anblick • kein erfreulicher Anblick sein
to be a sorry sight
The new playground is a sorry sight – almost everything has already been vandalised.

anbrennen • nichts anbrennen lassen
not to let the grass grow under one's feet
If you want to make money out of the property market you mustn't afford to let the grass grow under your feet.

andrehen • jmd etwas andrehen
to fob sth off on sbd, to palm sth off on sbd (coll)
Someone had tried to fob her off with a forged ten pound note.

anecken • bei jmd / mit etwas anecken
to put sbd's back up (coll), to rub sbd up the wrong way (coll), to get on sbd's wick (coll).
He really put my back up with his constant moaning.

Anfang • Aller Anfang ist schwer. (prov)
If at first you don't succeed, try, try again. (Hickson)
A job begun is a job half done. (prov)

Anfang • der Anfang vom Ende
the beginning of the end
The couple next door are spending their holiday separately. If you ask me, it's the beginning of the end.

anfeuern • jmd anfeuern
to spur sbd on
The commanders in the field tried to spur their troops on to greater efforts.

angebunden • kurz angebunden sein
to be a man/woman of few words, to be tight-lipped
He is a man of few words: he came in for the first time in days, gave his orders and went away again.

angenehm • das Angenehme mit dem Nützlichen verbinden
to combine business with pleasure
I was able to combine business with pleasure this afternoon – I went with a new client to a nice Italian restaurant.

angeschrieben • bei jdm gut/schlecht angeschrieben sein
to be in sbd's good/bad books (coll)
The question is, how do I get back into her good books?

angewurzelt • wie angewurzelt stehen
to be rooted to the spot
Fear rooted me to the spot – neither the tiger nor I moved an inch.

Angst • Angst ist ein schlechter Ratgeber. (prov)
Fear is a bad counselor. (prov)

angst und bange • Da kann einem ja angst und bange werden.
to be scared stiff (coll), to be scared to death (coll), to be frightened out of one's mind (coll), to be scared to bits (coll), to be scared shitless (vulg), to brick it (vulg)
When the police came and started asking me questions I was really bricking it.

Angsthase
scaredy-cat (coll)
That child is a real scaredy-cat – she is too frightened to jump into the pool.

Anhieb • auf Anhieb
<u>ohne nähere Prüfung:</u> off the top of one's head (coll), off-hand (coll), on the spur of the moment, off the cuff (coll)
I can't give you the correct figure off the top of my head.
<u>beim ersten Versuch:</u> first shot (coll), at the first attempt
He got a bike for the first time last weekend and was able to ride it first shot.

ankreiden • jmd etwas ankreiden
to hold sth against sbd
He was once very rude to my mother and she will hold that against him for the rest of her life.

ankurbeln • die Wirtschaft ankurbeln
to stimulate the economy
One can always stimulate an economy, but the long term consequences are often inflationary.

Anmarsch • im Anmarsch sein
to be in the offing (coll), to be just around the corner (coll), to be coming up
There are more problems just around the corner.

Annalen • in die Annalen eingehen
to go down in history, to be entered in the annals
He will go down in history as one of the greatest physicists of all time.

Anno • Anno Tobak
the year dot (coll)
That happened ages ago, way back in the year dot.

anpumpen • jmd anpumpen
to bum money from/off sbd (coll), to cadge money from/off sbd, to touch sbd for money (coll) (dated)
I bummed the taxi fare home off my friend.

Anschluß • den Anschluß verpassen
<u>nur im Sinne von einer vertanen Chance:</u> to miss the bus (coll)
Anybody who has not already completed and sent off their entry forms for the competition has missed the bus.

anschmieren • jmd anschmieren
to diddle (coll), to do sbd (esp. We have been done) (coll), to trick sbd (out of sth), to con sbd (coll)
The fraudster managed to con them out of thirty thousand dollars.

anschwärzen • jmd anschwärzen
to inform on sbd, to grass on sbd (coll), to put the finger on sbd (coll), to denounce sbd (to police)
A neighbour denounced the dissident to the Security Service.

anspielen • auf etwas anspielen
to drive at (coll), to hint at, to insinuate
What are you driving at?

Anstands-Wauwau • den Anstands-Wauwau spielen
to be a chaperon, to chaperon
I never get to be alone with my boyfriend – my mother chaperons me everywhere.

anstiften • jmd zu etwas anstiften
to put sbd up to sth (coll)
The young shoplifter had been put up to it by his own mother.

Anstoß • Anstoß an etwas nehmen
to take offence at sth, to be offended by sth, to get one's back up because of sth (coll)
Don't get your back up because of her behaviour – she's like that with everyone.

Antwort • Wer viel fragt, kriegt viel Antwort. (prov)
Ask a silly question, get a silly answer. (prov)

Apfel • in den sauren Apfel beißen müssen
to have to bite the bullet (coll)
If my company transfers me to the new factory, we'll have to bite the bullet and move away from our old home.

Apfel • Der Apfel fällt nicht weit vom Stamm. (prov)
Like father, like son. (prov) Like mother, like daughter. (prov)
to be a chip off the old block
"He came down here and started playing with the children just like his father. He looks like him, too! He is a real chip off the old block!"

Apfel • für n'Appel und n'Ei
for a song
They bought the house for a song.

April • jmd in den April schicken
to make an April fool of sbd
They made an April fool of him by telling him his father was waiting at the front door when he had left for Australia the day before.

Arbeit • Erst die Arbeit, dann das Vergnügen. (prov)
Business before pleasure.

Arbeitstier • ein Arbeitstier sein
to be a demon for work, to have a great appetite for work, to be a workaholic (coll)
He has a tremendous appetite for work, staying in the office until midnight most nights and never seeing his family.

Ärger • seinen Ärger runterschlucken
to swallow one's resentment; to suppress one's anger, one's irritation, one's annoyance
As usual, everybody waited until the text was in print before they complained. I suppressed my irritation as best I could and set to work on the alterations.

Arm • jmd auf den Arm nehmen
to pull sbd's leg (coll), to fool sbd, to kid sbd (coll), to have sbd on (coll), to take sbd for a ride (coll), to lead sbd up the garden path (coll), to wind sbd up (coll)
They took him for a complete ride, making him think Sarah was in love with him when in fact she can't stand him.

Arme • jmd unter die Arme greifen
to sub sbd
Luckily their parents subbed them so they could afford a new car.

Ärmel • die Ärmel hochkrempeln
to pull one's sleeves up
Let's pull our sleeves up and settle the problem.

Ärmel • etwas aus dem Ärmel schütteln
to do sth just like that (coll), to do sth off the cuff (coll)
In the exam he was able to answer even the most difficult questions just like that.

Arsch • sich den Arsch aufreißen
to work one's balls off (vulg), to work one's arse off (vulg)
He's been working his balls off trying to meet the deadline.

Arsch • sich in den Arsch beißen
to kick oneself (coll)
I could have kicked myself when I realised we were just doing the same work twice.

Arsch • Er kann mich mal am Arsch lecken.
He can get fucked (vulg). / He can get knotted (coll).

Arschkriecher • ein Arschkriecher sein
to suck up to sbd, to be a bootlicker
He is the biggest bootlicker I've ever met.

Arschloch • ein Arschloch sein
to be an arsehole
Their boss is the biggest arsehole in creation.

Art • aus der Art schlagen
<u>neutral:</u> to be the odd man out (coll)
We are all lawyers in my family except for my uncle. He is the odd man out: he is a doctor.
<u>im schlechten Sinne:</u> to be the black sheep
They are a perfectly respectable family except for the youngest son. He is the black sheep: he is in prison for theft.

As • ein Mathe-As sein
to be an ace at maths (coll), to be ace at maths (coll), to be a whizz at maths (coll), to be a genius at maths, to be a mathematical genius.
He is a mathematical genius and his brother is a whizz in classical archaeology.

Asche • sich Asche aufs Haupt streuen
to pour dust and ashes on one's head, to dress in sackcloth and ashes, to eat humble pie (coll)
The wine here is always bad. If you complain the waiter pours dust and ashes on his head and goes about in sackcloth for a week and then everything goes on as before.

Aschenputtel
Cinderella

Ast • sich einen Ast lachen
to kill oneself laughing (coll), to laugh oneself to death (coll), to roar with laughter
Angela told jokes all evening and we killed ourselves laughing.

Ast • Man sägt nicht den Ast ab, auf dem man sitzt. (prov)
Don't kill the goose that lays the golden eggs. (prov)

astrein • nicht astrein sein
not to be all above board (coll), not to be kosher (coll), not to be quite one hundred per cent (coll), to be fishy (coll)
I looked at his remortgaging scheme and I thought it was all a bit fishy, so I wouldn't have anything to do with it.

Atemzug • bis zum letzten Atemzug
to one's last breath, to one's last gasp, to one's dying breath
Desdemona loved Othello to her dying breath.

auf • das Auf und Ab
the ups and downs (coll)
A big problem for her is getting used to the ups and downs of life. She seems to think that everything normally runs smoothly.

auffliegen • mit etwas auffliegen
to come out, to come into the open
The whole dirty business came out in the House of Commons and the minister responsible had to resign.

aufgeschoben • Aufgeschoben ist nicht aufgehoben.
We'll make up for it another time.

aufhalsen • sich etwas aufhalsen
to saddle oneself with sth (coll), to land oneself with sth (coll)
I landed myself with an awful lot of trouble when I agreed to put her up for a few nights. I can't get rid of her anymore and she occupies every corner of my flat.

Aufhebens • (nicht) viel Aufhebens von etwas machen
(not) to make a great fuss about sth (coll), (not) to make a great to-do about sth (coll), (not) to make a great song and dance about sth (coll), (not) to make a great hullabaloo about sth (coll)
It was a lot of work, but he didn't make a great song and dance about it, he just went off and did it.

aufkreuzen
to turn up (coll), to show up (coll), to show (U.S.) (coll), to drop round (<u>nur Besuch abstatten</u>) (coll)
My cousin didn't come to see me for years until she had a problem – then she showed up all right.

aufmöbeln • jmd aufmöbeln
to pep up, buck up, cheer up, to jolly up (coll)
Julie was very depressed again yesterday, so I went round to her place to try to cheer her up.

aufmucken
to kick against the pricks (bibl), to grouse (coll), to moan (coll), to complain, to be a moaner (coll)
If you didn't want the job you shouldn't have taken it. Don't start kicking against the pricks now.

aufschnappen • etwas aufschnappen
to pick up (coll)
"Where did you pick up all this stuff about the theatre?" – "I worked as a stage hand while I was at university."

aufschneiden
to show off, to boast, to brag (coll)
Colin is a frightful bore. He spent the whole evening bragging about his new car.

auftragen • dick auftragen
to lay it on thick (coll), to go over the top (coll)
Simon was telling us about how well his children played in the football match – laying it on thick, as usual.

aufziehen • jmd aufziehen ▷ jmd auf den Arm nehmen

Augapfel • etwas / jmd wie seinen Augapfel hüten
to guard someone as the apple of one's eye
The Crown Prince is coming to the front line tomorrow, and we must guard him as the apple of our eyes.

Augapfel • der Augapfel von jmd sein ▷ jmd abgöttisch lieben

Auge • Aus den Augen, aus dem Sinn. (prov)
Out of sight, out of mind. (prov)

Auge • mit einem blauen Auge davonkommen
to get off lightly (coll)
The judge gave him only six months, so he got off lightly.

Auge • das Auge des Gesetzes
the long arm of the law (coll)
He had stolen a trifle from his employers some years before, but the long arm of the law caught him in the end.

Auge • ins Auge gehen
to end in tears (coll)
James and Sandra have moved into a flat together – but they don't really care for each other, they have no jobs, no plans to marry, and it'll all end in tears.

Auge • ins Auge springen
to leap to the eye
I looked at the translation and the mistake leapt to the eye at once. He had muddled up "legen" and "liegen".

Auge • Auge um Auge, Zahn um Zahn.
An eye for an eye, a tooth for a tooth. (bibl)

Auge • ein Auge zudrücken
to turn a blind eye to sth
Some schools turn a blind eye to pupils' cheating in exams, others take it very seriously.

Auge • kein Auge zutun
not to get a wink of sleep (coll)
I was so worried about the news from home that I didn't get a wink of sleep all night.

Augen • unter vier Augen
in confidence
We spoke to each other in confidence about the problem.

Augen • sich die Augen ausweinen
to cry one's eyes out (coll)
When her boyfriend left her she spent hours lying on the sofa crying her eyes out.

Augen • jmd schöne Augen machen
to make eyes at sbd (coll)
Simon is a bore in restaurants – he invariably makes eyes at the waitresses.

Augen • die Augen sind größer als der Magen
one's eyes are bigger than one's tummy (coll)
Children often feel hungrier than they really are and take more than they can eat: their eyes are larger than their tummy.

Augen • aus den Augen verlieren
to lose sight of sbd / sth, to lose track of sbd / sth (coll), to lose contact with sbd
I knew him very well at college, but we lost track of each other years ago.

Augen • schwarz vor Augen werden
to have everything go black, to black out (coll)
The hockey stick hit me so hard that everything went black for a second.

Augenweide • eine Augenweide sein
to be a feast for the eyes
The exhibition of Dutch painting is a feast for the eyes.

August • den dummen August spielen
to clown around (coll), to play the fool (coll)
We would have been all right if Harris hadn't played the fool and upset the boat.

ausbaden • etwas ausbaden müssen
to face the music (coll), to take the rap (coll) (U.S.), to take the consequences
He was caught committing burglary, and now he has to face the music.

ausbooten • jmd ausbooten
to get rid of, to oust, to put out of the running (coll)
In the struggle for the succession to the throne, the junior branch of the Royal Family were swiftly put out of the running.

ausbrüten
<u>eine Krankheit:</u> to be sickening for…
I think David is sickening for influenza; there's been an epidemic at his school.
<u>eine Gemeinheit:</u> to cook up (coll) + Substantiv, to plot + Substantiv/Verb
The MPs are plotting to depose the Prime Minister.

ausbügeln • etwas ausbügeln
to iron out (coll)
We had a final meeting last week to iron out any remaining problems before we started the operation.

ausfechten • etwas ausfechten
to fight sth out (coll), to have something out with sbd (coll)
They are quarrelling about politics again and I have left them to fight it out on their own.

ausfragen • jmd ausfragen
to cross-question, to quiz (coll), to interrogate, to cross-examine
After the children got home we cross-questioned them about where they had been.

ausgebrannt • ausgebrannt sein
to be burnt out
Female tennis players are often burnt out by the time they are twenty.

Ausgeburt • eine Ausgeburt der Hölle sein
to be a fiend
That prison guard is a perfect fiend.

ausgekocht • ausgekocht sein
clever, sly, crafty, cunning
You want to be careful about that lawyer, he is very sly.

ausgeschissen • wie ausgeschissen aussehen
to look like death warmed up (coll), to look shitty (vulg), to look washed-out (coll)
David has flu; he came to the office looking really shitty and I sent him home again.

Ausnahme • Ausnahmen bestätigen die Regel. (prov)
The exception proves the rule. (prov)

auspacken • auspacken (mit der Sprache herauskommen)
to spill the beans (coll), to tell the whole story, to unburden oneself
He looked very miserable and said nothing for a time, but in the end he told us the whole story.

Ausrede • nie um eine Ausrede verlegen sein
to be never at a loss for an excuse
That girl is invariably late for class, but she is never at a loss for an excuse of some kind.

aussteigen • aussteigen / ein Aussteiger sein
to drop out (coll), to be a dropout (coll)
It is nothing new for young people to wish to drop out of society, nor for them in due course to regret having done so.

außer • (vor Wut, vor Entsetzen) außer sich sein
to be beside oneself (with rage, with fear)
I was beside myself with rage when I heard of the mess that had been made of my project.

Axt • sich wie die Axt im Walde benehmen
to be a bull in a china shop
It was a delicate job, and he went at it like a bull in a china shop. The results were catastrophic.

B

Backfisch • ein Backfisch sein
to be a flapper (coll) (dated, 1920s)
Look at that flapper dancing the foxtrot. Isn't she divine!

Backpfeife • jmd eine Backpfeife geben
to clout sbd (coll) (dated), to give sbd a slap in the face
She gave the naughty child a slap in the face.

baden • als Kind zu heiß gebadet worden sein
to have been dropped on one's head by one's mother (coll)
You mean you're going to sign that document? What's the matter with you? Did your mother drop you on your head?

baff • baff sein
to be astonished, to be amazed, to be flabbergasted, to be gobsmacked (by sth) (coll), to be bowled over (coll)
The teacher listened to the entire discussion and was bowled over by the amount the youngsters knew.

Bahn • sich Bahn brechen
to make one's way, to carve a path for oneself, to force one's way, to forge (ahead)
He carved a path for himself triumphantly through life, advancing from success to success.
<u>nur in Beziehung auf die Wahrheit:</u> *Truth will out, sooner or later.*

Bahn • auf die schiefe Bahn geraten
to leave the straight and narrow (coll) (bibl), to get into bad company, to go to the bad
When he got to University he went right off the straight and narrow and in the end was sent down (=expelled from University). The whole problem was that he got into bad company.

Bahn • aus der Bahn geworfen werden
to be thrown off balance
The bad news from home threw him completely off balance.

Bahnhof • nur Bahnhof verstehen
It is Greek to me. (Shakespeare: Julius Caesar)

Balken • lügen, daß sich die Balken biegen
to tell a pack of lies (coll), to lie oneself blue in the face (coll), to tell thumping lies (coll), to tell whopping lies (coll), to tell porkies (coll), to tell whoppers (coll) (dated), to tell crammers (coll) (dated)
The defendant's whole case was a pack of thumping lies from beginning to end.

Balken • den Balken im eigenen Auge nicht sehen
not to see the plank in one's own eye, not to see the beam in one's own eye (bibl)
to be a case of the pot calling the kettle black (coll), to be a hypocrite
When this government criticises the opposition for making over-generous promises it really is a case of the pot calling the kettle black.

Bammel haben ▷ angst und bange.

Band • am laufenden Band
to have an endless supply
He has an endless supply of bright ideas.

Bandagen • mit harten Bandagen kämpfen
to have a bare-knuckle fight (coll), to have a fight with no holds barred (coll)
In the struggle for the European market American and Japanese companies are engaged in a bare-knuckle fight.
<u>bevor der Kampf anfängt:</u> to take the gloves off (coll)
We are going to have to take the gloves off if we are going to preserve our position as the leading manufacturers of this product.

Bände • Sein Gesicht sprach Bände.
His face spoke volumes.
He did not reply, but his face spoke volumes.

Bank • durch die Bank
all, without exception, the whole lot of them (coll)
If we offer the children a choice between Russian and music they will all take Russian.

Bank • etwas auf die lange Bank schieben
to put into cold storage (coll), to postpone indefinitely, to shelve (coll), to put into mothballs (coll)
The Government's plans to improve the education system have been put into cold storage because of financial difficulties.

Bann • jmd in seinen Bann ziehen
to bewitch, to spellbind
That girl bewitches all the men she meets quite automatically.

bärbeißig
to be snappy (coll), short-tempered
Some workers in British public services are sadly short-tempered when dealing with people who cannot speak English.

Bären • jmd einen Bären aufbinden ▷ jmd auf den Arm nehmen

Bärendienst • jmd einen Bärendienst leisten
to be no help at all (coll)
He tried to help with the washing up but he was no help at all because he put everything away in the wrong places.

Bärenhunger • einen Bärenhunger haben
to be able to eat a horse (could), to be ravenous (coll), to be starving (coll), to be famished
My son always comes home ravenous after playing football.

Bargeld • Bargeld lacht
Money talks. (prov)

Bart • jmd um den Bart gehen
to sweet-talk sbd (into doing sth) (coll), to butter sbd up (coll).
He'll do anything for you provided you butter him up first.

Bart • einen Bart haben
to be as old as the hills (coll), to be old hat (coll)
That idea is as old as the hills – it was first thought of years ago.

Bart • Der Bart ist ab!
The game's up. / It's all over. / It's all up.

Batzen • ein schöner Batzen Geld
a tidy sum of money (coll), a packet (coll)
When did you buy that car? It must have cost you a packet.

Bauch • sich den Bauch vollschlagen
to pig oneself (on) (coll), to gorge oneself (on, with) (coll), to stuff oneself (with) (coll), to stuff one's face with (coll)
That little girl has been pigging herself on ice cream all afternoon.

Bauch • sich gebauchpinselt fühlen
to be tickled pink (coll)
The deputy was tickled pink when his boss asked him to help him with his project.

Bauchlandung • eine Bauchlandung machen
to blow something (coll), to make a hash of sth (coll), to foul sth up (coll), to make a botch of sth (coll)
He tried to do an exam in Ancient Chinese, but he blew it.

Bausch • in Bausch und Bogen
lock, stock and barrel (coll)
He didn't bother to examine our scheme in detail, he just rejected it lock, stock and barrel.

bauen • auf jemand bauen können
to be able to count on sbd
If she's said she'll do it, then she'll do it – you can count on her.

Bauer • Die dümmsten Bauern haben die größten Kartoffeln!
Fools' luck!

Bauernfänger
to be a shark (coll), a fraudster (coll), a trickster (coll), a con-man (coll), a con artist (coll)
Lots of property dealers are absolute sharks.

Bauernschläue
native cunning
He had amassed a small fortune through native cunning although he had hardly any formal education.

Bauerntölpel
country bumpkin
He is an absolute country bumpkin and couldn't understand what the people from the big city expected of him.

Baum • zwischen Baum und Borke stehen
to be between the devil and the deep blue sea, to be between two fires, to be between a rock and a hard place (coll)
His business is going badly and he hasn't much money to spare, but his wife insists he must keep on inviting possible new clients out to dinner – so he is really caught between the devil and the deep blue sea.

Becher • den Becher bis zur Neige leeren
to drain the cup of bitterness to the dregs
I'm afraid we'll have to drain the cup of bitterness to the dregs: not only do we have to send our boss good wishes, but we also have to eat her birthday cake!

Becher • zu tief in den Becher geguckt haben
to have had one (drink) too many (coll)
He wasn't completely drunk but he had had one drink too many after lunch for the work he had to do in the afternoon.

bechern • einen bechern
to booze (coll), to drink, to raise the elbow (coll) (dated)
Lucy goes out boozing with her boyfriend every night.

bedeppert

<u>verlegen:</u> sheepish (coll)
When the conversation turned to the missing chocolate the boy stood there looking terribly sheepish.

<u>niedergeschlagen:</u> crestfallen, disappointed, damped
Claire stood there looking terribly disappointed when the election result came through.

<u>verwirrt:</u> dazed, knocked silly (coll)
He stood there dazed by the news and for a moment could not follow what we were saying to him.

Begriff · schwer von Begriff sein
to be slow on the uptake (coll), to be slow to cotton on (coll), to be dim (coll), to be thick (coll)
If you want to explain it to Simon you will have to be prepared to spend an hour on the job; he is incredibly thick.

beieinander · gut beieinander sein
strapping (<u>nur junge Frauen</u>) (coll), hefty (coll)
Jane is a strapping girl of seventeen who has played hockey for her school for three years.

Beigeschmack · einen (bitteren) Beigeschmack haben
to be tinged with, to have a touch of
His memories of the army are tinged with bitterness because he was never promoted beyond major, despite an excellent record.

beileibe · beileibe nicht
Certainly not! / Absolutely not! / Definitely not! / Out of the question! / Not by a long chalk (coll)! / No way (coll)!

Bein · sich kein Bein ausreißen
not to work oneself to death (coll), not to break one's neck (coll), not to overdo it (coll)
It's taken him six days to draft a three page document – he doesn't believe in breaking his neck to get things done, does he?

Bein • etwas ans Bein binden
to cut one's losses
They spent a lot of money trying to break into the Japanese market but in the end they decided to cut their losses and give up.

Bein • mit dem falschen / verkehrten Bein aufgestanden sein
to have got out of bed on the wrong side (coll)
Sarah was very short-tempered with her secretary today. But it was nothing serious; she admitted she just got out of bed on the wrong side this morning.

Bein • Auf einem Bein kann man nicht stehen. (prov)
Have one more for the road.

Bein • jmd ein Bein stellen
to trip sbd up (nur mündlich) (coll), to put a spoke in sbd's wheel (coll)
The barrister repeatedly tried to trip the witness up, but without success.
He reached the position of Vice-President in the company despite many attempts by rivals to put a spoke in his wheel.

Beine • mit beiden Beinen auf der Erde (im Leben / auf dem Boden der Realität) stehen
to have both feet planted firmly on the ground
He has both feet planted firmly on the ground and never suffers from any illusion that things are going to be straightforward.

Beine • immer wieder auf die Beine fallen
always to fall on one's feet
He has been sacked from several jobs but he always manages to fall on his feet and find a better one almost at once.

Beine • sich die Beine in den Bauch stehen
to stand until one is ready to drop
We stood in the queue until we were ready to drop but we still didn't get tickets.

Beine

Beine • die Beine in die Hand nehmen
to take to one's heels, to take off (coll), to leg it (coll), to gap it (coll), to scarper (coll), to skedaddle (coll)
We legged it as soon as we saw the police arrive.

Beine • wieder auf die Beine kommen
to get back on one's feet
After the war it took a long time for the economy to get back on its feet.

Beine • jmd Beine machen
to chase sbd up (coll)
I have not yet received a letter from the other side's solicitors. I will chase them up next week.

Beine • früh auf den Beinen sein
to be up early, to be up betimes (dated), to be up at the crack of dawn
I had to be up very early today to get the train to Birmingham.

Beispiel • mit gutem Beispiel vorangehen
to set a good example
He set her a good example by settling down to work at once.

Beispiele • Schlechte Beispiele verderben gute Sitten. (prov)
Bad conversation destroys good morals. (prov)

beißen • die Farben beißen sich
to clash
The wallpaper and the carpet in this restaurant clash horribly.

bemänteln • etwas bemänteln
<u>beschönigen:</u> to gloss over
<u>geheimhalten:</u> to hush up (coll)
The Minister tried to hush the matter up but the papers had a hold of it and the results were most unfortunate.

Benimm • kein Benimm haben
to have no manners
It's quite unfair to blame the present generation for having no manners – the problem lay with their parents.

berappen • etwas berappen müssen
to shell out (coll) (dated), to fork out (coll) (dated), to cough up (coll)
He's shelled out five hundred pounds for a new car.

Berg • hinterm Berg halten
to beat about the bush (coll), to hem and haw (coll), to prevaricate
Stop beating about the bush and come to the point!

Berg • nicht hinterm Berg halten
Out with it!
She always says what she thinks. She doesn't beat about the bush.

Berg • Wenn der Berg nicht zum Propheten kommt, muß der Prophet zum Berge gehen. (prov)
If the mountain won't come to Mohammed, Mohammed must go to the mountain.

Berg • über den Berg sein
to be out of the wood (coll)
The firm has managed to cut its losses considerably in the last quarter, but it is not out of the wood yet.

Berg • über alle Berge sein
to be over the hills and far away (coll), to be miles away (coll)
By the time the security forces had arrived the terrorists were miles away.

Berg • goldene Berge versprechen
to promise someone the moon (coll)
They promised him the moon to try to get him to join the firm.

bergab • mit jmd / etwas geht es bergab
to be going downhill, to be going to the dogs (coll), to be going down the drain (coll), to be going down the tubes (coll), to be going down the pan (coll)
The school has been going down the drain ever since they made that ass Smythe the headmaster.

bergauf • mit jmd / etwas geht es bergauf
to be getting better, to be recovering, to be on the up (coll), to be on the mend (coll)
The school has been on the up ever since they made Peter Smith headmaster.

Berserker • wie ein Berserker
to go berserk (coll)
Shortly after the quarrel started Steve went berserk and started attacking Tom with a billiard cue.

Bescherung • eine schöne Bescherung
a fine mess (coll), a nice mess (coll), a pretty kettle of fish
"Here's another nice mess you've got me into!" (Laurel and Hardy)

beschlagen • beschlagen sein
to be well up in sth (coll), to know one's onions (coll)
If you know your onions you can do this translation in half an hour. If you don't, it can take two hours.

Beschreibung • (Die Zustände) spotten jeder Beschreibung.
to beggar all description, to be beyond words
"For her own person,/It beggared all description." (Shakespeare: Antony and Cleopatra)

Besen • Da freß ich einen Besen.
I'll eat my hat if... (coll) (dated) / I'll be damned if...(coll)

Besen • Neue Besen kehren gut. (prov)
A new broom sweeps clean. (prov)

Besenstiel • einen Besenstiel verschluckt haben
to have swallowed a poker (coll), to be stiff as a poker, to be ramrod straight
The honour guard stood there, stiff as pokers, during the general's inspection.

besorgen • Was du heute kannst besorgen, das verschiebe nicht auf morgen. (prov)
Never put off till tomorrow what you can do today. (prov)

besser • Besser spät als nie. (prov)
Better late than never. (prov)

bestellen • wie bestellt und nicht abgeholt
all dressed up and nowhere to go (coll)
The girl who thought she was going to win the prize stood there all dressed up with nowhere to go when another person was called to receive it.

bestrickend sein
to be captivating, to be enchanting, to be seductive (verführerisch)
She is a simply captivating girl and I could have stayed talking to her for hours.

Bett • ans Bett gefesselt sein
to be confined to bed
He has been confined to bed for two weeks with influenza.

Bett • sich ins gemachte Bett legen
to walk into a ready-made position (coll)
After all the work building up the department had been done by Jenkins the boss gave the job to Sanderson, who walked into a ready-made position.

Bettelstab • jmd an den Bettelstab bringen
to reduce sbd to beggary, to reduce sbd to penury, to beggar sbd
After losing a series of legal actions he was reduced to beggary.

betten • Wie man sich bettet, so liegt man. (prov)
As you make your bed, so you must lie on it.

Bettschwere • die nötige Bettschwere haben
to be ready for bed, to be ready to crash out (coll), to be ready to hit the sack (coll)
If we don't rest at all during the day we'll be ready for bed by nine.

betucht • gut betucht sein
to be well-off (coll), to be comfortably off, not to be short of a bob or two (coll)
They complain endlessly of not being paid enough but most of them aren't short of a bob or two.

beweihräuchern
to praise fulsomely, to lay on the praise with a trowel (coll), to lay it on thick (schmeichelnd) (coll)
When it came to congratulating Sanderson for his work the boss laid it on pretty thick.

bibbern • (vor Kälte) bibbern
to shiver with cold
It was freezing outside – as soon as we went out we started shivering.

biegen • auf Biegen und Brechen
by hook or by crook (coll)
We need an extra $10,000 by Tuesday, but we'll get it, by hook or by crook.

bienenfleißig
as busy as a bee (coll)
Five minutes before the guests arrived she was still as busy as a bee in the kitchen.

Bier • etwas wie saures Bier anbieten
You're going to need a lot of sales talk to flog that.

Bierkutscher • fluchen wie ein Bierkutscher
to swear like a trooper (coll)
Whenever you ask the caretaker for help he swears like a trooper and tells you that he has no time.

Bild • Das ist ein Bild für die Götter.
That is a sight for the Gods.
That is a sight for sore eyes.

Bild • Setz mich mal ins Bild.
Put me in the picture (about sbd, sth).
Give me the low-down (on sbd, sth).

Bild • sich selbst ein Bild von etwas machen
to form a view of sth
It didn't take him long to form a view of what was going on and to decide how to put things right.

Bildfläche • von der Bildfläche verschwinden
to vanish into thin air
We spent hours looking for the suspicious girl, but she had vanished into thin air.

Bindfäden • Es regnet Bindfäden.
it's raining cats and dogs, it's chucking it (coll), it's pissing down (vulg).

Binsen • in die Binsen gehen
<u>Pläne, Hoffnungen:</u> to go phut (coll), to fall through (coll), to come to nothing
The bank refused to lend us the money so the whole project fell through.
<u>Geld:</u> to be money down the drain (coll)
The high speed rail project has proved to be money down the drain.
<u>Gegenstände:</u> to be ruined
My dress was absolutely ruined when I spilt coffee on it.

Binsenwahrheit
truism, platitude
It is a truism that nobody does greater harm than those who try to set the world to rights.

Bissen • ein fetter Bissen sein
to be a windfall (<u>nur Geld</u>)
Winning the lottery prize was a real windfall.

bitten • Da muß ich doch sehr bitten!
I really must protest!

bitterböse
livid, furious (<u>zornig</u>), evil (<u>schlimm</u>)
He was livid with rage when he found out that his daughter had been skipping school to visit a boyfriend.

Blatt • Das steht auf einem anderen Blatt.
to be quite another matter, to be a different story
In his dealings with Austria he was always fair and honest; with Spain it was quite another story.

Blatt • Das Blatt hat sich gewendet.
The tide has turned.
It is hard to date the beginning of an economic recovery. But after the event sooner or later everyone can see that the tide has turned, even if they can't say when it happened.

Blatt • ein unbeschriebenes Blatt sein
to be an unknown quantity
When the new Prime Minister came to power he was an unknown quantity – few knew what he wanted and none anticipated what he did.

Blatt • kein Blatt vor den Mund nehmen
not to mince one's words, to pull one's punches (coll)
My colleague doesn't mince her words. She always tells people exactly what she thinks of them.

blau • eine Fahrt ins Blaue machen
to go off on a jolly (coll) (dated), to go off on a jaunt (coll) (dated)
He has gone off on a jolly with the rest of the dominoes team.

blau • blau machen
to skive (coll), to play hookey (coll) (U.S.) (from school), to play truant (from school), to cut (coll) (dated), to be AWOL (Absent Without Leave) (coll)
At my school anyone who wanted could skive games.

blau • blau sein ▷ einen Affen haben

blau • das Blaue vom Himmel lügen ▷ Balken: lügen, daß sich die Balken biegen

blauäugig
naïve
He was so naïve he attached importance to party political broadcasts as actual declarations of intent.

blechen • blechen müssen ▷ berappen

Blick • mit Blicken durchbohren
<u>jmd wütend anschauen:</u> to look daggers at sbd
<u>jmd mißtrauisch anschauen:</u> to bore holes in sbd's face with one's gaze
He looked daggers at me when he realised I was going to vote against him.

Blick • den bösen Blick haben
to be able to put the evil eye on sbd
People say that that woman is able to put the evil eye on her enemies to make them ill.

Blick • einen Blick hinter die Kulissen werfen
to see what goes on behind the scenes, to look behind the scenes
He is a journalist who always looks behind the scenes of parliamentary politics, he's not satisfied with just following debates.

Blick • keines Blickes würdigen
not even to look at, not to deign to glance at
I showed him the proposed draft, but he did not even deign to glance at it.

blind • Unter den Blinden ist der Einäugige König. (prov)
In the country of the blind the one-eyed man is king. (prov)

Blitz • wie ein geölter Blitz
like greased lightning (coll)
He jumped into the car and drove off like greased lightning.

Blitz • wie ein Blitz aus heiterem Himmel
like a bolt from the blue
The news that the two battleships had been lost was like a bolt from the blue.

Blitz

Blitz • wie vom Blitz getroffen
to be thunderstruck (at/by), stunned (at/by), staggered (at/by) (coll)
I was stunned by the news of the loss of the two battleships.

blitzblank
to be as bright as a new pin (dated), to be in apple pie order (dated), to be as clean as a whistle (coll), to be all shipshape and Bristol fashion (coll), to be spick and span (coll)
After the English au pair had tidied up the kitchen it looked very spick and span.

Blitzesschnelle • in Blitzesschnelle
like lightning, like wildfire (Verbreitung einer Nachricht usw.)
The news spread like wildfire that the enemy had invaded.

blond • ein kühles Blondes
a glass of lager, a lager, a pint of piss (vulg)
"Pint of piss please, mate."

Blöße • sich keine Blöße geben
not to lay oneself open to attack (coll), to drop one's guard, not to expose oneself to criticism
He was careful not to expose himself to criticism by mentioning any of the less successful parts of his project.

Blücher • rangehen wie Blücher
to go at it hammer and tongs
When we first gave him this job to do he was really enthusiastic and went at it hammer and tongs, but soon he lost his interest in it and left it unfinished.

Blume • durch die Blume sagen
to hint at sth, to say sth in veiled language
He asked me how I liked his town, and I told me in veiled language that I couldn't wait to get away.

Blumentopf • keinen Blumentopf mit etwas gewinnen können
not to get any brownie points for sth (coll), not to get many marks for sth, not to get any prizes for sth (coll)
You don't get many brownie points for simply remembering to bring the right books to class – you should have done the homework as well.

Blut • Nur ruhig Blut!
Don't panic! (coll) / Stay cool (coll) / Don't get your knickers in a twist! (vulg)

Blut • blaues Blut haben
to have blue blood in one's veins
In English society it is far less useful than it used to be to have blue blood in one's veins.

Blut • das Blut in Wallung bringen
to make sbd's blood boil (coll), to make sbd see red (coll)
All the propaganda he read in the opposition press made his blood boil.

Blut • böses Blut machen
to create bad blood
She creates bad blood between all her friends by saying horrid things about them behind their backs.

Blut • Blut und Wasser schwitzen
to be in a cold sweat
At the thought of the ghost he broke into a cold sweat.

Blüte • eine Blüte sein
a forged banknote, a dud note (coll), a bad note
He gave me a dud fiver in the change.

Blutsbruder
blood brother
They grew up in the same street, went to the same school and worked for the same firm. Everyone regarded them as blood brothers.

Bock • einen Bock haben / bockig sein
to have a tantrum
Her son had a tantrum because she wouldn't buy him an ice cream.

Bock • Null Bock haben
to be fed up (coll), cheesed off (coll), pissed off (vulg)
At lot of schoolkids get cheesed off with school at about the age of sixteen.

Bock • einen Bock schießen
to put one's foot in it (coll), to drop a brick (coll), to drop a clanger (coll), to goof (coll), to boob (coll)
I dropped a fearful clanger asking her when she was finally going to marry Ben. Apparently they had called the whole thing off two weeks before.

Bockshorn • jmd ins Bockshorn jagen
to put the wind up sbd (coll), to scare sbd stiff (coll), to scare the pants off sbd (coll), to scare sbd shitless (vulg)
The police came and started asking questions. It put the wind up him and now he's disappeared.

Boden • auf fruchtbaren Boden fallen
to fall on fertile ground, to fall on fertile soil
The suggestion fell on fertile ground, for it was taken up with enthusiasm by the entire committee.

Boden • an Boden gewinnen
to gain ground
The view that Shakespeare occasionally collaborated with another writer has steadily gained ground over the last few years.

Boden • jmd den Boden unter den Füßen wegziehen
to cut the ground from under sbd's feet
By making this concession to the other side without warning us he cut the ground from under our feet.

bodenständig
to have put down roots (coll)
He has put down roots in Panama now and doesn't want to come home.

Bogen • den Bogen überspannen
to aim too high
He would have done the firm a great service with his new ideas if he had not been over-ambitious. As it was he aimed too high and we lost a lot of money.

Bogen • einen großen Bogen um jmd machen
to give sbd a wide berth, to steer clear of sbd (coll)
I'm steering clear of Simon at the moment, because I still owe him a hundred pounds and I can't pay him till next month.

Bohnenstange • eine Bohnenstange sein
<u>dünn:</u> beanpole (coll), rake (coll)
<u>lang:</u> lamppost (coll)
She is as thin as a rake and he is as tall as a lamppost.

Bohnenstroh • dumm wie Bohnenstroh sein
to be as thick as two short planks
He is really good-looking but as thick as two short planks.

Bombe • wie eine Bombe einschlagen
to land like a bombshell, to go off like a bombshell (coll), to explode like a bomb
The news of the stock market collapse exploded like a bomb in the midst of the cabinet meeting.

Bombe • eine Bombe platzen lassen
to put the fat in the fire (coll), to make the shit hit the fan (vulg), to pour oil on troubled waters
When the Annual Report comes out it'll really make the shit hit the fan.

Bombenerfolg
to be a great success, to be a roaring success, to be smash hit (coll)
There have been a stream of smash hit musicals produced in London over the past few years.

Bombengeschäft
roaring trade
The pubs did a roaring trade in the hot weather.

Boot

Boot • in einem Boot sitzen
to be in the same boat
All the schools are in the same boat as far as shortage of cash is concerned.

Bord • (gute Vorsätze) über Bord werfen
to throw overboard, to throw to the winds, to jettison, to cast aside
With one wild move he cast aside all his good intentions and put the same pressure on his brother as his father had put upon him.

Braten • den Braten riechen
to smell a rat (coll), to sense something fishy (coll)
As soon as I realised how generous their offer was I smelt a rat and decided the whole thing must be a trick.

Brechmittel
to be enough to make one sick (coll), to make one throw up (coll), to make one puke (up) (vulg)
The arrogance of her brother is enough to make you puke up on the carpet.

Brei • (nicht) um den heißen Brei herumreden ▷ Berg: (nicht) hinterm Berg halten

breitschlagen • sich breitschlagen lassen
to let oneself be won over, persuaded, talked into sth (coll)
I didn't want to take on an extra job, but I let myself be talked into it.

bremsen • nicht zu bremsen sein
there is no stopping sbd / sth (coll)
Once he has got an idea into his head there is no stopping him.

brennen • auf etwas brennen
to be burning to do sth, to be itching to do sth (coll), to be dying to do sth (coll)
I'm dying to see my parents again.

Brennpunkt • im Brennpunkt stehen
to be the focal point of interest, to be the focus of all interest, to be in the limelight, to be the cynosure of all eyes
The recently promoted bishop was the focal point of interest at the party.

Bresche • in die Bresche springen
to leap into the breach
The soprano who was supposed to sing fell ill half way through the concert, but an amateur singer in the audience leaped into the breach and sang for the second half.

Brett • ein Brett vorm Kopf haben
to have a mental blackout (coll)
Though he prepared very well for the exam, he had a mental blackout as soon as he opened the exam paper. For the first fifteen minutes he couldn't answer a single question.

Bretter • die Bretter, die die Welt bedeuten
the boards (coll)
He decided to go to the boards and become a famous actor.

Brief • Dafür geb ich dir Brief und Siegel.
I give you my (Bible) oath on that.

Brille • (alles) durch die rosarote Brille sehen
to see everything through rose tinted spectacles (coll)
He has only just arrived and sees everything through rose-tinted spectacles. Those of us who have been in the country longer aren't so optimistic any more.

Brillenschlange • eine Brillenschlange sein
to be a four-eyes (<u>normalerweise als Beleidigung</u>) (vulg)
What do you want, four-eyes?

Brocken • ein harter Brocken sein
to be a tough nut to crack (coll), to be a tough cookie
This is a tough nut to crack, but I know a specialist who could probably solve the problem.

Brot • sein Brot verdienen
to earn one's living, to earn one's crust (coll)
But now you've stopped working for the firm how do you earn your crust?

Brücken • jmd goldene Brücken bauen
to smooth sbd's path
I'm sure he feels he ought to apologise and we ought to smooth his path a bit to make it easy.

Brücken • alle Brücken hinter sich abbrechen
to burn one's boats (coll), to burn one's bridges (coll)
We have no choice but to go on. We have burned our boats behind us.

Brüder • Gleiche Brüder, gleiche Kappen. (prov)
Birds of a feather flock together. (prov)

brühwarm • etwas brühwarm erzählen
to tell sth as hot news (coll)
He told us last week when it was still hot news.

Brummschädel
a head (coll), a (splitting) (coll) headache
<u>Kater:</u> hangover (coll)
He had an awful hangover after drinking too much whisky.

Brust • aus voller Brust
at the top of one's voice (coll), at the top of one's lungs (coll)
He sang the National Anthem at the top of his voice.

Brust • sich einen zur Brust nehmen
to get one down oneself (coll), to get one down one's neck (coll), to have one for the road (coll)
Let us pop into the "Seven Stars" and get one down our necks before we go home.

Brust • sich jmd zur Brust nehmen
to give someone hell (coll)
The caretaker gave us hell for forgetting to return the keys.

Brust • sich in die Brust werfen
to stick out one's chest (coll), to puff out one's chest (coll)
As soon as he got his result he stuck out his chest and walked off proudly homewards.

Brustton • mit dem Brustton der Überzeugung
with the ring of conviction
He told the tale with such a ring of conviction in his voice that we all believed him without question.

Buch • reden wie ein Buch
to talk endlessly, to talk on and on (coll)
MIND FF: to talk like a book: gestelzt reden

Buch • ein Buch mit sieben Siegeln sein
That is a sealed book to me.
It is Greek to me (coll) (Shakespeare: Julius Caesar).
Physics is and will always remain a sealed book to me. I listened to all the lecturer said, but it was Greek to me.

Buchstaben • sich an die Buchstaben des Gesetzes halten
to stick to the letter of the law, to go by the book (coll)
He always goes by the book and never makes any exceptions for anyone.

Buchstaben • sich auf seine vier Buchstaben setzen
to sit down on one's behind (coll), to sit down on one's bottom (coll), to sit down on one's backside (coll), to sit down on one's bum (vulg)
He just sat down on his backside and waited while everyone else did all the work.

Bude • die Bude auf den Kopf stellen
to turn the place upside down (coll)
I turned my room upside down but I couldn't find our manuscript.

Bug • einen vor den Bug bekommen
to get a shot across one's bows (coll)
He got a shot across his bows from the police about the way he was driving his car the other day – and I think he will be more careful in future.

Bund • den Bund fürs Leben schließen
to tie the knot for life (coll)
They lived together for a year before they decided to tie the knot for life.

Bündel • sein Bündel schnüren
to pack up and go / leave (coll)
After a final row with her parents the girl packed up and left home for good.

bunt • Das wird mir zu bunt!
That's too much! / That's going too far! / That's out of order!

Busch • auf den Busch klopfen
to see how the land lies (coll), to find out what the form is (coll), to sound things out (coll)
I did not know how they would receive my suggestion and so I sounded the committee members out individually before I made my formal proposal.
MIND FF: to beat about the bush: um etwas herumreden

Busenfreund / in
bosom friend, bosom pal (coll), bosom chum (coll)
They have been bosom pals all their lives.

Butter • nicht die Butter vom Brot nehmen lassen
to know which side one's bread is buttered (coll), to know what is good for one (coll), to stick up for number one (coll)
She knows which side her bread is buttered.

Butterbrot • für ein Butterbrot ▷ Apfel: für 'n Appel

Butterbrot • jmd etwas aufs Butterbrot schmieren
to rub sth in (coll), to go on and on about sth (coll)
All right, I was a bit late again – you needn't rub it in.

Buxtehude • aus Buxtehude kommen
to come from the back of beyond (coll), to come from (somewhere in) the sticks (coll)
He comes from the sticks and doesn't know London at all.

C

Canossa • den Gang nach Canossa machen
to do penance
When the mistake was pointed out I realised I was going to have to do penance and spend half an hour apologising.

Chlorodont • sein Chlorodontlächeln zeigen
to smile like a toothpaste-advertisement (coll), to grin like a toothpaste advertisement (coll)
The young popstar grinned like a toothpaste advertisement at his admiring fans.

Chorknabe • kein Chorknabe sein
to be no angel (coll)
He looks like a charming young man, but as the girls know, he is no angel.

Creme • die Creme der Gesellschaft
the creme de la creme (Fr.)
Not all the early party members were the creme de la creme.

D

Dach • etwas unter Dach und Fach bringen
<u>arrangieren:</u> to get sth fixed (coll), to get sth organized
At long last we got it fixed: We meet him in Brussels on Wednesday and go on together to Cologne.
<u>fertigstellen:</u> to get sth sewn up (coll) (<u>einen Plan, Vereinbarung</u>), to get sth finished off (coll), to get sth done
The lawyers worked all night trying to sew up the deal, but they got it done in the end.

Dachs • ein junger Dachs sein
to be a pushy youngster (coll)
Who is that pushy youngster? He seems to think he can set us all to rights without having had any experience himself at all.

Dachschaden • einen Dachschaden haben
to be not all there (coll), to be a few bricks short of a load (coll), to be a few sandwiches short of a picnic (coll), to have a screw loose (coll), to be bonkers (coll), to be crackers (coll), to be barking (coll), to be out of one's tree (coll), to be off one's head (coll), to be off the wall (coll), to be as nutty as a fruitcake
I listened to his idea, but I couldn't understand it at all. I don't think he's all there.

Dachstübchen • nicht ganz richtig im Dachstübchen sein ▷ Dachschaden

dahinterstecken • Wer / was steckt da dahinter?
What's the catch? / What's behind this? / Who's behind this?

dalli! • Nun mal dalli dalli!
Buck up! (coll) / Get a move on!

Damoklesschwert • wie ein Damoklesschwert über jmd schweben
to loom over sbd like a sword of Damocles
The possibility of dismissal looms over him like a sword of Damocles.

Dampf • Dampf ablassen
to let off steam (coll)
He threw his slippers at the children – he didn't want to hit them, it was just to let off steam.

Dampf • Dampf dahinter machen
<u>mit Volldampf:</u> to (really) go (at / for) it (coll), to go at it flat out (coll), to go at it hell for leather (coll) (dated)), to do it with a will
He wasn't interested in this line of research at first, but now he's going at it hell for leather.

mehr Energie einsetzen: to put some oomphh into sth (coll)
The whole project was way behind schedule but the new manager has really put some oomphh into it.

Dampfer • auf dem falschen Dampfer sein
to be on the wrong track (coll)
You are on the wrong track there!

Dämpfer • einen Dämpfer bekommen
to receive a dampener (coll), to be dampened, to be damped
Our spirits were much damped by the news of the defeat.

daneben • sich daneben benehmen
to behave badly, to misbehave (bes. Kinder), to be out of order (coll)
At the party he got drunk and behaved very badly.

darstellen • etwas darstellen wollen
to want to be (really) somebody (coll), to want to be a big noise (coll), to want to be a big cheese (coll) (dated), to want to be a big shot (U.S.) (coll)
He wants to be a big shot around here, but if we give him enough work to do he'll soon settle down.

Dasein • sein Dasein fristen
to lead a miserable life; to eke out a miserable existence, to eke out one's days (in Armut)
After his wife left him he eked out a miserable existence living alone in a cottage.

Daumen • Däumchen drehen
to twiddle one's thumbs (coll)
The teachers were on strike and the students were left with nothing to do but twiddle their thumbs.

Daumen • den grünen Daumen haben
to have green fingers (coll)
She has plants all over her flat – all of them flourishing. She must have green fingers.

Daumen • die Daumen halten (drücken)
to keep one's fingers crossed (coll)
All my family kept their fingers crossed for me during my exams.

Daumen • über den Daumen peilen
to hazard a rough guess at (coll), to make a rough estimate of (coll), to give a ball-park figure (U.S.) (coll) (<u>nur Anzahl</u>)
I can hazard a rough guess at what it might cost.

Daumenschrauben • die Daumenschrauben anziehen
to put the screws on sbd (coll)
My tenant was so often in arrears with her rent that in the end I had to put the screws on her and threaten her with eviction.

davon • auf und davon
off, off and away (coll), up and off (coll)
As soon as school was over the children were off and away.

auf Deck sein
to be up and about (again)
He has been in bed with flu for a week, but now he is up and about again.

Decke • die Decke fällt jmd auf den Kopf
to feel shut in
It had been raining all day, and it was impossible to go outdoors. By five o'clock the children were beginning to feel shut in.

Decke • an die Decke gehen
to go through the roof (coll), to blow one's top (coll), to do a wobbly (coll), to fly off the handle (coll)
When he found out how badly his son had behaved at school he went through the roof.

Decke • vor Freude an die Decke springen
(to be ready) to jump for joy
When we heard the news about the baby we were ready to jump for joy.

Decke • unter einer Decke stecken
to be hand in glove with sbd (coll), to be in cahoots with sbd (coll), to be in league with sbd
It was only later on that we realised that the two of them had been in cahoots with each other from the very beginning.

Decke • sich nach der Decke strecken
to make the best of it (coll), to make the best of a bad job (coll), to cut one's coat according to one's cloth (<u>dem vorhandenen Geld entsprechend handeln</u>)
When the government reduced the department's research grant we had to cut our coat according to our cloth and make the best of a bad job.

Deckmantel • unter dem Deckmantel
under the guise of
He was able to flirt with the daughter under the guise of visiting her parents.

Denkste!
Says you! (coll)

Deut • keinen Deut besser als jmd sein
to be no whit better than sbd
You can learn this book off by heart and still be no whit better than anybody else taking the exam.

deutsch • auf gut deutsch gesagt
in plain English (coll), putting it bluntly (coll), to be perfectly frank (coll)
They're being polite about it, but in plain English they are saying they don't want to come.

dicht • dichthalten
to keep sth dark (coll) (dated), to keep mum (coll) (dated), to keep sth under one's chest (coll)
When I gave him the news I told him to keep it dark. That's why he kept mum when you were all talking about it.

dick • gemeinsam durch dick und dünn gehen
to stick together through thick and thin (coll)
The two friends were resolved to stick together through thick and thin.

dick • dick auftragen
to lay it on thick (coll), to lay it on with a shovel, to exaggerate, to show off (coll)
He told us about his daughter's violin playing at the concert – exaggerating wildly as usual.

Dickkopf • einen Dickkopf haben
to be pigheaded (coll), pigheadedness (coll)
He prolonged the negotiations for four hours through sheer pigheadedness.

Dieb • Man hängt keinen Dieb, bevor man ihn hat. (prov)
Don't count your chickens before they are hatched. (prov)

diebisch • sich diebisch freuen
to gloat, to take malicious pleasure in sth
He gloated over their misfortunes.

Diener • einen Diener machen
to take a bow, to bow
Little boys were taught to bow and little girls were taught to curtsey.

Diener • Diener zweier Herren sein
to be a servant of two masters (bibl), to have divided loyalties
"No man can be a servant of two masters."

Dienst • Ein Dienst ist des anderen wert. (prov)
One good turn deserves another. (prov)

Dienst • Dienst ist Dienst, und Schnaps ist Schnaps.
Don't mix business and pleasure.

Ding • ein krummes Ding drehen
to commit a criminal offence:
<u>Einbruch:</u> to do a job (coll), <u>Raub mit Waffen:</u> to blag (coll), <u>Raub mit oder ohne Waffen:</u> to do a snatch (coll), <u>Geld vom Arbeit-</u>

geber zu stehlen: to have one's hand in the till (coll), to be on the fiddle (coll)
That burglar was so clever he did one job a week for twelve years without getting caught.

Ding • Jedes Ding hat zwei Seiten. (prov)
There are always two sides to the coin. (prov)

Ding • Gut Ding will Weile haben. (prov)
All in good time. Rome wasn't built in a day.

Dinge • Große Dinge haben kleine Anfänge. (prov)
Great oak trees from small acorns grow. (prov)

Dinge • guter Dinge sein
to be in a really good mood (coll)
I was in a really good mood today, until you came to me with that piece of news.

Dinge • über den Dingen stehen
to be above it all (coll)
Whenever we have to talk about practical details he is simply above it all and can't be bothered with it.

Dinge • nicht mit rechten Dingen zugehen
to work sth (for sbd) (coll), to pull strings (coll), to fiddle sth (for sbd) (coll)
His uncle worked that promotion for him.

dingfest • jmd dingfest machen
to arrest, to pull (in) (coll), to bang up (coll)
The police pulled in Fred.

Dingsbums
What's his/her/its name (coll), what's his/her/its face (coll), thingummy (coll), what-do-you-call-it (coll)

Doktor • herumdoktern
to doctor; to doctor up (coll), to try to patch up (nur Personen)
He spent ages doctoring up his car, but it was no better afterwards.

Dolch • den Dolch in die Brust gestoßen bekommen / jmd einen Dolchstoß versetzen
to be stabbed in the back (coll) / to do a hatchet job on sbd (coll), to stab sbd in the back (coll), to do the dirty on sbd (coll)
I was stabbed in the back by one of my supporters on the committee. He suddenly changed sides and started arguing against my proposal.

Don • ein Don Juan sein
to be a Don Juan / casanova
He is a real Don Juan; he has at least four girlfriends at a time.

Donner • wie vom Donner gerührt sein ▷ Blitz

doppelt • Doppelt (genäht) hält besser. (prov)
to do a belt-and-braces job (coll), to make assurance doubly sure (Shakespeare: Macbeth)
I'll do a belt-and-braces job and send a telegram and leave a message on his answerphone machine.

Dörfer • böhmische Dörfer
to be double Dutch
It's Greek to me. (Shakespeare: Julius Caesar)

Dorn • ein Dorn im Auge sein
<u>Anblick:</u> to be an eyesore
That is a thorn in my flesh!

Drache • ein Drache sein
to be a dragon (coll), to be an old battle-axe (coll)
His mother is a real old battle-axe, and even now she orders him about as if he was twelve years old.

Draht • auf Draht sein
to be mustard (coll)
<u>wachsam:</u> to be on one's toes (coll), to be on the ball (coll)
We shall have to be really on our toes at this meeting – the other side have got plenty of clever ideas and we mustn't let them trick us.
<u>wissensmäßig:</u> to know one's stuff / onions (coll), to be well up in sth (coll)

I need a lawyer who really knows his stuff in the field of professional negligence.

Draht • einen Draht zu jmd haben
to have a direct / hot line to sbd (coll)
I've got a direct line to the Vice President because my girlfriend is best friends with his daughter.

Drahtseile • Nerven wie Drahtseile haben
to have nerves of steel
At numerous points in the course of the negotiations the leader of the party displayed nerves of steel and wrung ever more concessions from the other side.

Drahtzieher • der Drahtzieher von etwas sein
to be the person who pulls the strings (coll), to be the power behind the scenes, to be the brains behind the operation
Yes, I know Trundlehumper is supposed to be chairman, but who pulls the strings round here?

Draufgänger • ein Draufgänger sein
to be a womanizer (coll), to be a ladykiller (coll)
The boss is a real womanizer – he is always going out to lunch with the younger secretaries.
to be a dare-devil
He's a bit of a dare-devil.

Dreck • Dreck am Stecken haben
to have blotted one's copy-book (coll), to have a skeleton in the cupboard (coll)
He is almost the only man in politics who didn't blot his copy-book in the corrruption scandals last year.

Dreck • sich einen Dreck um etwas scheren
not to give a damn (coll)
The armchair idealists of most political parties are only interested in theories – they don't give a damn about the wellbeing of actual human beings.

Dreck • jmd wie den letzten Dreck behandeln
to treat sbd like dirt / like a dogsbody (coll), to treat sbd like shit (vulg)
He had worked for the firm for twenty years and yet they treated him like dirt and sacked him for one trivial mistake.

Dreck • jmd mit Dreck bewerfen
to sling mud at sbd (coll)
The election campaign speedily degenerated and the leading men of both parties started slinging mud at each other in the usual way.

Dreck • sich um jeden Dreck kümmern
to look after everything o.s., to do everything o.s., to do every last (little) thing (coll)
It's high time somebody else around here did something, so far I've had to do every last little thing myself.

Dreck • jmd / etwas in den Dreck ziehen
to drag sbd's name through the dirt (coll), through the mud (coll), through the shit (vulg)
I know he behaved badly but did you really have to drag his name through the mud like that?

Dreh • den Dreh raushaben
to get the hang of sth (coll), to get the knack for sth (coll)
I showed him how to work the machine and he soon got the hang of it.

drehen • Daran hat jemand gedreht.
to pull strings, to fiddle sth (coll)
Someone fiddled that!

drehen • Worum dreht es sich?
What's it all about?

drehen • sich drehen und wenden ▷ Aal: sich winden wie ein Aal

drei • aussehen, als ob man nicht bis drei zählen kann
to look as if butter couldn't melt in one's mouth (coll)
That young man looks as if butter wouldn't melt in his mouth, but he is actually very cunning.

Dreikäsehoch
midget (coll), runt (vulg), half pint (coll), titch (coll)
His brothers are quite big, but he is still only a half-pint.

dreizehn • Nun schlägt's dreizehn!
That's the last straw! / Now you've done it!

Druck • jmd unter Druck setzen
to put sbd under pressure (coll), to turn the screws on sbd (coll)
The barrister put the witness under a lot of pressure during the cross-examination, but still didn't get the answer he wanted.

Drückeberger
<u>faul:</u> skiver (coll), slacker (dated)
This whole departmment is full of skivers. Nobody ever does anything.
<u>feig:</u> chicken (coll), quitter (U.S.) (coll)
He abandoned the struggle half way through, and was accused of being a mere quitter.

Drücker • auf den letzten Drücker
in the nick of time (coll), at the last minute
He managed to finish the job in the nick of time – he only had seconds to spare.

drum • mit allem Drum und Dran
with all the trimmings (coll)
He was invited to a formal dinner party with all the trimmings that the English upper classes are accustomed to provide.

drum • drum herum kommen
to get (a)round sth (coll), to get out of sth (coll)
It will be very difficult to get people to invest in a scheme like this. That will be the main problem, but we shall get round that somehow.

drunter • drunter und drüber gehen
to be complete / total chaos (coll), to be a pig's breakfast (coll), to be a shambles (coll), to be at sixes and sevens (coll), to be topsy turvy
I went to the meeting in London and it is quite clear that everything there is in a complete shambles.

Duckmäuser
to be a moral coward
He showed that he was a moral coward by refusing to stand up for his beliefs.

dumm • jmd dummkommen
to cheek sbd, to come it (funny with sbd) (coll)
Don't you come it funny with me, mate. I haven't time.

dumm • sich nicht für dumm verkaufen lassen
not to let oneself be taken for a ride (coll)
I'm certainly not going to buy one of those things! I'm not going to let myself be taken for a ride like that.

dumm • dümmer als die Polizei erlaubt ▷ Bohnenstroh

Dummenfang • auf Dummenfang gehen
to look for a sucker (coll), to look for a mug (coll)
Many salesmen simply spend their time looking for suckers who are fool enough to buy their goods.

Dummkopf
to be a (complete) fool / idiot / ass / twit / twerp / chump (coll), to be a prat / prick / pillock / twat / cunt (vulg)
You should never have given him that job to do – you know he is a complete fool.

dunkel • im dunkeln tappen
to be completely in the dark (coll), to be at a loss
We're completely in the dark as to who can have done this.

dünn • sich dünn(e)machen
to make o.s. scarce, to clear off (coll), to beat it (coll), to fuck off (vulg), to piss off (vulg)
I saw they were only going to argue all evening so I pissed off and left them to it.

Dunst • keinen blassen Dunst haben
not to have the faintest (idea) (coll), not to have the foggiest (idea) (coll), not to have a clue (coll),

I haven't got the faintest idea how they propose to put this project through.

durch • durch und durch (völlig/total)
through and through, out-and-out, one hundred per cent, twenty-two carat (coll)
He is a twenty-two carat idiot – only an out-and-out clown could have done such a thing.

durch • etwas geht einem durch und durch
to send shivers down one's spine

durchbeißen • sich durchbeißen (im Leben)
to fight one's way through, to stick it out (coll), to hang in there (coll)
He hated life at university, but he hung in there and got his degree.

durchbrennen
to run off with another man/woman (coll)
His wife ran off with another man.

durchbringen • (sein Geld) durchbringen
to chuck away money (coll)
He's been chucking all his money away and he'll probably end up hopelessly in debt.

durchfüttern • sich von jdm durchfüttern lassen
to freeload off (coll), to sponge off (coll)
He doesn't have any money, but his brother's quite successful and he freeloads off him all the time.

durchkämmen • etwas durchkämmen
to comb
The police combed the wood, but they couldn't find the murderer.

durchmachen • viel durchmachen müssen
to go through a lot (coll)
In his years of poverty while studying at university he went through a lot.

Durchmarsch • den Durchmarsch haben / kriegen
to have (get) gippy tummy (coll), to have (get) Delhi belly (coll), to suffer from Montezuma's revenge (coll), to have (get) the runs (vulg), to have (get) the trots (vulg)
He'd have an awful time if he went to India – he always gets the runs after eating curry.

durchsehen • nicht durchsehen
<u>nicht alles im Griff haben:</u> not to have everything under control
He's been in charge of this department for six months and he still doesn't have everything under control.
<u>nicht verstehen:</u> *Well, I heard what he said, but I didn't get it.*

durchstehen • etwas durchstehen müssen
to have to go through sth, to have to face it out
The fourth day of the trial will bring out some embarrassing things which we shall just have to face out.

durchtrieben
cunning
Baldrick has a cunning plan.

Dusche • wie eine kalte Dusche
to be like a slap in the face
The news hit him like a slap in the face, and he lost his enthusiasm almost immediately.

Dusel • Dusel haben
to be a jammy doughnut (coll), to be a jammy bastard (vulg)
Some people have all the luck.
He got 160 points in three darts, the jammy doughnut.

E

Ecke • jmd um die Ecke bringen
to bump sbd off (coll), to do sbd in (coll), to off sbd (coll)
The Mafia have bumped off fourteen policemen this year.

Ecken • an allen Ecken und Enden
everywhere, down the line (coll), at every turn (coll)
We are being beaten right down the line.
We are having to economize at every turn.

Effeff • etwas aus dem Effeff können
to know sth backwards (coll), to be able to do sth backwards (coll), to have sth sussed (coll)
She didn't understand a word about computers before, but she has got it sussed now.

Ehre • Ehre, wem Ehre gebührt. (prov)
Honour to whom honour is due. (prov)
Credit where credit is due.

Ehre • auf Ehre und Gewissen
(with) (my) hand on (my) heart (coll), on one's honour,
He told me hand on heart that it was true, so of course I believed him.

ehrlich • Ehrlich währt am längsten. (prov)
Honesty is the best policy. (prov)

Ei • jmd wie ein rohes Ei behandeln
to handle sbd with kid gloves (coll)
I had the impression throughout the debate that the opposition were handling us with kid gloves, as if afraid of what we might say if they pressed us too hard.

Ei • sich gleichen wie ein Ei dem anderen
to be as like as two peas (coll), to be the spitting image of each other (coll)
He and his brother are as like as two peas, even though they are not twins.

Ei • Das Ei will klüger als die Henne sein.
Teach your grandmother (to suck eggs)!

Eier • sich um ungelegte Eier kümmern
to cross one's bridges before one comes to them (coll), to count one's chickens before they're hatched
He is already worrying about the budget for the year after next – he loves to cross bridges before he comes to them.

Eifer • im Eifer des Gefechtes
in the heat of the fray, in the heat of the moment
We had a violent argument and I said a lot of things in the heat of the moment which I regretted afterwards.

Eifer • Blinder Eifer schadet nur. (prov)
Don't try to run before you can walk. (prov)

eigen • etwas eigen sein
to be odd (coll), to be peculiar
I like him well enough, but he is a bit odd.

Eigenlob • Eigenlob stinkt. (prov)
Don't blow your own trumpet.

Eile • Eile mit Weile. (prov)
More haste less speed. (prov)

Eimer • im Eimer sein
<u>dahin:</u> to go / to be down the drain (coll)
The computer deleted the whole thing and all our work was down the drain.
<u>kaputt:</u> to be kaput (coll), to be bust (coll), to have had it (coll), to a be a write-off (coll)
I think this television has about had it – it's fifteen years old.
<u>Plan:</u> to be a washout (coll), to be a frost (coll)
His proposal would have cost an extra five thousand pounds which we didn't have, so that plan was a washout.

ein • nicht ein noch aus wissen
to be at one's wit's end (coll), not to know which way to turn (coll)
After this disastrous news I don't know which way to turn.

ein • ein und alles für jmd sein ▷ Augapfel

einbrocken • Da hab' ich mir ja was eingebrockt.
to let oneself in for something (coll)
I really let myself in for something there.

Eindruck • Der erste Eindruck ist der beste. (prov)
First impressions are important.
It's the first impression which counts.

Eindruck • Eindruck schinden
to draw attention to oneself, to push oneself forward
That colleague of mine is always drawing attention to himself and trying to make an impression.

Einfaltspinsel ▷ Dummkopf

Einigkeit • Einigkeit macht stark. (prov)
United we stand, divided we fall. (prov)

Einkehr • innere Einkehr halten
to search one's heart, to commune with o.s., <u>oft Substantiv:</u> heart-searching
You must search your heart long and hard before you proceed to ordination to the priesthood.
After much heartsearching the young couple decided not to marry.

Einklang • im Einklang stehen mit jmd / etwas
to be in full agreement with sbd, to be of one mind with sbd, to be in full accord with sbd, to square with sth (coll)
I am in full agreement with him, but all the same his theory doesn't square with the Professor's.

einkratzen • sich bei jmd einkratzen
to grease up to sbd (coll), to be a creep (coll), to butter sbd up (coll)
He didn't get that promotion by being any good at his last job – he got it by being a creep.

einlullen • jmd einlullen wollen
<u>Argwohn:</u> to lull sbd's suspicions
She tried to lull his suspicions by making references to a male cousin, but she was not convincing, and his jealousy grew.
<u>in Sicherheit wiegen:</u> to lull sbd into a false sense of security
Early and easy victories in East and West lulled some Germans into a false sense of security which was first shaken by the reverses before Moscow in December 1941.

Eis • Das Eis ist gebrochen.
the ice is broken (coll); <u>oft Präsens:</u> to break the ice (coll)
After weeks of not speaking to her mother she finally offered to carry some shopping home and then the ice was broken.
Foreign language teachers are expected to spend an awful lot of time learning techniques to break the ice between students meeting for the first time.

Eis • etwas auf Eis legen
to put something on ice (coll)
The project wasn't cancelled but it was put on ice for a while.

Eisen • Schmiede das Eisen, solange es heiß ist. (prov)
Strike while the iron is hot. (prov)
Make hay while the sun shines. (prov)

Eisen • ein heißes Eisen
to be a dodgy business (coll), to be a ticklish business (coll), to be a dicey business. (dated)
It is always a ticklish business trying to rescue people from the consequences of their own actions.

Eisen • noch ein Eisen im Feuer haben
to have another iron in the fire (coll), <u>oft:</u> to have two (several) irons in the fire (coll), to have another string to one's bow (coll)

If this attempt fails we have another iron in the fire.
We have got two irons in the fire: the conference next week and the committee meeting next Thursday. We're not likely to be turned down twice.

Eisen • jmd zum alten Eisen werfen
to dump sbd on the economic scrap-heap (coll), to discard sbd like an old toy
The workers in the coal industry feel themselves to have been dumped on the economic scrap-heap.

Eisenbahn • höchste Eisenbahn
high time (coll)
It is high time you sent that letter, otherwise it will arrive too late.

Elefant • sich wie ein Elefant im Porzellanladen benehmen
to behave like a bull in a china shop (coll)
Although the whole situation was very awkward he did not stop to find out any of the details or background and went at the job like a bull in a china shop, upsetting everybody.

Element • in seinem/ihrem Element sein
to be in one's element
As soon as the conversation turned to Mozart's operas the music teacher was in his element.

Ellbogen • Ellbogen haben/benutzen
to use one's elbows (coll), to elbow one's way forward (coll), to be pushy (coll)
He used his elbows throughout his life and ended up with lots of money and no friends.

Elle • alles mit der gleichen Elle messen
not to apply double standards
The British judiciary take great care not to apply double standards and to treat all defendants alike, from whatever background they come.

Elster • eine diebische Elster sein
to have sticky fingers (coll), to nick things (coll)
Don't leave anything valuable on your desk – the people in this office have sticky fingers.

Ende • Ende gut, alles gut. (prov)
All's well that ends well. (prov)

Ende • Das dicke Ende kommt nach.
The sting is in the tail.

Ende • Lieber ein Ende mit Schrecken, als ein Schrecken ohne Ende. (prov)
Better an end with terror than terror without end. (prov)

Ende • das Ende vom Lied
the end of the matter, <u>oft:</u> that was that (coll), that is that (coll), that finishes it (coll), that finished it
The firm kept on investing in unsuccessful foreign ventures. Eventually it went bankrupt and that was the end of the matter.
The car had been running badly for some time, then finally it struck a big stone at the edge of the road, and that was that: we had to go the rest of the way on foot.

Enge • in die Enge getrieben werden
to be forced into a corner, to be cornered (coll); <u>oft aktiv:</u> to corner sbd (coll)
The government was forced into a corner by the Opposition economic spokesman's relentless questioning, and finally admitted that a further devaluation of the currency could not be ruled out.
The oppositon cornered the government in the House of Commons on the unemployment issue.

Ente • wie eine bleierne Ente schwimmen
to swim like a brick (coll)
He swims like a brick, he will never reach the other side.

Ente • eine lahme Ente sein
to be a slowcoach (coll), to be a person who'd be late for his/her own funeral (coll)

Get a move on, don't be such a slowcoach!
MIND FF: to be a lame duck: Niete, Versager

entpuppen • sich entpuppen
to turn out to be
We thought it would be a good idea, but it turned out to be disastrous.

Entsetzen • nicht mit Entsetzen Scherz treiben
It's not a joking matter.

Erdboden • dem Erdboden gleichmachen
to raze to the ground, to level to the ground
The Romans razed Carthage to the ground.

Erdboden • wie vom Erdboden verschwunden
to disappear as if the earth had swallowed one up, to vanish from the face of the Earth
The three soldiers disappeared as if the earth had swallowed them up.

Ereignisse • Kommende Ereignisse werfen ihre Schatten voraus. (prov)
Coming events cast their shadow before. (prov)

Erfahrenheit • Erfahrenheit macht Narren gescheit. (prov)
Nothing teaches like experience. (prov)

Erfahrung • Erfahrung ist ein teurer Lehrmeister. (prov)
<u>englisches Sprichwort sagt das Gegenteil:</u> *Experience is always cheap at the price. (prov)*

Erfolg • Ein Erfolg führt zum nächsten. (prov)
Nothing succeds like success. (prov)

erhöhen • Wer sich selbst erhöht wird erniedrigt werden. (prov)
Pride goeth before a fall. (bibl, prov)

erstunken • erstunken und erlogen
a pack of lies (coll), to be (a load of) balls (vulg), (to be a load of) bullshit (vulg)

The whole story about the prize is a load of bullshit. I don't believe it for a moment.

erwärmen • sich für etwas (nicht) erwärmen können
<u>Begeisterung, Interesse:</u> to work up an enthusiasm for, to work up an interest for, to work up an interest in
I have tried repeatedly, but I cannot work up any enthusiasm for opera.
<u>Zuneigung:</u> to warm towards (oft ohne *can*, außer im Negativ:)
I warmed towards him in the end, but I had to get to know him first.
I could never warm towards him.

Esel • störrisch wie ein Esel sein
to be as stubborn as a mule / a donkey's hind leg, to be muleheaded (coll), to be mulish (coll)
He can see the point, but he's too muleheaded to admit it.

Eselsbrücke • jmd eine Eselsbrücke bauen
a mnemonic
'Richard of York gained battles in vain' is a useful mnemonic for the colours of the rainbow.

Eselsohr • das Buch hat Eselsohren
to have / to get dog-ears, to be dog-eared
The children love that book so much that it's getting dog-ears.
He leafed through a dog-eared volume.

Espenlaub • zittern wie Espenlaub
to quiver like an aspen (coll)
The girl stood quivering like an aspen until the judge made his decision.

Eulen • Eulen nach Athen tragen
to carry (to take, to bring, to send) coals to Newcastle
It's like sending coals to Newcastle to appoint another computer expert to that office.

F

fackeln • nicht lange fackeln
not to dilly-dally (coll), not to let the grass grow under one's feet
Our boss doesn't dilly-dally when people repeatedly turn up late at the office. He sacks them after the second or third time.

Faden • an einem (am seidenen) Faden hängen
to hang by a thread
His life hung by a thread for the first two days after the accident.

Faden • ein roter Faden
the thread, the connecting idea
I couldn't follow the thread of his argument at all.

Faden • keinen trockenen Faden am Leib haben ▷ patschnaß

Faden • keinen guten Faden an jmd lassen
not to have a good word to say for someone (coll)
She doesn't have a good word to say for her sister, simply because they had a quarrel about money a few years ago.

Faden • den Faden verlieren
to lose the thread (of one's thoughts) (coll), to lose one's train of thought (coll)
The speaker paused for almost fifteen seconds having clearly lost his train of thought.

Faden • den Faden wieder aufnehmen
to take up the thread (of the argument), to take up the argument
After a long discussion of an unrelated matter he took up the thread of the argument afresh.

Fäden • alle Fäden in der Hand halten
to have everything under control, to have all the threads in one's hand (coll)
She thinks she has all the threads in her hand, but in fact her subordinates are just doing what they like.

Fadenkreuz • ins Fadenkreuz geraten
to get/take flak (coll), to get/take stick (coll), to come under fire (coll), to be criticised
We made a bad mistake and we can expect to get some flak because of it.

Fahne • eine Fahne haben
to reek of liquor, to reek of booze (coll), to reek of the stuff (coll)
Her husband came home late from the pub, reeking of liquor.

Fahne • die Fahne hochhalten
to keep the flag flying
"We'll keep the Red Flag flying here." (British Labour Party Song)

Fahne • die Fahne nach dem Wind drehen
to be a sheep (coll), to go with the crowd (coll), to follow the mob (coll), to trim one's sails to the wind, to be a weathercock, to be a trimmer, to trim
The Liberal Party is repeatedly accused of trimming.

Fahnen • mit fliegenden Fahnen untergehen
to go down fighting (coll), to go down with all guns blazing (coll)
The trial soon turned against the defence, but they fought on and finally went down with all guns blazing.

Fährte • auf der falschen Fährte sein
to bark up the wrong tree (coll), to get hold of the wrong end of the stick (coll)
It's no good telling them that we're only trying to help – they'll get hold of the wrong end of the stick and think we're competing.

Fahrwasser • im Fahrwasser von jmd plätschern
to follow in sbd's train, to follow in sbd's wake, to ride on sbd's coat-tails (coll)
The Prime Minister rode to power on the coat-tails of his predecessor.

Fall • ein klarer Fall
to be a clear case
It is a clear case of tax evasion.

Fall • jmd zu Fall bringen
to bring sbd down (coll), to cause sbd's downfall, to bring about sbd's downfall
They were determined to bring about the successful newcomer's downfall before he revealed their lack of ability.

fallen • jmd fallenlassen
to drop sbd (like a hot potato) (coll)
When I find somebody's deceived me in an important matter I drop them like a hot potato.

Fallstricke • jmd Fallstricke legen
to set a trap, to lay a trap
The prosecution lawyer laid many traps for the witness in the course of the cross-examination.

Farbe • etwas in dunklen/düsteren Farben malen
to paint a black picture, to paint a gloomy picture
The economic research bureau painted a gloomy picture of the economic prospects for the coming year.

Fassung • jmd aus der Fassung bringen
to throw sbd (coll)
The last question threw him completely. He had not been expecting it at all.

Faß • ein Faß ohne Boden
a bottomless pit (coll)
Helping that foreign government with economic development is like pouring money into a bottomless pit.

Faulheit • vor Faulheit stinken
to be bone idle (coll), to be a layabout (coll), to be an uncorrigible lazybones
He has sat around all day and done nothing. He is bone idle.

Faust • auf eigene Faust
off one's own bat (coll)
After wasting three years trying to get someone qualified to organise

some help for the young people I decided to try and do it off my own bat. Then the qualified people said I should be doing it differently.

Faust • mit der Faust auf den Tisch hauen
to put one's foot down (coll), to lay down the law
It is high time you put your foot down and stopped the students cheating in exams. Soon no-one will take the results seriously any more.

Faust • wie die Faust aufs Auge passen
to be bang on (coll)
His argument was bang on.

Faust • die Faust im Nacken spüren
to feel sbd breathing down one's neck (coll)
I cannot do my best work with my boss breathing down my neck the whole time.

Fäustchen • sich ins Fäustchen lachen
to laugh in one's sleeve
All the schoolboys were laughing in their sleeves while the headmaster tried to show them how one plays an electric guitar.

faustdick • es faustdick hinter den Ohren haben
to be no fool (coll)
He is no fool. He will be able to get out of this problem without any difficulty.

Faxen • Mach keine Faxen!
No funny business! / No messing about!

Federn • Federn lassen müssen
to receive a hard knock (coll), to receive a hard blow (coll)
He received a hard knock when a rival company started to produce a similar product.

Federn • sich mit fremden Federn schmücken
to strut in borrowed plumes
This writer is always strutting in borrowed plumes. He has no ideas of his own and simply strings together erudite quotations.

Fehdehandschuh • jmd den Fehdehandschuh hinwerfen
to throw down the gauntlet
When he started criticising my work I threw down the gauntlet at once and told him to do better himself if he could.

feierlich • Das ist nicht mehr feierlich!
to be beyond a joke (coll), (positiv:) to be too much of a good thing (coll)
My son works far too hard at his homework. Five hours every evening is too much of a good thing.

Feile • die letzte Feile anlegen
to put the finishing touches to sth
He put the finishing touches to the Fourth Symphony whilst on a visit to Vienna.

fein • fein raus sein
to have got out of sth (coll), to have got out of a difficulty
He was in a mess – unemployed and in debt – but he has got out of the mess now, because he has had a win on the pools.

Feinde • Wer drei Feinde hat, muß sich mit zweien vertragen. (prov)
nur folgendes Sprichwort annähernd möglich: *The enemy of my enemy is my friend. (prov)*

Feld • das Feld räumen
to make way for sbd, to hand over to sbd (coll)
An American President hands over to his successor in the month of January.

Feld • etwas ins Feld führen
Argument: to adduce
In the course of the long and exhausting debate the Government spokesmen were able to adduce a series of arguments in support of their policy.

Feld • gegen jmd / etwas zu Felde ziehen
to hit out at, to combat, to crusade against, to embark on a campaign against
Government spokesmen hit out against immorality in private life.

Fell • jmd juckt das Fell
to be asking for it (coll), to be asking for trouble (coll)
In sending police onto the streets in such numbers so soon after the riots the Home Secretary was simply asking for trouble.

Fell • Man soll das Fell des Bären nicht verkaufen, bevor man ihn erlegt hat. (prov) ▷ Tag: Tag nicht vor dem Abend loben

Fell • jmd das Fell gerben
to give sbd a good hiding, to thrash sbd, to tan sbd's hide (dated)
I gave him a good hiding for bullying his little sister.

Fell • ein dickes Fell haben
to have a thick skin (coll)
We told the salesman to his face we wanted him to go and leave us in peace, but he had a very thick skin and carried on telling us about how good his company's detergents were.

Fell • jmd das Fell über die Ohren ziehen
to rip sbd off (coll)
He was badly ripped off by someone who sold him a forgery.

Felle • all seine Felle davonschwimmen sehen
to see all one's hopes go up in smoke (coll)
When the company went into liquidation he saw all his hopes go up in smoke.

Fels • wie ein Fels in der Brandung
as firm as a rock, a tower of strength
Belisarius stood as firm as a rock, a tower of strength in the midst of his infantry.

festnageln • jmd auf etwas festnageln
<u>jmd an ein Versprechen, usw erinnern:</u> to hold sbd to sth
You promised me last week that you would help, and I hold you to that.

<u>konkret werden:</u> to pin sbd down to sth
I couldn't pin her down to a definite time, but she should turn up sometime this week.

Festtagslaune • in Festtagslaune sein
to be in a holiday mood
After the news of the victory at the front the whole town was in a holiday mood.

Fett • Da hast du dein Fett weg!
That serves you right! / That'll teach you!

Fettnäpfchen • ins Fettnäpfchen treten
<u>ungewollt etwas Verkehrtes sagen, etwas, das beim Gesprächspartner negativ angkommt:</u> to drop a clanger (coll), to put one's foot in it (coll)
I dropped a fearful clanger when I asked him to give his wife my best wishes – she had left him the week before.

Fetzen • daß die Fetzen fliegen
to make the sparks fly (coll)
The two sisters quarrelled with each other and really made the sparks fly.

Feuer • Feuer fangen
to have one's imagination fired, to be fired with enthusiasm
Once the idea of a teaching career had fired his imagination he lost all interest in doing anything else.

Feuer • für jmd durchs Feuer gehen
to go through fire and water for sbd
I'd go through fire and water for that family, they have been so good to me.

Feuer • zwischen zwei Feuer sitzen ▷ Baum: zwischen Baum und Borke stehen

Feuer • mit dem Feuer spielen
to play with fire
If we try to get rid of the Vice President without knowing what the President's attitude is we shall simply be playing with fire.

Feuer • Feuer und Flamme sein ▷ Feuer fangen

Feuerwehr • fahren wie die Feuerwehr
to drive like the clappers (coll), to drive like a demon (coll)
He drove like the clappers, well over the speed limit, and the police stopped him.

fiebern • vor Erregung / Ungeduld fiebern, etwas entgegenfiebern
to be in a fever of excitement / impatience
I waited for the phone call in a fever of impatience.

Filmriß • einen Filmriß haben
to have one's mind a complete blank (coll)
His mind was a complete blank as far as the previous evening was concerned, because he had had so much to drink.

Finger • es juckt in den Fingern
to be itching to do sth (coll), to be aching to do sth (coll)
I was aching to point out their error, but I had no right to speak at that meeting.

Finger • etwas an allen fünf Fingern abzählen können
to be blindingly obvious (coll), to be as clear as daylight (coll), to be crystal clear, to be as plain as a pike-staff (coll), to go without saying (coll), to stand to reason (coll)
It goes without saying that you will only get a job like that if you have the proper qualifications for it.
MIND FF: to be able to count sth on the fingers of one's hand: an einer Hand abzählen können

Finger • wenn man jmd den kleinen Finger gibt, dann nimmt er die ganz Hand
Give him an inch and he'll take a mile.

Finger • keinen Finger krummmachen
not to lift a finger (coll), not to do a hand's turn (coll)
You might at least help with the washing up – you haven't done a hand's turn all day.

Finger • lange Finger machen ▷ Elster

Finger • sich alle Finger nach etwas lecken
to lick one's lips at sth (coll), to lick one's chops at sth (coll)
Anyone would lick their chops at a job like his.

Finger • sich nicht die Finger schmutzig machen
<u>die eigene unmoralische Handlung nicht selbst tun:</u> not to do one's own dirty work (coll)
He did not do his own dirty work, but hired a professional thief to steal the incriminating documents.
<u>bestimmte primitive, niedrige Arbeit vermeiden:</u> not to dirty one's hands with sth (coll)
He thinks himself far too important to dirty his hands with manual labour.

Finger • jmd um den kleinen Finger wickeln
to twist sbd round one's little finger (coll)
She can twist her boyfriend round her little finger; he always does what she wants.

Finger • sich etwas aus den Fingern saugen
to concoct, to dream up (coll), to make up (coll)
The two defendants had together concocted a plausible explanation but the jury disbelieved them.
<u>In Beziehung auf strafrechtliche Anklagen:</u> to trump up charges (= anklagen)
He was arrested and tried on trumped-up charges of blackmail.

Fisch • stumm wie ein Fisch
to be mute, to be as quiet as a mouse
He sat there all the time as quiet as a mouse.

Fisch • gesund wie ein Fisch im Wasser
to be as fit as a fiddle (coll), to be as sound as a bell (dated), to be as sound as a dollar (dated)
"How is your guinea pig?" – "Fit as a fiddle!"

Fisch • weder Fisch noch Fleisch
neither fish nor fowl
This book is something between a novel and an autobiography. It is neither fish nor fowl.

Fische • kleine Fische
peanuts (coll)
A million pounds is peanuts to a major international bank.

Fisimatenten • keine Fisimatenten machen ▷ Faxen machen

Fittiche • jmd unter seine Fittiche nehmen
to take sbd under one's wing (coll)
The well-established lawyers took the trainees under their wings as articled clerks.

fix • fix und fertig sein
to be knackered (coll), to be all in (coll), to be done in (coll), to be worn out
I came home absolutely knackered after my day's work.

Flagge • unter falscher Flagge segeln
to masquerade, to sail under false colours
This is a political pressure group masquerading as a charitable enterprise.

Flamme • eine (alte) Flamme von jmd sein
to be sbd's old flame (coll)
That girl over there is an old flame of mine – do you mind if we say hello to her?

Flappe • eine Flappe ziehen
to pout, to make a face (coll)
Don't pout! You can't always have your own way.

Flaum • noch Flaum hinter den Ohren haben
to be wet behind the ears (coll)
Pete is not the right chap for that business in Germany – he is still wet behind the ears and it needs somebody experienced in charge.

Flausen • jmd die Flausen austreiben
to drive / knock the nonsense out of sbd's head (coll), auch: to knock some sense into you (coll)
If you marry her she will knock the nonsense out of your head in no time.

Fleisch • sein eigen Fleisch und Blut
one's own flesh and blood
To be betrayed by your own flesh and blood is worse than being betrayed by friends.

Fleisch • in Fleisch und Blut übergehen
to become second nature to sbd, <u>oft:</u> to be second nature to sbd
It is second nature to me to write down all my appointments in my memorandum book.

Fleisch • sich ins eigene Fleisch schneiden
to cut off one's nose to spite one's face
If you refuse to allow your neighbour to get rid of that tree just because of your old quarrel with him you are cutting off your nose to spite your face because the roots will soon be damaging the foundations of your own house.

Fleiß • Ohne Fleiß kein Preis. (prov)
There is no such thing as a free lunch. (coll, prov)

Fliege • keiner Fliege etwas zuleide tun können
to be unable to hurt a fly (coll), <u>oft mit *would*:</u> He wouldn't hurt a fly.
They accused him of murder, but all his friends knew that he wouldn't hurt a fly.

Fliege • jmd stört die Fliege an der Wand
to be bothered by the smallest thing (coll)
He is impossible to work with. He gets bothered by the smallest thing.

Fliegen • zwei Fliegen mit einer Klappe schlagen
to kill two birds with one stone (coll)
Can't we kill two birds with one stone and buy the food and the books in the department store at the same time, rather than going to two different shops?

fliegen • jmd fliegt alles zu
everything comes easily to one, everything is child's play to one (coll)
That student can do everything: maths, physics, football. It's all child's play to him.

Flinte • nicht die Flinte ins Korn werfen
Don't give up.

Floh • jmd einen Floh ins Ohr setzen
to put an idea/ideas in sbd's head (coll), to give sbd ideas (coll)
Don't put ideas in my daughter's head! You know she'll never be able to marry him however much she wants to.
MIND FF: to put a flea in sbd's ear: jdn schelten, ausschimpfen

Flügel • jmd die Flügel stutzen
to clip sbd's wings (coll)
The new chief assistant was very overbearing until the boss clipped her wings.

Flunder • platt wie 'ne Flunder sein
<u>Gegenstand:</u> to be as flat as a pancake (coll)
I sat on the hat and squashed it so that it was as flat as a pancake.
<u>Frau/Mädchen:</u> to be as flat as an ironing-board (coll)
That poor girl is eighteen and still as flat as an ironing-board.

Folter • jmd auf die Folter spannen
to keep sbd on tenterhooks (coll), to be on tenterhooks (coll), to keep sbd in suspense
We were on tenterhooks to know what had happened but the messenger refused to speak to anyone but the boss.

Frage • Kommt nicht in Frage!
Out of the question!

Frage • Eine Frage ist keine Klage. (prov)
I'm only asking!

fragen • Wer viel fragt...(kriegt viele Antworten)
Ask a silly question, get a silly answer

französisch • sich auf französisch empfehlen
to take French leave (coll), to go AWOL (Absent Without Leave)
My secretary has disappeared again. She goes AWOL practically every afternoon.

freihalten • jmd freihalten
to take somebody out, to treat sbd (dated)
She took him out to the opera three times and then asked him to marry her.

Fressen • ein gefundenes Fressen
a juicy titbit (coll)
The scandal about the Duchess's love affair was a juicy titbit for the gutter press.

Freud • in Freud und Leid
for better or worse
We've decided to stay together, for better or worse.

Freund • jedermanns Freund sein
to run with the hare and hunt with the hounds (coll)
I don't trust him at all. He runs with the hare and hunts with the hounds.

Freunde • Freunde in der Not gehen tausend auf ein Lot. (prov)
A friend in need is a friend indeed. (prov)

Freundschaft • jmd die Freundschaft kündigen
to sever relations with sbd, to part brass rags with sbd (coll)
George was a very good friend of mine and then suddenly he decided to part brass rags. I don't know why.

Friedenspfeife • mit jmd die Friedenspfeife rauchen
to call it pax (coll), to bury the hatchet
The two opponents quarrelled for hours and then finally decided to call it pax and look for another victim instead.

frisch • Frisch gewagt ist halb gewonnen. (prov)
Nothing ventured nothing gained. (prov)

frisieren • einen Motor/Bericht frisieren
<u>Motor:</u> to soup up (coll)
The motor of the little car had been souped up so that it was able to overtake a sports car.

einen Bericht: to doctor (coll), to fiddle (coll)
The accounts had been fiddled to cover up the firm's insolvency.

Front • gegen jmd / etwas Front machen
to take (make) a stand against
It is high time we made a stand against the entrepreneurs building all these new houses around here.

Frosch • Sei kein Frosch!
Don't be such a wimp!

Frosch • einen Frosch in der Kehle (im Hals) haben
to have a frog in one's throat
I must have a drink of water; I've got a frog in my throat.

Fuchs • wo sich Fuchs und Hase gute Nacht sagen
the back of beyond (coll), right out in the sticks (coll)
He lives somewhere in the back of beyond and commutes to London every day.

Fuchtel • unter der Fuchtel von jmd stehen
to be under sbd's thumb, (nur unter der Fuchtel von Ehefrau oder Mutter:) to be tied to sbd's apron strings (coll)
He is completely under his mother's thumb.

Fuffzehn • 'n Fuffzehn machen
to take a break (coll), to have a breather (coll)
We took a break halfway up the hill to look at the view.

Fug • mit Fug und Recht
with every justification
He was dismissed from his job with every justification.

Fühler • seine Fühler ausstrecken
to put out a feeler (coll), to sound out a situation (coll), to see what the form is (coll)
I haven't seen the documents yet, but I'll put out a feeler and try to get the necessary information about the project.

Fundgrube • eine Fundgrube sein
a mine of sth (normalerweise Information)
The Encyclopaedia Britannica is a mine of information on all subjects.

funkelnagelneu
brand new (coll)
He came driving up in his brand new car and made us all jealous.

Funken • keinen Funken Verstand haben
not to have a grain/glimmer of sense (coll)
He hasn't got a glimmer of sense, otherwise he wouldn't hang around in pubs all the time.

fürstlich • fürstlich speisen
to feast like a king, to feast royally (coll), to dine/lunch/breakfast royally (coll)
We breakfasted royally off gammon, eggs, toast and croissants.

Fuß • stehenden Fußes
on the spot (coll), there and then (coll)
After looking at the brochure they decided there and then they didn't want to go to Spain for a holiday.

Fuß • mit dem falschen Fuß aufstehen/mit dem linken Fuß zuerst aufstehen
to get out of bed the wrong side (coll)
"What's wrong with him?" – "He just got out of bed the wrong side, that's all."

Fuß • mit einem Fuß im Grabe stehen
to have one foot in the grave (coll)
Why on earth doesn't he retire? He's got one foot in the grave and it's high time he stopped working.

Fuß • auf großem Fuße leben
to live in style (coll), to live in the grand manner, to live like a king (coll), to live high on the hog (coll)
You can live like a king there for next to nothing as long as you have got the right currency.

Fuß

Fuß • auf freiem Fuß sein
to be at liberty
After three years in custody he is again at liberty.

Fuß • mit jmd auf gutem Fuße stehen
to be on good terms with sbd, to be well in with sbd (coll) (bes. nachdem man sich bei jdm eingekratzt hat)
I should be able to persuade them to help – I'm fairly well in with them.

Füße • kalte Füße bekommen
to get cold feet (coll)
We were ready to go parachuting for the first time, but then we all got cold feet.

Füße • auf die Füße fallen
to fall on one's feet (coll)
He lost that job, but he fell on his feet and got another almost at once.

Füße • jmd die Füße küssen
to grovel with gratitude
After the police decided not to press charges they almost grovelled with gratitude.

Füße • auf eigenen Füßen stehen
to be independent, to stand on one's own two feet (coll)
He needed some help from his friends when he first gave up his job, but now he is standing on his own two feet.

Füße • etwas mit Füßen treten
to pour contumely on sth, to tear sth to pieces
I don't want to pour contumely on your work, but I don't think you have done the best you could.

Füße • sich die Füße vertreten
to stretch one's legs (coll)
After sitting in the library for four hours I went out to stretch my legs.

Füße • jmd etwas vor die Füße werfen
to throw sth in sbd's face (coll)
I sometimes feel like throwing the whole job in the boss's face.

futsch • Futsch ist futsch und hin ist hin.
What's done is done.
It's no use crying over spilt milk. (prov)

G

Galgenfrist
period of grace (oft mit Fristangabe+Genitiv+grace)
The landlord will give him one week's grace to pay the rent.

Galgenhumor
gallows humour
Convicted criminals only very seldom indulge in gallows humour before they are sentenced.

Galle • jmd läuft die Galle über
to be livid, to boil with rage (coll), sbd's blood boils
When I heard what she said about the future of our company, I just boiled with rage.

gang • gang und gäbe sein
to be a matter of course, to be the usual thing (coll), to be the usual procedure / standard practice / the done thing
It used to be a matter of course that parents decided who their daughter was to marry.

Gängelband • jmd am Gängelband führen
to have sbd on a string (coll)
It's ridiculous that our boss tries to have us on a string all the time. We get more and more demotivated by that.

Gänsehaut
gooseflesh, goosepimples
The last movement of this symphony always gives me gooseflesh.

Gänsemarsch
to walk in single file, to walk in Indian file (coll)
It's so narrow that you have to walk in single file.

Gardinen • hinter schwedischen Gardinen sitzen
to do time (coll), to be inside (coll), to do one's bird (coll)
It's no fun doing time.

Gardinenpredigt • jmd eine Gardinenpredigt halten
to give sbd a lecture (coll), to give sbd a talking-to (coll), to read sbd a sermon (coll), to give sbd a dressing-down (coll)
I had to give the children another lecture about going to bed in time.

Garn • jmd ins Garn gehen
to be caught in sbd's net, to get tangled with sbd
I'm surprised you got caught in his net like that – he only wants you for your money.

Gaul • Einem geschenkten Gaul schaut man nicht ins Maul. (prov)
Never look a gift horse in the mouth. (prov)

Gaumen • einen feinen Gaumen haben
to have a discriminating palate, to have a fastidious palate
He has a very discriminating palate – he can tell the difference between the wine from neighbouring vineyards.

geben • Dem hab ich es aber gegeben!
I've told him what I think.

geben • Geben ist seeliger denn Nehmen. (prov)
It is more blessed to give than to receive (bibl).

Gebet • jmd ins Gebet nehmen
to speak seriously to sbd about sth, to have a serious talk with sbd about sth
I decided to speak seriously to my friend about the amount he was drinking.

Gedächtnis • ein Gedächtnis wie ein Sieb haben
to have a brain like a sieve (coll)
I told you yesterday! If you've forgotten again you must have a brain like a sieve.

Gedeih • auf Gedeih und Verderb(en) ▷ Freud und Leid

Geduldsfaden • jmd reißt der Geduldsfaden
to have one's patience exhausted
If this pointless discussion goes on much longer my patience will be exhausted.

gefärbt • eine gefärbte Darstellung / ein gefärbter Bericht
coloured, slanted, one-sided
His report is coloured by his own wishful thinking.
His report is slanted towards the Government side.
His report is completely one-sided.

gefressen • jmd / etwas gefressen haben
to be unable to stand the sight of (coll), to be unable to stomach the sight of (coll)
I can't stomach the sight of people who speak with their mouths full.

Gefühle • mit gemischten Gefühlen
with mixed feelings
I heard about the success of my ex-wife's new boyfriend with very mixed feelings.

Gegensätze • Gegensätze ziehen sich an.
Opposites attract.

geharnischt • eine geharnischte Rede halten / ein geharnischter Brief
to haul sbd over the coals (coll), a stiff letter, a stinker (coll)
I hauled my neighbour over the coals because of his son's noisy parties.
I wrote him a stinker the other day, but he still hasn't sent us the money he owes us.

Gehege • jmd ins Gehege kommen
to cross sbd, to get in sbd's way (coll), to cross swords with sbd, (<u>die Rechte von jmd verletzen:</u>) to encroach on sbd's preserves, to be on sbd's patch (coll)
Don't cross swords with the boss – he is in a very bad mood today.

gehenkt • wie gehenkt aussehen
to look like a tramp (coll), to look scruffy (coll), to look as if one has been pulled through a hedge backwards (coll)
He turned up at an elegant dinner party looking as if he had been pulled through a hedge backwards. What he needs is a wife.

gehupft • gehupft wie gesprungen
It's as broad as it's long.
It's six of one and half a dozen of the other.

Geier • weiß der Geier
God knows. / Heaven only knows.

Geier • hol's der Geier
To hell with it!

Geige • die erste Geige spielen
not to play second fiddle (coll)
That woman there refuses to play second fiddle to anyone.

Geist • seinen Geist aufgeben
<u>nur Person:</u> to kick the bucket (coll), to snuff it (coll), to peg out (coll), to breathe one's last, to draw one's last breath, to give up the ghost (coll)
He breathed his last on 15th February after a long illness.
Halfway up a steep hill the engine of the old car gave up the ghost completely.

Geist • Der Geist ist willig, doch das Fleisch ist schwach.
The spirit is willing but the flesh is weak. (bibl)

Geist • Das zeigt, wes Geistes Kind sie ist.
That shows what sort of a person she is.

Geister • von allen guten Geistern verlassen sein
to have gone out of one's mind (coll), to have taken leave of one's senses
How can you give up your job now, when you have all these debts? Have you gone out of your mind?

Geld • Geld allein macht nicht glücklich.
You can't buy happiness. / Money isn't everything.

Geld • Geld auf die hohe Kante legen
to put money by, to put money aside
I have been putting money by for a new car for three months.

Geld • Geld regiert die Welt.
Money makes the world go round. (ursprünglich *"Love makes the world go round."*)

Geld • im Geld schwimmen
to be loaded (coll), to be rolling in it (coll), to be rolling (coll), to be made of money (coll), to have money to burn (coll)
His family are absolutely rolling, you should see some of the pictures they have on their walls at home.

Geld • sich für Geld sehen lassen können
to be a sight to see (coll), to be a sight worth seeing (coll)
Our guinea pig can swim, which is a sight worth seeing.

Geld • nicht für Geld und gute Worte
not for love nor money (coll)
I could not persuade them to move for love nor money.

Geld • Geld wie Heu haben ▷ im Geld schwimmen

Geld • Geld zum Fenster hinauswerfen
to throw money down the drain (coll), to throw money out of the window (coll), to throw money away (coll)
The money I invested in his new theatrical project was just money thrown down the drain.

Gelegenheit • die Gelegenheit beim Schopfe packen
to grab a chance (coll), to jump at an opportunity, to seize an opportunity with both hands (coll)
I saw they were going cheap, so I grabbed the chance and bought ten to sell at a profit.

Gelegenheit • Gelegenheit macht Diebe.
Opportunity makes the thief.

Geleit • das letzte Geleit geben
to pay one's last respects
I went to my grandmother's funeral to pay my last respects.

gemünzt • auf jmd gemünzt sein
to be aimed at, to be directed at, to be a dig at (coll), to be meant for
That remark was directed at you.

Gemüse • junges Gemüse
<u>negativ:</u> sprogs (coll), plebs (coll Public School)
<u>nur weiblich:</u> spring chicken
It is no good expecting to get any sense out of those plebs for another year or two.

genäht • Doppelt genäht hält besser. ▷ doppelt

Genick • jmd/etwas das Genick brechen
to be sbd's downfall, to do for sbd (coll)
It was the question about the Armenian monarchy that did for me in the exam.

Genie • Das Genie beherrscht das Chaos.
Organisation is the last refuge of a tired mind.

gerädert • wie gerädert sein
to be fagged out (coll), to be knackered (coll), to be exhausted, to be worn out
I worked fourteen hours non-stop and came home completely knackered.

Geratewohl • aufs Geratewohl
on the off chance (coll)
We called round on the off chance that he might be at home.

Gericht • bis zum jüngsten Gericht
until doomsday, until the Day of Judgment, until hell freezes over (coll)
We can work on this until doomsday, but we can't improve it any more.

gertenschlank
sylph-like
The girl had a sylph-like figure she was over-anxious to keep, and she didn't eat properly.

gerufen • wie gerufen kommen
to be the very person wanted, to be just the person one wanted to see (coll)
You are just the person I wanted to see: can you tell me the answer to this question?

Geschäft • Beim Geschäft hört die Freundschaft auf.
Don't mix business with pleasure.

Geschenke • Kleine Geschenke erhalten die Freundschaft.
It's the thought that counts.

Geschmack • Über Geschmack läßt sich (nicht) streiten.
Chacun à son gout. (Fr.)
There's no accounting for tastes.

geschniegelt • geschniegelt und gebügelt
spick and span (coll), dressed up to the nines (coll), spruced up (coll)
He appeared for the interview looking very spick and span in a new suit.

Gesicht • wie aus dem Gesicht geschnitten
to be the spitting image of sbd (coll)
He is the spitting image of his father – you can hardly tell them apart.

Gesicht • **jmd steht etwas im Gesicht geschrieben**
to be written all over one's face (coll)
Look – he's failed. It's written all over his face.

Gesicht • **zwei Gesichter haben**
to be two faced (coll)
You cannot rely on what he says – he is completely two faced.

Gesicht • **ein langes Gesicht machen**
to pull a long face (coll)
I pulled a long face when I saw my poor exam result.

Gesicht • **sein Gesicht verlieren**
to lose face
The diplomats were mostly anxious about the danger of losing face.

Gesicht • **sein Gesicht wahren**
to save face
The diplomats tried to save face, but it was perfectly clear that the conference had been a failure.

Gesicht • **sein wahres Gesicht zeigen**
to show one's true colours, to reveal one's true nature
This affair has made him reveal his true colours.

Gespann • **ein gutes Gespann sein**
to make a good team (coll)
Those two make a good team. They work very well together.

Gespenster • **Gespenster sehen**
to see things (coll)
"Look, there's your brother!" – "You're seeing things. He's in America."

Gespött • **sich zum Gespött der Leute machen**
to make oneself a laughing stock
He made a laughing stock of himself with his foolish proposal.

gestern • **nicht von gestern sein**
not to be born yesterday (coll)
You must think I was born yesterday if you expect me to agree to something like that.

gestiefelt • gestiefelt und gespornt
booted and spurred (coll)
There we were, all booted and spurred and ready to go and then they told us the trip was cancelled.

gestochen • wie gestochen schreiben
(als Substantiv:) copperplate writing
Whose is that copperplate writing?

gestohlen • Der kann mir gestohlen bleiben!
He can get fucked! (vulg)

gestorben • Der ist für mich gestorben!
I have nothing more to do with him.

gesund • gesund und munter
to be fit and well, to be on top form (coll), to be in fine fettle (coll) (dated), to be as fit as a fiddle (coll) (dated)
My son was ill in bed last week, but now he is fit and well again.

Gevatter • Gevatter Tod
the Grim Reaper, the Old Man with the Scythe
The Grim Reaper came upon him as he will come upon us all.

Gewalt • Gewalt geht vor Recht. (prov)
Might is Right. (prov)

gewaschen • Das hat sich gewaschen.
to strike home (coll)
That remark struck home, and upset a lot of the participants.

Gewissen • jmd/etwas auf dem Gewissen haben
to have sbd's death on one's conscience
He drove his car while drunk and killed three people. He had their deaths on his conscience for the rest of his life.

Gewissensbisse • sich Gewissensbisse machen
to have a guilty conscience (coll)

I have got a guilty conscience because I sent my daughter to the shops in the pouring rain and now she has caught a cold.

gewonnen • Wie gewonnen, so zerronnen. (prov)
Easy come, easy go. (prov)

Gift • Darauf kannst du Gift nehmen.
You can bet your (sweet) life on that. (coll)
You can stake your life on that. (coll)
You can bet your buttocks on that. (vulg)

Giftpfeile • Giftpfeile schleudern
to make barbed remarks
His barbed remarks reduced her to tears.

Glacéhandschuhe • jmd mit Glacéhandschuhen anfassen
to handle sbd with kid gloves (coll)
He is a nice enough fellow, but you have to handle him with kid gloves; he has a terrible temper.

Glanz • mit Glanz und Gloria
with pomp and circumstance
The birthday of Her Majesty the Queen is celebrated with pomp and circumstance twice a year.

Glashaus • Wer selbst im Glashaus sitzt, soll nicht mit Steinen werfen. (prov)
People who live in glass houses shouldn't throw stones. (prov)

Glaube • Der Glaube kann Berge versetzen. (prov)
Faith moves mountains. (bibl)

glauben • Wer's glaubt, wird selig.
If you believe that, you'll believe anything. (coll)

gleich • Gleich und Gleich gesellt sich gern. (prov)
Birds of a feather flock together. (prov)

Glück

gleich • Gleiches mit Gleichem vergelten
to pay sbd back in his own coin, to give sbd tit for tat (coll) (auch: <u>*tit for tat* als Adjektiv</u>)
After the allied raids on German cities, the Luftwaffe tried to pay them back in their own coin in the "Baedeker Raids" on British cultural centres.
Sectarian killings in Northern Ireland continued on a tit for tat basis.

Gleise • sich in ausgefahrenen Gleisen bewegen
to be (stuck) in a rut (coll), to have got into a rut (coll)
The whole department is in a rut; nobody has tried to do anything new or different for ages.

Glocke • wissen, was die Glocke geschlagen hat
to know how matters stand (coll)
As soon as we saw our head of department coming weeping out of the Director's office we knew how matters stood. She resigned the very next day.

Glocke • etwas an die große Glocke hängen
to shout / trumpet sth from the housetops (coll), to broadcast, to trumpet abroad
The Party press trumpeted every success from the housetops.

Glück • auf gut Glück ▷ aufs Geratewohl

Glück • mehr Glück als Verstand haben
to have more luck than judgment
More by luck than judgment he managed to land the damaged plane on the jungle airstrip.

Glück • dem Glück ein wenig nachhelfen
to load the dice
We can load the dice in favour of the applicant we want by requiring qualifications which she has, and which very few other people have.

Glück • Glück im Spiel, Pech in der Liebe. (prov)
Lucky at cards, unlucky in love. (prov)

Glück • Glück im Unglück haben
to be a blessing in disguise
It was a blessing in disguise that we missed our plane, because a civil war broke out in the country we were heading for on the very next day.

Glück • das Glück ist jmd hold
to be in luck (coll), to have one's luck hold
I wonder how long her luck will hold – she's been taking things without paying for them for months.

Glück • Jeder ist seines eigenen Glückes Schmied.
The fault…is not in our stars, / But in ourselves, that we are underlings. (Shakespeare: Julius Caesar.)

Glück • Man kann niemanden zu seinem Glück zwingen.
You can take a horse to water but you can't make it drink. (prov)

glücklich • Dem Glücklichen schlägt keine Stunde.
Time flies when you're enjoying yourself.

Glücksstern • unter einem Glücksstern geboren sein
to have been born under a lucky star
He has been very successful all his life, but I don't think he is particularly able – just born under a lucky star.

Glückssträhne
a run of luck (coll), a lucky streak (coll)
He had a run of luck at cards and won $1000 in a single night.

Gnade • Gnade vor Recht ergehen lassen
to temper justice with mercy
He tempered justice with mercy and sentenced the defendant to a relatively short term of imprisonment.

Gnadenbrot • jmd Gnadenbrot geben
to look after one's own (coll)
What are we going to do about the old porter? He's far too old to carry on – but one does look after one's own, I suppose.

Gold • Es ist nicht alles Gold, was glänzt. (prov)
All is not gold that glitters. (prov)

Gold • sich nicht mit Gold aufwiegen lassen
to be worth one's / it's weight in gold (coll)
That girl is worth her weight in gold. We couldn't do without her.

Gold • nicht für alles Gold in der Welt
not for all the tea in China (coll)
I wouldn't go through it again for all the tea in China.

Gold • treu wie Gold sein
to be as true as steel
He was as true as steel to me, and lent me money all through the difficult period I went through last year.

Goldgrube
gold mine
That pub is a real gold mine; it's always full of customers.

Goldwaage • (nicht) alles auf die Goldwaage legen
(not) to take everything literally / seriously
You shouldn't take all he says literally.

Gosse • aus der Gosse kommen
to come from the gutter
Though he is rich now, his manners show you that he has come up from the gutter.

Gott • Hilf dir selbst, so hilft dir Gott.
God helps those who help themselves.

Gott • Gottes Mühlen mahlen langsam, aber gerecht. (prov)
The mills of God grind slow, yet they grind exceeding small. (Longfellow)

Gott • über Gott und die Welt reden
about life / life, the universe and everything (coll), about everything under the sun
We sat for hours on the beach talking about everything under the sun.

Gott • ganz und gar von Gott verlassen sein ▷ Geister: von allen guten Geistern verlassen sein

Gott • Was Gott zusammengefügt hat, soll der Mensch nicht scheiden. (bibl, Trauungsfeier Liturgie)
Those whom God hath joined, let no man put asunder.

Götter • das wissen die Götter
Heaven knows! / God alone knows! / God knows!

Götter • ein Bild für die Götter sein
a sight for the Gods (coll)
He was a sight for the Gods – short trousers, braces, a top hat and an umbrella.

Grab • sein eigenes Grab schaufeln
to dig one's own grave (coll)
The defendant lied so unskilfully in the witness box that he dug his own grave.

Grab • sich im Grabe umdrehen
to turn in one's grave (coll)
Your father would turn in his grave if he knew what you are doing.

Granit • bei jmd auf Granit beißen
to beat one's head against a brick wall (coll)
He argued with them for hours, but he was beating his head against a brick wall.

Gras • Das Gras auf der anderen Seite ist immer grüner. (prov)
The grass is always greener on the other side (of the hill). (prov)

Gras • ins Gras beißen
to bite the dust
The film was a Western, in which plenty of cowboys bit the dust.

Gras • Gras über eine Sache wachsen lassen
to let bygones be bygones
We must let bygones be bygones if we are ever going to be able to work together in the future.

Gras • das Gras wachsen hören
to read too much into things (coll), to start at shadows (coll)
There was a nasty argument the other day in our department, but he read far too much into it, and now he thinks that half of us are going to leave.

grau • grau in grau
sombre, gloomy, in sombre colours
He painted a gloomy picture of our future economic prospects.

Grausen • das kalte Grausen kriegen
to get the heebie-jeebies (coll)
When I had to sleep in the empty house I really got the heebie-jeebies.

Grenze • an seine/ihre Grenzen stoßen
to reach the limit of one's abilities/powers
Once we had given her more than two files to look after she very quickly reached the limit of her abilities.

Gretchenfrage • die Gretchenfrage stellen
to put the 64,000 dollar question (coll)
After we had discussed the details of the project for some time I decided to put the 64,000 dollar question and asked him if he would be prepared to work with us permanently.

grob • aus dem Gröbsten heraus sein
to be over the worst (coll), to be out of the wood (coll)
"We're not out of the wood yet," said the captain after his team had scored fifteen points. "They are still twenty points ahead."

Groschen • der Groschen ist gefallen
the penny has dropped (coll)
After I had listened to his explanation for a few minutes the penny suddenly dropped and I understood what he was talking about.

grün • jmd nicht grün sein
to be on bad terms with sbd (coll), to have a grudge against sbd
They have been on bad terms for years even though they have to work in the same department.

grün • jmd grün und blau schlagen
to beat sbd black and blue (coll)
The bigger boys beat the newcomer black and blue.

Grund • Nichts geschieht ohne Grund. ▷ Rauch: kein Rauch ohne Feuer

Grund • jmd in Grund und Boden verdammen
to condemn sbd outright / out of hand
The press would have condemned the man outright, before the trial had even started.

Gunst • die Gunst der Stunde nutzen
to take time by the fetlock, to seize one's chance / the moment, to improve the shining hour (Isaac Watts)
As our boss was in a good temper I seized the moment and asked him for an increase in my wages.

Gurgel • jmd an die Gurgel gehen
to fly at sbd's throat, to be at sbd's throat
After the defeat, all the leaders were at each other's throats, blaming each other.

Gürtel • den Gürtel enger schnallen
to tighten one's belt (coll)
Now that I have lost my job, everybody in the family will have to tighten their belt.

Gut • Unrecht Gut gedeihet nicht.
Crime doesn't pay.

gut • Es hat alles sein Gutes.
There's some good in everything.
Every cloud has a silver lining.

H

Haar • um ein Haar
all but (coll), within a hair's breadth of (coll), by the skin of one's teeth (coll), to come within an ace of (coll), to be a near (run) thing (coll), to be a close (run) thing (<u>Schlacht, Wettkampf</u>) (coll); to be a close shave (coll)
He all but fell.
He was within a hair's breadth of falling.
The German armies came within an ace of capturing Moscow.
The Battle of Waterloo was a near run thing.
That was a close shave!

Haar • ein Haar in der Suppe finden
to find a fly in the ointment
However good things seem you can rely on her to find a fly in the ointment. She is never satisfied.

Haar • jmd aufs Haar gleichen
to be as like as two peas (in a pad) (coll)
The twins are as like as two peas.

Haare • Haare auf den Zähnen haben
to have gubs (coll), to be not an easy customer
It's hard to get one over on her.

Haare • etwas ist an den Haaren herbeigezogen
to be far-fetched (coll)
The whole story is so far-fetched that I don't believe a word of it.

Haare • sich in den Haaren liegen
<u>Feindschaft:</u> to be at daggers drawn with sbd, to have one's knife into sbd (coll)
Those two have really got their knives into each other. It's no good expecting them to work together any longer.
<u>Uneinigkeit:</u> to be at loggerheads with sbd over sth (coll), not to see eye to eye with sbd about sth (coll)
I've never seen eye to eye with him about the new investment portfolio.

Haare • sich die Haare raufen
to tear one's hair (coll), to go up the wall (coll)
He went right up the wall when he heard the new plan had failed.

Haare • jmd die Haare vom Kopf fressen
to eat sbd out of house and home (coll)
If you go on tucking in like that, you will eat us out of house and home.

Haare • sich keine grauen Haare wachsen lassen
to lose no sleep over / about sth (coll), not to worry one's head about sth (coll), not to do one's nut (in) about sth (coll)
There's no point in losing any sleep over it; it'll be all right in time.

Haare • jmd stehen die Haare zu Berge
sbd's hair stands on end
The tale he told was enough to make your hair stand on end.
<u>Adjektiv:</u> hair-raising: *It's a hair-raising story.*

Haaresbreite • um Haaresbreite ▷ um ein Haar

haargenau
to be bang on (coll), to be dead right (coll), to be correct to a T (coll), to be correct to the last detail
The boy's solution to the problem was bang on.

Haarspalterei • Haarspalterei betreiben
to split hairs (coll), to quibble
It is splitting hairs to worry about whether the money is paid by the Housing Department or by the Social Security – it all comes out of the same budget.

Hab • Hab und Gut
all one's worldly wealth
Having lost all their worldly wealth in the war they fled to a country where they remained for the rest of their lives.

Habenichts • ein Habenichts sein
to be a have-not (usually only together with the haves) (coll), to be skint (coll), to be penniless
We won't get any financial help out of him. He is penniless.

Hackhuhn • das Hackhuhn sein
to be the last in the pecking order (coll)
When I was a child I was the last in the pecking order in my family. I always had to do the washing-up.

Hafer • jmd sticht der Hafer ▷ Decke: an die Decke gehen

Hahn • Hahn im Korbe sein
to be the lion of the party (coll), to rule the roost (coll), be cock of the walk (coll), to be cock of the roost (coll) (dated)
As the only man in the department he was at first treated as the cock of the walk, but his female colleagues soon turned to persecuting him.

Hahn • Danach kräht kein Hahn mehr!
nobody gives a damn about sth (coll), nobody gives a shit (vulg)/ fuck (vulg) about sth
Nobody gives a shit about your previous successes.

Hahnenschrei • beim ersten Hahnenschrei aufstehen
to get up at cock-crow, to rise with the lark, to get up at the crack (of dawn) (coll)
I always get up at the crack during the week and then stay in bed half the weekend.

Häkchen • Früh krümmt sich, was ein Häkchen werden will. (prov)
You can't teach an old dog new tricks. (prov)

Haken • Das ist der Haken!
That is the snag! / That is the catch!
There's the rub! (Shakespeare: Hamlet)

halb • nichts halbes und nichts ganzes ▷ Fisch: weder Fisch noch Fleisch

halbgebildet • Der Halbgebildete ist schlimmer als der Unwissende. (prov)
A little knowledge is a dangerous thing. (prov)

Halle • in diesen heiligen Hallen
in these hallowed halls
He was educated in the hallowed halls of Eton and Trinity College Cambridge.

Hals • etwas in den falschen Hals bekommen
to take sth the wrong way (coll), to get one's back up (coll), to get the wrong end of the stick
She took his words the wrong way, and thought that he meant that he didn't want to work with her any more.

Hals • jmd / etwas auf dem / am Hals haben
to be lumbered with sbd / sth (coll), to be saddled with sbd / sth (coll), to have sbd / sth on one's hands
First of all my daughter said she wanted a dog, but now I'm lumbered with him – she never takes him for walks.

Hals • zum Hals heraushängen
to be sick and tired of (coll), to be sick to death of (coll), to be cheesed off with (coll), to be pissed off with (vulg)
I'm pissed off with cricket – I'm going to take up tennis instead.

Hals • den Hals nicht voll kriegen
to be insatiable, never to have one's fill, never to have enough
He's quite insatiable in his demands for luxury.

Hals • Hals über Kopf
<u>verlieben:</u> to fall head-over-heels in love with sbd
She fell head over heels in love with him.
<u>eilig:</u> precipitately
They left the town precipitately. / They suddenly upped and left. / They couldn't leave fast enough. / Before we knew it, they'd left.

Hals • sich jmd an den Hals werfen
to pour oneself over sbd, to flaunt o.s., to force oneself on sbd's attention
As a modern girl she was not one to force herself on a man. And wise men did not force themselves on her.

Hals • jmd Hals- und Beinbruch wünschen
to wish sbd luck, to wish sbd all the best (coll)
They wished him all the best when he emigrated to New Zealand. Break a leg!

Halsabschneider • ein Halsabschneider sein
to be a shark (coll)
Don't go near those estate agents. They are all sharks.

Hammer • unter den Hammer kommen
to come under the hammer (coll), to be sold by auction
After all his goods were seized by his creditors they came under the hammer and raised more than enough to pay off his debts.

Hand • Hand in Hand
<u>nur hinterlistig:</u> hand in glove with, in cahoots with (coll)
This firm of lawyers is no good; they work hand in glove with the police.
<u>direkter Sinn:</u> hand in hand
The young man and the girl walked hand in hand along the street.

Hand • Hand an sich legen
to take one's own life
When they saw that their position was hopeless they took their own lives.

Hand • die Hand auf der Tasche haben
to have short arms (and deep pockets)
She's got short arms and won't let him spend any money on extras for the car.

Hand • Hand aufs Herz!
Cross your heart? / On the level?

Hand • etwas unter der Hand bekommen
to get sth on the black market, to get sth under the counter (coll), through channels (coll)
We got the food on the black market. We paid for it with American cigarettes.

Hand

Hand • jmd aus der Hand fressen
to eat out of sbd's hand (coll)
As soon as we showed them how useful we could be they started eating out of our hands.

Hand • jmd zur Hand gehen
to lend sbd a hand (coll)
Can you lend me a hand and peel the potatoes?

Hand • freie Hand haben
to have a free hand
He had a free hand as to whom he employed in the firm.

Hand • etwas aus erster Hand haben
to have sth first hand (coll), to have sth straight from source (coll), to have sth straight from the horse's mouth (dated) (coll), to have sth hot off the press (coll)
Caroline is getting married! I heard it at first hand, from her own lips.

Hand • jmd in der Hand haben
to have sbd at one's mercy
He knows too much about us, and so has us at his mercy.

Hand • seine Hand im Spiel haben
to have a finger in the pie (<u>negativ</u>) (coll), to have a say in the business (coll)
That fellow always wants to know what's going on. He likes to have a finger in every pie.

Hand • für jmd/etwas die Hand ins Feuer legen
to stake one's life on sth
She won't let you down. I'd stake my life on that.

Hand • weder Hand noch Fuß haben
to make no sense, not to hang together (coll), not to add up (coll)
His ideas are really hair-brained. They make no sense at all.

Hand • die rechte Hand von jmd sein
to be sbd's right hand/man, to be sbd's right arm
You cannot move her out of my department: she is my right arm.

Hand • von langer Hand vorbereiten
to be prepared well in advance, to be prepared well beforehand
The takeover of the company had clearly been prepared well in advance.

Hand • Eine Hand wäscht die andere. (prov)
I scratch your back – you scratch mine. (prov)

Hände • zwei linke Hände haben
to be all thumbs (coll)
You clumsy ass, you're all thumbs today. Can't you even tighten a screw?

Hände • die Hände in den Schoß legen
to sit with folded hands, to sit with one's hands in one's lap (coll)
Don't just sit there with your hands in your lap – get up and do something!

Hände • (nicht) mit leeren Händen kommen
(not) to come empty-handed
Whenever Aunty visits us, she never comes empty-handed. She always brings us sweets.

Hände • Viele Hände machen der Arbeit bald ein Ende. (prov)
Many hands make light work. (prov)

Hände • sich die Hände reiben
to rub one's hands
He rubbed his hands with delight when he heard the news.

Hände • jmd in die Hände spielen
to play into sbd's hands (<u>nur intransitiv</u>)
We played into the hands of our opponents by taking that risk. – It was exactly what they were hoping, and they immediately took advantage.

Hände • in die Hände spucken
to start work with enthusiasm, to get / knuckle down to sth (coll)
He started work with enthusiasm, but lost interest when things got difficult.

Hände

Hände • alle Hände voll zu tun haben
to have one's hands full (coll)
I have my hands full with this new project and I can't take on anything else at the moment.

händeringend • händeringend nach etwas / jmd suchen
to search for sbd / sth high and low (coll)
Where have you been? I've been searching for you high and low.

Handgelenk • etwas aus dem Handgelenk schütteln
to reel sth off (coll), to toss sth off (coll)
Nowadays the Brahms piano concerti are tossed off by the young – as though they were as easy as peanuts.

Handschlag • keinen Handschlag tun
<u>Faulheit:</u> not to do a hand's turn (coll)
<u>unterlassene Hilfe:</u> not to lift a finger (coll)
He hasn't done a hand's turn. He left me alone with all the work.

Handtuch • das Handtuch werfen
to throw in the towel (coll)
Sometimes I feel like throwing in the towel. I do all this for these people, and I never get one word of thanks.

Handumdrehen • im Handumdrehen
in less than no time (coll), in next to no time (coll), in a jiffy (coll), in two ticks (coll), in a trice, in a (split) second (coll), in a twinkling (coll)
With his help we got the work done in less than no time.

Handwerk • jmd das Handwerk legen
to put an end to (sbd's activity), to put a stop to (sbd's activity)
When the police found out what he was doing they put a stop to it at once.

Handwerk • jmd ins Handwerk pfuschen
to queer sbd's pitch (coll), to poach on sbd's preserves
I'd prefer to do everything myself than have other people coming in and queering the pitch for me.

Hänschen • Was Hänschen nicht lernt, lernt Hans nimmermehr. (prov)
You can't teach an old dog new tricks. (prov)

Hansdampf • Hansdampf in allen Gassen sein
to be a jack-of-all-trades (coll)
He calls himself an electrician, but he is really a jack-of-all-trades. He can do most repairs.

Harke • jmd zeigen, was eine Harke ist
to show sbd what's what (coll), to teach sbd a lesson
When he heard that his younger brother had been bullied he taught the bullies a lesson by thrashing them all.

Harnisch • in Harnisch geraten
to fly into a rage
When he heard about the debt his son was in he flew into a rage and threw him out of the house.

hart • wenn es hart auf hart kommt
if push comes to shove (coll), if it comes down to it (coll), when it comes to the crunch (coll)
He'll help us if push comes to shove and we're really desperate.

hart • hart gesotten sein
to be hard-boiled (coll) (dated)
Only the most hard-boiled of men could carry out the ruthless task.

Hase • ein alter Hase sein
to be an old campaigner (coll), to be an old hand (coll)
None of us had tackled such a job before so we listened closely to what the old campaigner had to say.

Hase • Da liegt der Hase im Pfeffer! ▷ Haken

Hasenfuß • ein Hasenfuß sein
to be yellow (coll), to be chicken (coll)
All the people in town called him yellow.

Hasenherz • ein Hasenherz sein ▷ Hasenfuß

Hast

Hast • Hast bricht Beine. (prov)
More haste less speed. (prov)

Haube • unter die Haube bringen
to get sbd suited (dated), to get sbd spliced (coll), to marry s.o. off
Her mother has been trying to get her only daughter spliced for years, and now that the girl's gone off with a man she complains about being alone all the time.

Haubitze • voll wie eine Haubitze sein
to be drunk as a lord (coll)
It's no use calling for the caretaker. He's drunk as a lord again.

Häufchen • wie ein Häufchen Elend
a picture of misery (coll)
The kitten sat there a picture of misery and I just had to take her home with me.

Haus • ein fideles Haus sein
to be a laugh (coll), to be a bundle of laughs (coll)
His brother is a laugh – he never takes anything seriously.

Haus • in etwas zu Hause sein ▷ beschlagen sein

hausbacken • hausbacken sein
<u>Personen:</u> to be simple, to be homely (MIND: U.S: "homely"= häßlich)
He is a simple, homely person. He is not at all interested in the great world.
<u>Sachen, bes. Ideen:</u> homespun
His homespun philosophy didn't impress the scholars one bit.

Häuschen • ganz aus dem Häuschen sein
to be over the moon (coll) (dated)

haushoch • jmd haushoch überlegen sein
to stand head and shoulders above sbd (in/at sth), to be miles/streets ahead of sbd (coll) (in/at sth), to knock sbd into a cocked hat (coll) (at sth), to be able to ... the socks off sbd (coll), to be sbd to whom you cannot hold a candle (coll)

He's miles ahead of the rest of us in his ability to reason sharply.
The visiting team can play the socks off the home side.

häuslich • sich häuslich niederlassen
to settle down
Our daughter's friend was always welcome to our flat. But when he started settling down in our living room for weeks we decided to tell him that he'd better go somewhere else.

Haut • mit heiler Haut davonkommen
to come through unscathed, to escape without a scratch, to come/get off without a scratch (coll)
It's a miracle how he came unscathed through the years of the war.

Haut • unter die Haut gehen
to be moving
His words were very moving and none of us was able to speak for quite a long time after he had finished.

Haut • nicht aus seiner Haut können
The leopard cannot change his spots. (prov)

Haut • seine Haut retten
to save one's skin (coll)
He puts all the blame on us in order to save his own skin.

Haut • eine ehrliche Haut sein
to be as honest as the day is long (coll)
The landlord is as honest as the day is long. He'll never overcharge us.

Haut • nur Haut und Knochen sein
just/no more than skin and bones (coll)
The refugees were just skin and bones when they arrived at the soup kitchen.

Haut • sich seiner Haut wehren
to stand up for o.s. (coll), to stand one's ground, not to give/budge an inch (coll)
When they wanted to reduce her salary she didn't give an inch and simply refused to agree.

Hebel • alle Hebel in Bewegung setzen
to leave no stone unturned
He left no stone unturned in his efforts to obtain a transfer to the London office.

Hefekloß • aufgehen wie ein Hefekloß
to balloon (coll)
That girl has really ballooned over the last couple of years.

Hehl • kein Hehl aus etwas machen ▷ Brei: nicht um den heißen Brei herumreden

hauen • Das haut nicht hin.
That won't work. / That doesn't make sense. / That doesn't add up.

Heim • Heim und Herd verlassen
to leave hearth and home
In the nineteenth century innumerable Irish peasantry left hearth and home to seek their fortune in America.

heimlich • heimlich, still und leise
in secret, on the quiet (coll) (<u>auch Adj:</u> hush-hush (coll))
We'll have to do it all on the quiet. If anybody finds out it could be very awkward.
Keep it hush-hush.

Heimlichkeiten • Heimlichkeiten – Schlechtigkeiten!
My ears are burning!

heimzahlen • jmd etwas heimzahlen
to get one's own back on sbd for sth (coll), to get even with sbd for sth (coll), to pay sbd back for sth (coll)
It's almost automatic to want to get your own back on someone who has done you wrong.

Heirat • Heirat in Eile bereut man mit Weile. (prov)
Marry in haste, repent at leisure. (prov)

heiß • Es wird nichts so heiß gegessen, wie es gekocht wird. (prov)
Things are not as black as they look.
Things are not as bad as they seem.

heiß • ganz heiß auf etwas sein
to be very keen on sth
They were really very keen to listen to the story but were afterwards disappointed.

heiß • zu heiß gebadet worden sein ▷ baden

Heißsporn • ein Heißsporn sein
to be a hothead (<u>auch Adj</u>: hotheaded)
The older leadership had some difficulty keeping the young hotheads of the movement under control.

Heller • jmd etwas auf Heller und Pfennig zurückzahlen
to the last farthing (bibl)
He paid his debts to the last farthing.

Heller • keinen roten Heller besitzen
not to have a penny to one's name, not to have a bean (coll), not to have a brass farthing (coll)
They do not have a penny to their names and cannnot possibly afford to do what you are suggesting.

Hemd • jmd das letzte Hemd ausziehen
to bleed sbd white (coll), to squeeze sbd dry (coll), to fleece sbd (coll), to have sbd for his eye teeth (coll)
If lawyers are ruthless enough they don't hesitate to have people for their eye teeth.

Hemd • Das letzte Hemd hat keine Taschen.
You can't take it with you when you go.

herablassen • jmd herablassend behandeln
to look down one's nose at sbd (coll)
I won't ask him for help, he always looks down his nose at me.

heranmachen • sich an jmd heranmachen ▷ anbändeln

Herd • Eigener Herd ist Goldes wert. (prov)
There's no place like home. (prov)

Herdentier • ein Herdentier sein
to be a sheep (coll), to be one of the common herd
I do not think he has had an original thought in his life. He is one of the common herd.

hereinfallen • auf jmd hereinfallen
to fall for sbd/sth hook, line and sinker (coll)
I fell for him hook, line and sinker.

hereinschneien
to blow in (coll), to drop in (coll), to come round (coll), to turn up unannounced
He turned up unannounced yesterday and stayed to supper.

Heringe • wie die Heringe
like sardines (coll)
We were too many people for the little car and were packed into it like sardines.

Herr • zeigen, wer der Herr im Hause ist
to show/make clear who is master in the house/who's boss/who's in charge
He very soon made clear who was master in the house.

Herr • Wie der Herr, so's Gescherr. (prov)
Like father like son. (prov)

Herren • aus aller Herren Länder
from everywhere under the sun (coll), from all corners of the earth
They came to the Olympic Games from all corners of the earth.

Herrgottsfrühe • in aller Herrgottsfrühe ▷ beim ersten Hahnenschrei

herunterputzen • jmd herunterputzen ▷ jmd abkanzeln

Herz • jmd blutet das Herz
one's heart bleeds (coll) (oft iron.)
So you've had to sell your car? My heart bleeds for you!

Herz • jmd bricht das Herz
one's heart breaks
His heart broke when she went off with another man.

Herz • sein Herz an etwas hängen
to set one's heart on sth
My son has set his heart on that horse and doesn't think of anything else but riding lessons.

Herz • das Herz auf dem rechten Fleck haben
to have one's heart in the right place (coll), sbd's heart is in the right place (coll)
Their mother was a good-natured woman with her heart in the right place.

Herz • das Herz auf der Zunge haben
to wear one's heart on one's sleeve (Shakespeare: Othello)
He wears his heart on his sleeve the whole time, so we all knew he was very upset.

Herz • ein Herz aus Gold haben
to have a heart of gold (coll)
That boy has a heart of gold: he visits his old grandmother every day.

Herz • sein Herz ausschütten
to pour out one's heart
She poured out her heart to me about her boyfriend's troubles, but I really did not see how I could help.

Herz • ein Herz aus Stein haben
to have a heart of stone
He has a heart of stone: he has never given anybody a helping hand in all his life.

Herz • etwas nicht über's Herz bringen
to be unable to bring oneself to do sth (coll)
I simply can't bring myself to kill that rabbit. Let's eat something else.

Herz • sich ein Herz fassen
to pluck up courage, to take one's courage in both hands (coll)
He took his courage in both hands and volunteered for the dangerous task.

Herz • jmd ans Herz gewachsen sein
to be near/dear to sbd's heart (coll)
This project is particularly dear to my heart because I know several of the people involved.

Herz • das Herz lacht einem im Leibe
one's heart leaps, one's heart gives a leap
Your heart will leap when you see Mary and Paul, they are really so happy together.

Herz • jmd etwas ans Herz legen
to impress sth on sbd, to bring sth home to sbd, to knock/drum sth into sbd's head (coll)
I tried to drum the dangers of the position into their heads but they didn't listen.

Herz • jmd/etwas auf Herz und Nieren prüfen
to put sbd/sth through his/her/its paces
We put the new computer programmme through its paces.

Herz • ein Herz und eine Seele
soulmates (coll)
They hadn't seen each other for years, but now they are soulmates.

Herz • sein Herz verlieren
to lose one's heart to sbd (coll)
It's not easy to realise that you've lost your heart to the wrong person.

Herzdrücken • nicht an Herzdrücken sterben ▷ Herzen: aus seinem Herzen keine Mördergrube machen

Herzen • mit dem Herzen dabei sein
to put one's heart into sth (coll)
His heart really isn't in his career.

Herzen • etwas auf dem Herzen haben
to have sth on one's mind (coll); Gewissensbisse: to have sth on one's conscience
I wish he had told me what he had on his mind – I might have been able to help.

Herzen • aus seinem Herzen keine Mördergrube machen
not to mince one's words
I did not mince my words, and I told her exactly what I thought of her dirty tricks.

Herzen • sich etwas zu Herzen nehmen
to take sth to heart (coll)
He takes the loss of his girlfriends very much to heart, every week.

Herzenslust • nach Herzenslust
to one's heart's content
You can watch tennis to your heart's content during Wimbledon fortnight.

Heulen • mit Heulen und Zähneklappern
with fear and trembling (bibl)
He confessed with fear and trembling that he was the father of the child.

Hexenjagd • Hexenjagd veranstalten
to have a witchhunt, to organize a witchhunt
The newspapers organized a tremendous witchhunt after the bribery scandal.

hieb • hieb- und stichfest sein
rock solid
His alibi is rock solid, and cannot be shaken.

Himmel • Das stinkt zum Himmel!
to cry to heaven
This monstrous atrocity cries to heaven for vengeance.

Himmel • Ach du lieber Himmel!
Good Lord! / Good Heavens! / Heaven! / Good Gracious! (dated) / My Goodness! (dated)! / My goodness gracious me! (dated) / Good God! / Good God Almighty! / Bless me! (dated) / Bless my soul! (dated) / Blow me (down with a feather)! / Blow me tight! / Strike me pink! / Blimey! / Cor Blimey! / My (only) sainted aunt! (dated) / Hell! / Bloody Hell! (vulg) / Fuck me! (vulg) / Fuck me sideways! (vulg) / Holy fuck! (vulg) / Holy shit! (vulg)

Himmel • jmd den Himmel auf Erden versprechen
to promise sbd the moon (coll), to promise sbd heaven on earth
As soon as the campaign begins the politicians will start promising everybody the moon.

Himmel • jmd in den Himmel heben
to sing sbd's praises, to praise sbd to the skies (coll)
Of course today nobody has a good word to say for him, but yesterday they were praising him to the skies.

Himmel • im siebenten Himmel sein
to be in the seventh heaven (bibl)
When she agreed to marry him he was in the seventh heaven.

Himmel • Himmel und Hölle in Bewegung setzen ▷ Hebel

Himmel • Um Himmels willen!
For heaven's sake! / For Goodness' sake! / For God's sake! / For Pete's sake! / For the love of Mike! / For fuck's sake! (vulg)

Himmeldonnerwetter
God damn!

Himmelfahrtskommando
suicide mission
You must be crazy to take part in a suicide mission like that!

Himmelfahrtsnase
a turned-up nose, a snub nose
My sister has a very turned-up nose – very pretty, especially from sideways on.

hin • hin- und hergerissen sein
to be torn
I'm really torn. I simply can't decide which of the two shirts I should wear.

hinten • jmd hintenan stellen
to be an also-ran (coll)
In her company she was an also-ran and never given a real chance of promotion.

hinten • nach hinten losgehen
to backfire (coll)
Their plan backfired and they were arrested and shot.

hinten • jmd hinten und vorn(e) bedienen
to wait on sbd hand and foot
My brother is so lazy. He expects everybody to wait on him hand and foot.

hinten • es jmd hinten und vorn reinstecken
to spoon-feed (coll)
Young people these days are spoon-fed so much that some of them hardly appreciate the value of anything.

Hinterhand • etwas in der Hinterhand haben
to have another shot in one's locker (coll), to have sth up one's sleeve (coll)
He is a tough cookie and you can never be sure that he hasn't got another shot in his locker.

Hintern • Ich könnte mich in den Hintern beißen!
I could kick myself!

Hintern • jmd in den Hintern kriechen ▷ Arschkriecher

Hintertreffen • ins Hintertreffen geraten
to get left behind, to get behindhand
If a lawyer does not read the daily law report he will soon find that he has got behindhand with the latest legal decisions.

Hintertürchen • sich ein Hintertürchen offenhalten
to leave oneself a loop-hole (coll), to leave oneself a way out (coll), to leave oneself a line of retreat, to find / exploit a loop-hole
He more or less committed himself but left himself a loop-hole, saying he would have to talk to his boss about it first.

Hinz • Hinz und Kunz
every Tom, Dick and Harry (coll), all and sundry (coll)
I don't want to have this project spoilt by letting every Tom, Dick and Harry stick his nose in.

Hiobsbotschaft • eine Hiobsbotschaft bringen
to be a bringer of bad news / tidings
I don't like to be a bringer of bad news, but the fridge has broken down again.

Hirn • sich das Hirn zermartern
to rack one's brains (coll)
I've been racking my brains for hours trying to think of a solution.

Hitze • in der Hitze des Gefechts
in the heat of the battle
The soldiers forgot their orders in the heat of the battle.

hochkommen • Wenn es hochkommt, ist es hundert Mark wert.
at (the) best, at (the) most, at the very best, at the very most, at the outside (coll), top whack (coll)
It's worth a hundred marks, top whack.

hochleben • jmd hochleben lassen
to give sbd three cheers
We gave the footballers three cheers after they came in from the field.

Hochmut • Hochmut kommt vor dem Fall. (prov)
Pride goeth before a fall. (bibl. prov)

hochnäsig sein
to give oneself airs, to be stuck-up (coll), to be snooty (coll)

I don't like her because she gives herself airs and thinks she can do everything better than I can.

Hochzeiten • auf zwei Hochzeiten tanzen
to be in two places at once (you normally resent having to be)
They want me to work in the accounts department and in the registry, but I can't be in two places at once.

Hof • jmd den Hof machen
to court sbd
In the past you had to court the girl you wanted to marry for quite a while before you could propose to her.

Hoffnung • guter Hoffnung sein
to be PG (coll), to be in the club (coll), to be in the family way (coll) (dated), to have a bun in the oven (coll) (dated), to be expecting a little stranger (coll)
Sandra is in the club again. This'll be her fifth.

Höhe • Das ist die Höhe!
That's the limit! / That caps the lot! / That takes the biscuit!

Höhe • auf der Höhe der Zeit sein
(the) state of the art, to keep abreast of new developments
Even experts find it hard to keep up with the state of the art in computer technology.

Höhe • nicht auf der Höhe sein
to feel lousy (coll), to feel (a bit) yuck (coll), to feel yucky (coll), to feel off-colour (coll), to feel under the weather (coll), not to feel oneself, not to feel a hundred per cent (coll)
I've got a cold and I feel a bit yucky.

Höhle • sich in die Höhle des Löwen begeben
to go into the lion's den
Well, now I have to go and see the managing director. Who is coming with me into the lion's den?

Hölle

Hölle • jmd die Hölle heiß machen
to give sbd hell (coll)
He's giving us hell because he wants his money back from us.

holterdiepolter
helter-skelter (coll)
The children ran helter-skelter down the beach into the sea.

Holz • aus einem Holz geschnitzt sein
to be cast in the same mould; to be tarred with the same brush (coll)
(<u>nur im schlechten Sinne</u>)
He was jailed for drugs dealing and I'm very much afraid that his brother is tarred with the same brush.

Holz • auf Holz klopfen
to touch wood, (<u>fast nur als Imperativ:</u>) Touch wood!
I have had perfect health for years – touch wood!

Holzweg ▷ auf dem falschen Dampfer sein

Honig • Das ist kein Honigschlecken.
not to be a bed of roses (coll), to be no doddle (coll)
Working together with him is really no doddle, he's a slave-driver.

Honigkuchenpferd • wie ein Honigkuchenpferd strahlen
to beam from ear to ear, to grin from ear to ear, to grin like a Cheshire cat (Lewis Carroll)
After he heard he had won the prize he went off grinning from ear to ear.

Hopfen • Da ist Hopfen und Malz verloren.
He is a hopeless case.

Hören • Da vergeht einem Hören und Sehen!
<u>beim Erstaunen:</u> *It's enough to take your breath away! / It takes your breath away!*
<u>beim Verwirren:</u> *It makes your head swim! / It makes your head go round and round!*

hören • Wer nicht hören will, muß fühlen. (prov)
to have to learn the hard way
You will have to learn the hard way – since you haven't done your homework yet, I won't let you go to the disco.

Horizont • Das geht über meinen Horizont.
It's beyond me. / It's out of my range.
It's Greek to me. (Shakespeare: Julius Caesar)

Horn • ins gleiche Horn blasen
to take the same line / view / attitude, to sing the same tune (coll)
Every party in the coalition has been singing the same tune for so long it's now very difficult to tell them apart.

Hörner • sich die Hörner abstoßen
to sow one's wild oats (coll)
He sowed his wild oats before his marriage, and now he is a most respectable husband.

Hörner • Sie setzt ihrem Ehemann Hörner auf.
to cuckold
She has been cuckolding her husband for years and he still doesn't know.

Hosen • die Hosen anhaben
to wear the trousers (coll)
His wife wears the trousers in that family.

Hosenboden • sich auf den Hosenboden setzen
to settle down to work, to buckle down to work (coll), to get down to work (coll)
My daughter decided to settle down to work at last and managed to pass the exam.

hü • Der eine sagt hü, der andere sagt hott.
to be just contrary
Whatever you ask them, they are just contrary.

huckepack • jmd huckepack tragen
to carry sbd piggy-back (coll), to give sbd a piggy-back (coll)
I am absolutely exhausted. I have been giving the children piggy-backs all day.

Hüfte • nicht aus der Hüfte kommen
not to get going (coll), not to get a move on
If you don't get going soon, we'll not manage to finish the job in time!

Huhn • wie ein gerupftes Huhn aussehen
to look as if one has been through a hedge backwards (coll)
Her new haircut is awful, she looks as if she's been through a hedge backwards.

Huhn • Ein blindes Huhn findet auch einmal ein Korn. (prov)
Every dog has his day. (Kingsley)

Huhn • das Huhn schlachten, das die goldenen Eier legt
to kill the goose that lays the golden eggs (coll)
In demanding large wage rises the workers soon found that they had killed the goose that laid the golden eggs as company after company went into liquidation.

Hühnchen • mit jmd noch ein Hühnchen zu rupfen haben
to have a bone to pick with sbd (coll)
Hey, I've got a bone to pick with you! Why didn't you turn up last week? I waited for an hour and a half.

Hühner • Da lachen ja die Hühner!
It's enough to make a cat laugh!

Hühner • mit den Hühnern aufstehen ▷ Hahnenschrei

Hülle • in Hülle und Fülle
heaps / masses / stacks of…(coll), … galore (coll), … in abundance, … in spades (coll)
We've got actors and actresses in spades, but we are still looking for a really capable stage manager.

Hund • bekannt sein wie ein bunter Hund
to be known far and wide, to be known all over (coll), to have a bit of a reputation
Everybody's heard of him; he's known all over.

Hund • Da liegt der Hund begraben! ▷ das ist der Haken

Hund • auf den Hund gekommen sein
to have gone down the drain (coll), to go to the dogs (coll), to have gone down the tubes (coll), to go to pot (coll)
Since his wife left him, his health has gone down the tubes.

Hund • ein krummer Hund sein
to be a crook (coll), to be bent (coll)
Don't trust him, he's a crook!

Hund • wie Hund und Katze sein
to be at it like cats and dogs (coll), to be at each other's throat
The children in that class quarrel about everything. They are at it like cats and dogs from the moment they arrive till home time.

Hunde • Hunde, die bellen, beißen nicht. (prov)
His bark is worse than his bite.

Hunde • vor die Hunde gehen
to be sent to the slaughter
In the First World War thousands of young men were sent uselessly to the slaughter.

Hunde • Das ist ja zum Junge-Hunde-Kriegen!
It's enough to drive you round the bend.
It's enough to drive you to distraction.

Hunde • keine schlafenden Hunde wecken
Let sleeping dogs lie. (prov)

hundemüde sein
to be dog-tired (coll), to be knackered (coll), to be bushed (coll), to be all in (coll)
I can't go out with you tonight, I'm dog-tired and only want to sleep.

Hundert • vom Hundertsten ins Tausendste kommen ▷ lang

Hungertuch • am Hungertuche nagen
to be unable to keep the wolf from the door (coll)
I have my income from my American investments and I earn a bit with my articles for the newspapers, and that is enough to keep the wolf from the door.

Hut • unter einen Hut bringen
to bring sbd/sth under one roof
British political parties are broad churches which attempt to bring a wide variety of opinions under one roof.

Hut • den Hut herumgehen lassen
to pass the hat (coll)
After the stranger had sung some songs in the inn, he passed the hat.

Hut • Da geht einem der Hut hoch!
It gets up my nostrils./It gets up my nose./It gets on my wick./It puts my back up./It drives me mad./It makes me see red.

Hut • seinen Hut nehmen müssen ▷ die Papiere bekommen

Hut • auf der Hut sein
to be on the alert, to be on one's guard, to be sur le qui vive (coll), on the qui vive (coll)
We have got to be on the qui vive with people like that. You never know what they are after.

Hut • Das kannst du dir an den Hut stecken!
You can stick that up your backside/arse/cunt (vulg)!

Hut • den Hut vor jmd ziehen
to take one's hat off to someone (coll)
I take my hat off to those who died in the fight for freedom.

Hutschnur • über die Hutschnur gehen
to overstep the mark, to go over the limit (coll), to be beyond a joke (coll)
He really overstepped the mark with his remark about my new haircut and I threw him out.

I

I • I bewahre!
Not a bit of it!/Not in the least!

ich • sein zweites Ich
his alter ego
My sister is my alter ego. She always understands exactly what I want without my having to explain at all.

ich • ein Ich-Mensch sein
to be an egotist, to only care about No. 1
He never shares anything with anybody but expects others to share with him. He is a complete egotist.

Idee • eine fixe Idee
(to have) a dream, (to build) a castle/castles in Spain (coll)
He thinks of paying off his debts and getting a sensible job, but he is simply building castles in Spain: he has no money and no-one will ever employ him again.

idiotensicher
fool-proof
It is so simple that it is foolproof – no-one could muck it up.

in • in sich gehen
to think long and hard, to think long and deeply
I thought long and hard over what he had to say, but in the end I decided against his proposal.

in • es in sich haben
to be harder than it looks, to be not so easy
<u>Problem/Aufgabe:</u> to be a pretty problem (coll)
This is a pretty problem! I don't see the answer to it at the moment.
<u>Vertrag:</u> to have a catch in it ▷ Haken
<u>Geschichte:</u> to have a sting to it (coll)
This story had a sting to it, and I was left feeling quite uncomfortable.

Getränk: to have a kick in it (coll)
His cocktails have quite a kick in them. You ought to start going slow after the first one.

Innerste • bis ins Innerste getroffen sein
to be cut to the quick
His remark about my daughter cut me to the quick.

Intimus • ein Intimus von jmd sein ▷ Busenfreund

Irren • Irren ist menschlich. (prov)
To err is human. (prov)

J

ja • ein Ja-Sager sein
to be a yes-man (coll)
The boss is surrounded by yes-men, and none of them is prepared to say what he really thinks.

ja • ja und amen zu etwas sagen ▷ seinen Segen zu etwas geben

Jacke • Die Jacke ziehe ich mir nicht an.
I'm not putting my hands up to that.
I'm not taking/admitting responsibility for that.
That is not down to me.

Jacke • das ist Jacke wie Hose ▷ das ist gehupft wie gesprungen

Jahre • alle Jahre wieder
year in, year out (coll)
Year in, year out, Uncle George came to stay for Christmas.

Jammerlappen • ein Jammerlappen sein
to be a cry-baby (coll) (wenn es zum Weinen kommt), to be a wimp (coll), to be a sissy (coll)

Jeder • Jeder ist sich selbst der Nächste.
Look after Number One. / Every man for himself!

Jordan • über den Jordan gehen
to vanish into thin air (for ever), to go West (coll)
That's what happens when you tidy up – half my papers vanish into thin air and I never see them again.

Jubeljahr • alle Jubeljahre (einmal)
once in a blue moon (coll), once in a month of Sundays (coll), once every million years (coll)
I've no idea how he is – I only see him about once every million years.

jucken • Das juckt mich gar nicht ▷ kratzen

Judas • ein Judas sein
to be a Judas (coll)
He is an absolute Judas – he has betrayed us completely.

Judaslohn • Judaslohn (bekommen)
(to get one's) thirty pieces of silver / blood money
After betraying his friends, he duly got his thirty pieces of silver.

Jugend • Jugend hat keine Tugend. (prov)
Boys will be boys. (prov)

jung • Jung gewohnt, alt getan. (prov)
Once learnt, never forgotten. (prov)

Jux • sich einen Jux aus etwas machen ▷ aus lauter Jux und Tollerei

Jux • aus lauter Jux und Tollerei
just for a joke / jape (coll), just for fun (coll)
Just for fun the students painted their faces red for the examinations.

jwd
in the sticks, North of Watford (<u>nur in London</u>) ▷ auch Buxtehude

K

Kacke • die Kacke ist am Dampfen
the shit is going to hit the fan (vulg)
The boss has just found out about the missing money, and now the shit is going to hit the fan.

Kaff
a dump (coll), a tip (coll) (<u>beziehen sich auch auf Kneipen, Bars usw.</u>)
She asked me what the hell you can do in the evenings in a dump like Klosterborn.

Kaffee • Das ist doch kalter Kaffee!
That is old hat. (coll)
Queen Anne's dead. (<u>Eine Nachricht, die man sehr lange erwartete.</u>)

Kaffee • Dem hat man wohl 'was in den Kaffee getan!
He must be joking! / He must be kidding! / He must be having you/me/them (usw.) on!

Käfig • im goldenen Käfig sitzen
to sit in a gilded cage
His wife is delightful, but she sits surrounded by his wealth like a bird in a gilded cage and doesn't feel she can do anything for herself.

Kainszeichen • das Kainszeichen tragen
to bear the mark of Cain (bibl), to be branded (as a ...), to carry the stigma of being a ...
He returned home after the Civil War, still bearing the mark of Cain.

Kaiser • sich um des Kaisers Bart streiten
to argue / quarrel about nothing (coll)
They are quarrelling about nothing, because there's not the slightest chance of their project getting off the ground.

Kaiser • Wo nichts ist, hat der Kaiser sein Recht verloren. (prov)
You can't get blood out of a stone.

Kaiser • Gebet dem Kaiser, was des Kaisers, und Gott, was Gottes ist. (prov)
Render unto Caesar what is Caesar's and unto God what is God's. (bibl)

Kaiser • Der/Er kommt sich vor wie der Kaiser von China.
He thinks he's really something./He thinks he's God./He thinks he's the cat's whiskers

Kaiser • wo der Kaiser zu Fuß hingeht
the privy (dated), the little boys'/girls' room (coll), the loo (coll), the bog (vulg), the bathroom (U.S.), the washroom (U.S.)
He spent an hour in the privy, reading the newspaper.

Kakao • jmd durch den Kakao ziehen
to tease sbd, to take the mickey out of sbd (coll), to take the piss out of sbd (vulg)
Everybody in the office told him what a wonderful help he was and how useful he had been, and he never saw they were only teasing him.

Kaliber • von gleichem Kaliber sein
to be cast in the same mould as sbd
He is cast in the same mould as his brother. They have very similar characters. For example, they are both very honest and both very stubborn.

kaltstellen • jmd kaltstellen ▷ Abstellgleis

Kamel • Du Kamel! ▷ Dummkopf

Kamellen • Das sind doch olle Kamellen!
That's old news!/That's nothing new!

Kamm • jmd ist der Kamm geschwollen
sbd's head has swollen, sbd has become/got (coll) very/all(coll) cocky/important (coll iron)
He's got all important since they elected him deputy supreme vice button pusher.

Kamm • nicht alles über einen Kamm scheren
to treat every case on its merits, to go on a case by case basis, not to generalize
Applications for political asylum are treated on a case by case basis.

Kampfhahn • ein Kampfhahn sein
to be a fighter (coll), to fight like an alley cat (coll), to be a fighting cock (coll)
The Leader of the Opposition is a fighter, and he won't give up until the returns have been counted, whatever the opinion polls say.

Kandare • jmd fest an die Kandare nehmen
to take sbd in hand
It is the sergeant's job to take the new recruits in hand.

Kaninchen • sich vermehren wie die Kaninchen
to breed like rabbits (coll)
Another baby? – Your cousins breed like rabbits!

Kanone • Das ist unter aller Kanone!
That is beneath contempt. / That's rather bad taste.

Kanonen • mit Kanonen auf Spatzen schießen
to use a sledge-hammer to crack a nut (coll), to go over the top (coll)
In calling out the army to deal with the rioting schoolchildren the authorities were using a sledge-hammer to crack a nut.

Kanonenfutter sein
to be cannon-fodder (coll)
Ill-trained infantry is good only as cannon-fodder.

Kanonenrohr • Heiliges Kanonenrohr!
Good grief!

Kantonist • ein unsicherer Kantonist sein
to be the nigger in the wood-pile (coll) (dated), to be the rotten apple (coll), to be the weak link (coll)
The rotten apple turned out to be one of the clerks, who admitted giving secret information to the newspapers.

Kapee • schwer von Kapee sein
to be slow on the uptake (coll), to be slow to cotton on (coll), to be thick-witted (coll), to be dim (coll), to be a dunce (coll), to be thick
It took me four hours to explain the rules of cricket to them, they were so slow on the uptake.

Kapitel • ein dunkles Kapitel
a dark chapter
The period of my divorce will always stay in my mind as a dark chapter in my life.

Kapitel • ein Kapitel für sich sein
to be a story in itself (coll), but that's another story
The tale of their final escape into safe territory would be a story in itself.

kapitelfest • kapitelfest sein ▷ beschlagen sein

Kappe • etwas auf seine Kappe nehmen
to take sth on one's own shoulders (coll), to answer for sth
If you carry out the orders I'll answer for having issued them.

Kappes • Kappes reden ▷ Quatsch

Karren • den Karren aus dem Dreck ziehen
to clean up the mess (coll), to put things straight (coll), to get things back on the rails (coll)
After my holiday it took me a couple of weeks to clean up the mess. My deputy had made every possible mistake while I had been away.

Karren • Wie man den Karren schmiert, so läuft er. (prov) ▷ betten

Karte • alles auf eine Karte setzen
to put all one's eggs in one basket (coll), to stake everything on one card (coll)
We have to succeed today because we have put all our eggs in one basket.

Karten • sich nicht in die Karten schauen lassen
not to show one's hand (coll), to play one's hand close to one's chest (coll)

He plays his hand so close to his chest I often don't know what it is he's trying to achieve.

Karten • seine Karten auf den Tisch legen
to put one's cards on the table (coll), to come clean (coll), to level (with sbd), to come into the open (coll)
I'll put my cards on the table and tell you exactly what I have in mind.

Kartenhaus • zusammenstürzen wie ein Kartenhaus
to collapse like a house of cards
The financial structure is like a house of cards – if one unexpected bill comes in the whole thing will collapse.

Kartoffeln • rin in die Kartoffeln, raus aus'n Kartoffeln
first one thing then another (coll), chopping and changing (coll)
It would be easier to work for this company if one knew what the management wanted for more than a week at a time, but they are constantly chopping and changing.

Käseblatt
rag (coll), scandal sheet (coll)
That newspaper once had pretentions to being a serious journal but it's nothing but a scandal sheet now – sport and sex.

käseweiß ▷ kreidebleich

Kasse • da klingelt die Kasse
The money is rolling in.

Kasse • jmd zur Kasse bitten
to ask sbd to pay up (coll), to ask sbd to shell out (coll), to ask sbd to fork out (coll)
Once the government has got its expensive social security system on the statute book the taxpayer will be asked to pay up to finance it.

Kasse • getrennte Kasse machen
to go Dutch
I can't afford to take you all out to dinner – we shall have to go Dutch.

Kasse • gut bei Kasse sein
to be rolling (coll), to be in funds (coll), to have the readies (coll)
Someone's got to pay for the next round. Who's got the readies?

Kasse • schlecht bei Kasse sein
to be hard up (coll), to be short of the readies (coll), to be on one's uppers
I'm sorry I can't come to the pub with you – I haven't got the readies.

Kastanien • für jmd die Kastanien aus dem Feuer holen
to pull sbd's chestnuts out of the fire (coll)
Fantasia disarmed and enjoyed the moral superiority of pacifism, confident that, if necessary, their well-armed allies would pull their chestnuts out of the fire for them.

Katze • für die Katz
There's no point! / It's pointless! / It's a waste of time!

Katze • Das trägt die Katze auf dem Schwanze weg.
That's nothing to write home about. (coll) / That's chicken feed. (coll) / That's peanuts. (coll)

Katze • Wenn die Katze aus dem Haus ist, tanzen die Mäuse auf dem Tisch. (prov)
When the cat's away, the mice will play. (prov)

Katze • die Katze aus dem Sack lassen
to let the cat out of the bag (coll), to spill the beans (coll), to give the game away (coll)
He gave the game away about our Christmas surprise for the children.

Katze • nicht die Katze im Sack kaufen (wollen)
not to buy a pig in a poke (coll)
We have to show the people what we're offering because nobody is buying a pig in a poke nowadays.

Katze • Die Katze läßt das Mausen nicht. (prov)
The leopard can't change his spots. (prov)

Katze

Katze • eine falsche Katze sein
to be two-faced (coll), to be double-dealing (coll)
My last girlfriend was a two-faced bitch. She was going out with my best friend at the same time.

Katze • wie die Katze um den heißen Brei herumschleichen
to pussyfoot, to beat about the bush
Stop pussyfooting around and say what you want.
Stop beating about the bush and tell me if I've won the price.

Katze • mit jmd Katz und Maus spielen
to play cat-and-mouse with sbd (coll), to give sbd the runaround (coll)
The lawyers on the other side are playing cat-and-mouse with us to try and get us to reduce our claim.

Katzensprung • Das ist ein Katzensprung von hier.
That is a stone's throw from here.

Kauderwelsch
gibberish (coll), double-Dutch (coll)
I cannot understand the instructions for my new computer. They are gibberish to me.

kauen • an etwas zu kauen haben
to have sth to think about (coll), one has not got over sth, to be still reeling after sth, sth keeps playing on one's mind
She has not got over that bad mark in Chemistry.
MIND FF: to chew sth over: noch einmal über etwas nachdenken / durch den Kopf gehen lassen

Kauz • ein komischer Kauz sein
weirdo, strange customer

Kehle • sich die Kehle aus dem Hals schreien
to yell / shout / scream one's head off (coll)
At the front of the meeting some politician was yelling his head off, and at the back sensible people were playing cards.
MIND FF: to shoot off one's mouth: dummes Zeug reden

Kehle • etwas in die falsche Kehle bekommen ▷ Hals: etwas in den falschen Hals bekommen

Kehrseite • die Kehrseite der Medaille
the other side of the coin (coll)
The other side of the coin is that even if taxes go up there may be an increase in net income.

Keil • einen Keil zwischen zwei Personen treiben
to drive a wedge between two people
We had to drive a wedge between the officials of the branch office and those of the area directorate before we could get anything done. It was a pity, because a lot of them had been good friends.

Keile • Keile kriegen
to get a good hiding (coll), to get a good thrashing (coll)
The boy got a good hiding from his angry father.

Keim • etwas im Keim ersticken
to nip sth in the bud
The rumour was nipped in the bud because all the interested parties denied the story.

Kelch • den Kelch bis zur bitteren Neige leeren
to drain / drink the bitter cup, to drain / drink the cup of suffering to the dregs (bibl)
Franz Josef of Austria experienced repeated defeat in war and the deaths of almost all his relatives, his wife, his son, his brother, and his nephew, forced him to drink the cup of suffering to the dregs.

Kelch • Der Kelch ist an mir noch einmal vorübergegangen.
I escaped that time. That one didn't have my number on it.

Kerbe • in die gleiche Kerbe hauen
to have the same aim / end in view, to have the same thought in mind (coll)
We both have the same end in view, but we are going at it from different directions.

Kerbholz • etwas auf dem Kerbholz haben
<u>wenn man schon einmal verurteilt worden ist:</u> to have form (coll), to have previous (coll)

The defendant received a heavy sentence for the shoplifting offence because he had a lot of form.

Kern • einen guten Kern in einer rauhen Schale haben
sbd's bark is worse than their bite (coll), to have a rough exterior concealing a heart of gold (coll), to have a heart of gold under a rough exterior
The judge had been very sharp in his remarks during the trial, but when he came to sentence the defendants it was clear that his bark was worse than his bite.

Kieker • jmd auf dem Kieker haben
to be in sbd's bad books (coll), to have got one's eye on sbd,
He's got it in for me. I daren't go near him.
I am really in his bad books and I have to watch my step.

Kies • Kies haben ▷ Kohle haben

Kind • das Kind beim Namen nennen
to call a spade a spade (coll), to be perfectly frank
I called a spade a spade and told him he had not been behaving honestly.

Kind • das Kind im Manne
All men are boys at heart.

Kind • sich bei jmd lieb Kind machen wollen
to pander to, to soft soap (coll), to truckle to
He isn't interested in working hard, just in pandering to the boss so that he gets that promotion.

Kind • das Kind mit dem Bade ausschütten
to throw the baby out with the bath water (coll), not to separate the wheat from the chaff (coll)
When he sacked the entire staff he was throwing the baby out with the bath water, because there is absolutely no-one left who is able to run our Frankfurt office.

Kind • Gebranntes Kind scheut das Feuer. (prov)
Once bitten, twice shy. (prov)

Kind • Wir werden das Kind schon schaukeln.
We'll soon have all that sorted (out).
We'll manage.

Kind • mit Kind und Kegel
me and mine / you and yours / he and his / she and hers / they and theirs
We set off on holiday with everything but the kitchen sink.
I am giving you notice to quit: you and yours must be out of this flat by the end of next month.

Kind • kein Kind von Traurigkeit sein
to be a jolly chap (coll) (dated), to be a cheerful character (coll) (dated), to be of a sunny disposition
The new clerk is a very jolly chap – he never seems to be depressed about anything.

Kindermund • Kindermund tut Wahrheit kund. (prov)
Out of the mouths of very babes and sucklings. (prov)

Kinderschuhe • noch in den Kinderschuhen stecken
to be still in the early stages, to be in embryo, to be still in diapers (U.S.) (coll)
The new project is still in the early stages and I don't think we can expect a return on our investment for some time yet.

Kinderstube • (k)eine gute Kinderstube gehabt haben
(not) to have been well brought up
It's perfectly clear that he is pleasant enough, but he has been badly brought up, so he keeps offending people unintentionally.

Kippe • etwas steht auf der Kippe
to hanging by a thread (coll), to be in the balance, to be on a knife edge (coll)
The patient's survival has been in the balance since the last operation.

Kirche • die Kirche im Dorf lassen
to draw the line somewhere (coll)
We can let the children drink and smoke if they must, but I'm not having them take drugs – you have to draw the line somewhere.

Kirchenmaus • arm wie eine Kirchenmaus sein
to be as poor as a church mouse
I visited him the other day, and found he has hardly any furniture in his rooms. He must be as poor as a church mouse.

Kirschen • mit jmd ist nicht gut Kirschen essen
to be an unclubbable person (dated)
He is very unclubbable, I'm afraid – and I don't feel like asking him to dinner.

klammheimlich • klammheimlich verschwinden ▷ französisch

Klapperstorch • vom Klapperstorch gebissen worden sein ▷ guter Hoffnung sein

Klapperstorch • an den Klapperstorch glauben
to believe in fairies (coll)
He is twelve and he still believes in fairies!

Klartext • Klartext mit jmd reden ▷ auf deutsch gesagt

Klasse • Das ist große Klasse!
That is fantastic!

Klatsch • Klatsch und Tratsch
tittle tattle (coll), chitchat (coll), gossip (coll), tit-bits (coll), scuttlebutt (U.S.) (coll)
The women's magazines are full of chitchat about the Royal Family.

Klatschweib • ein altes Klatschweib sein / eine Klatschtante sein
a gossip, gossipmonger (coll), scandal merchant (coll)
She is a dreadful gossip – if something has happened to any of her neighbours the whole street knows about it before the day is out.

Klee • jmd/etwas über den grünen Klee loben ▷ Himmel: jmd in den Himmel heben

klein • klein aber mein
A small thing, but mine own. (Shakespeare)

klein • klein beigeben
to give way, to climb down (coll), to give in (coll)
We offered them forty; they demanded sixty. But after a long argument they climbed down.

Kleinholz • aus jmd Kleinholz machen
to make mincemeat of s.o.

Kleinvieh • Kleinvieh macht auch Mist. (prov)
It mounts up. / Where there's muck, there's brass.
If you look after the pennies, the pounds will look after themselves.

Klemme • in der Klemme sein / sitzen
to be in a spot (coll), to be in a fix (coll), to be in a tight corner (coll), to be in a jam (coll), to be up a gum-tree (coll), to be in the shit (vulg), to be in deep shit (vulg), to be up shit creek (without a paddle) (vulg)
If we can't get help we shall be up shit creek without a paddle.

Klette • sich wie eine Klette an jmd hängen / eine Klette sein
to stick to sbd like glue / a limpet (coll)
My daughter's new boyfriend sticks to her like a limpet and doesn't give her any time on her own at all.

Klinge • jmd über die Klinge springen lassen
to send sbd to his doom, to send to the slaughter
Hundreds of thousands were sent to their doom on the Western Front.

klingeln • Jetzt hat's geklingelt! ▷ Groschen

Klinke • sich die Klinke in die Hand geben
I've had a lot of guests today, coming in one after the other.
People have been streaming in.
The doorbell hasn't stopped ringing all day.

Klinken • Klinken putzen
to go in search of work
He has been going around town in search of work for months now.

klipp • klipp und klar sagen
to be quite frank, to be clear about sth, to tell sbd bluntly, to tell sbd straight (coll)
Let's be clear about it!
They told him straight that they wouldn't do it.

Kloß • einen Kloß im Hals haben ▷ Frosch

Kloßbrühe • klar wie Kloßbrühe sein ▷ Finger: etwas an allen fünf Fingern abzählen können

Klotz • jmd ein Klotz am Bein sein
to be a millstone round sbd's neck
The present organisation is a millstone round our neck. We shall have to get rid of it and start from scratch if we want to get anything done.

Klotz • ein ungehobelter Klotz sein
to be a thug (coll), to be a rough diamond (coll)
He is a complete thug, who has never been taught any manners.

klug • Der Klügere gibt nach. (prov)
Discretion is the better part of valour. (prov)

Klugscheißer • ein Klugscheißer sein
a know-all (coll)
He is an insufferable know-all. He was lecturing me about German literature today – yesterday it was about the interior of the sun and tomorrow it will probably be Chinese porcelain.

Knie • etwas (nicht) übers Knie brechen
not to make an instant decision about sth
I'm not prepared to make an instant decision – I need time to think about it. / I want to sleep on it.

Knie • seine Knie waren wie Wachs
his knees turned to jelly (coll)
When he heard that the headmaster wanted to speak to him his knees turned to jelly.

Knie • jmd auf Knien danken ▷ Füße: jmd die Füße küssen

Knie • jmd übers Knie legen
to put sbd over one's knee
He put his younger brother over his knee and spanked him.

Kniff • den Kniff bei etwas heraushaben
to have got the hang / knack of sth (coll)
I'll just see how you get on with this machine until I know you've got the hang of it.

Knirps • ein Knirps sein ▷ Dreikäsehoch

knochentrocken
to be bone dry (coll), to be as dry as a bone (coll)
The wind off the desert is as dry as a bone.

Knöpfe • etwas an den Knöpfen abzählen
to let fortune decide, to leave sth to fate
I decided to leave to fate whether or not I would ever see the girl again.

Knoten • einen Knoten ins Taschentuch machen
to tie a knot in one's handkerchief (in G.B. nicht im übertragenen Sinne, sondern praktisch umgesetzt)
I tied a knot in my handkerchief to remind myself to buy some fish.

Knoten • Der Knoten ist bei ihm / ihr noch nicht geplatzt
He is not quite there yet. / She's a late developer.

Knüppel • jmd einen Knüppel zwischen die Beine werfen
to put a spoke in sbd's wheel (coll)
I put a spoke in his wheel by telling the boss how he had made a mess of the deal with XYZ Co.

Knute • unter der Knute von jmd stehen ▷ Fuchtel

Knute • die Knute zu spüren bekommen
to feel the knout (coll)
As soon as the new managers had taken charge they made the workforce feel the knout by cutting down on holidays and extra allowances.

Köche • Viele Köche verderben den Brei. (prov)
Too many cooks spoil the broth. (prov)

Koffer • aus dem Koffer leben
to live out of a suitcase (coll)
After several weeks travelling through Europe I got tired of living out of a suitcase.

Koffer • die Koffer packen
to pack one's bags (coll)
After yet another violent quarrel his girlfriend packed her bags and left him.

Kohl • Das macht den Kohl nicht fett.
That won't help you much. / That won't get you very far. / You won't get very far on that.

Kohldampf • Kohldampf schieben
to live off scraps (coll)
In the years immediately after the war most of the population of Germany had to live off scraps.
<u>Kohldampf haben:</u> to be very hungry
I could eat a horse! / I'm famished!

Kohle • (keine) Kohle haben
to be skint (coll)
I can't come to the pub with you, because I'm completely skint.

Kohlen • feurige Kohlen auf jmds Haupt sammeln
to heap burning coals / coals of fire on sbd's head (bibl)
By accepting his rival's insults without complaint and remaining invariably polite and good-natured he heaped burning coals on the other's head.

Kohlen • wie auf (glühenden) Kohlen sitzen
to be like a cat on hot bricks / on a hot tin roof (coll), to sit as if on burning coals
When they asked the accountant where all the money had gone he sat as if on burning coals.

Koks • wie Graf Koks (von der Gasanstalt) auftreten
to behave like one of the nouveau riche (Fr)
He turned up driving a flashy car, with an expensive-looking woman, behaving altogether like one of the nouveau riche.

kommen • komme, was da wolle
come what may
I will stand by you, come what may.

Komödie • jmd eine Komödie vorspielen
to pretend to be sth, to act sth
He came in here acting sick, but I wasn't fooled. I sent him straight back to work.

König • der König der Lüfte
the eagle

König • der König der Tiere
the King of Beasts (lion)

Kopf • jmd raucht der Kopf
s.o.'s head is in a whirl (coll) / is buzzing (coll) / is going round and round (coll)
The children had so much to tell me that my head was soon in a whirl.

Kopf • seinen Kopf aus der Schlinge ziehen
to get out of a tight spot (coll), to get out of a difficult situation
He is no fool. He will be able to get out of that tight spot

Kopf • Ihr (ihm, ihnen) ist es zu Kopf gestiegen.
to turn sbd's head (coll)
His first success turned his head and he then became over-ambitious.

Kopf • einen kühlen Kopf bewahren
to keep a cool head (coll), to keep cool (coll)
Despite the flurry of bad news pouring in from every side the General kept a cool head.

Kopf • mit dem Kopf durch die Wand wollen ▷ seinen Kopf durchsetzen wollen

Kopf

Kopf • seinen Kopf durchsetzen (wollen)
to insist on having one's own way (coll), to dig in one's heels (coll), to get one's own way
He insisted on having his own way, so I let him get on with it without my help.

Kopf • nicht auf den Kopf gefallen sein
to be no fool (coll), not to have been born yesterday (coll), to have no flies on one (coll)
They won't be able to trick him, he is no fool.

Kopf • Es muß alles nach ihrem (seinem) Kopf gehen!
Everything has to be done his way.
He likes to get his way.

Kopf • sich etwas durch den Kopf gehen lassen
to think about sth, to think sth over, to turn sth over in one's mind, to chew sth over (coll)
I've been turning your idea over in my mind, and I think we can probably do some useful work together.

Kopf • wie vor den Kopf geschlagen sein ▷ baff sein

Kopf • Was man nicht im Kopf hat, hat man in den Beinen. (prov)
Use your head to save your legs. (prov)

Kopf • den Kopf in den Sand stecken
to bury one's head in the sand (coll), to shut one's eyes to the facts
There eventually came a time when it was no longer possible for us to shut our eyes to the facts and we asked for more time to pay.

Kopf • den Kopf kosten
to cost one one's head
That little oversight could cost you your head.

Kopf • jmd einen Kopf kürzer machen
to make sbd shorter by a head (coll)
Robespierre was made shorter by a head in the end, like most revolutionary leaders.

Kopf • Kopf und Kragen riskieren
to risk one's neck (coll)

The firemen risked their necks trying to save the children on the top floor.

Kopf • sich etwas aus dem Kopf schlagen
to put sth out of one's head (coll), to forget all about sth (coll)
I told the children they could forget all about going to the sea tomorrow unless they started to behave themselves.

Kopf • nicht wissen, wo einem der Kopf steht
not to know if one is coming or going (coll) / whether one is on one's head or one's heels (coll)
My friends came and went so often over Christmas that I didn't know if I was on my head or my heels.

Kopf • etwas auf den Kopf stellen
to turn sth upside down / topsy-turvy (coll)
I turned the bottle upside down to make sure it was empty.

Kopf • jmd vor den Kopf stoßen
to turn sbd down flat (coll)
I'm afraid I had to turn his interesting proposal down flat because it was too expensive.

Kopf • jmd den Kopf verdrehen
to turn sbd's head (coll)
That girl has turned everybody's head round here.

Kopf • über den Kopf wachsen
to get out of hand (coll) (ohne Objekt), to overwhelm sbd, to get on top of (coll), to get the better of (coll)
The whole situation with my sick father at home and my job in America is beginning to get on top of me.

Kopf • jmd den Kopf waschen ▷ abkanzeln

Kopf • sich den Kopf zerbrechen
to rack one's brains (coll)
We racked our brains trying to find a solution to the problem, but without success.

Köpfchen • Köpfchen haben
to be bright (coll) / brainy (coll)
Some of the new students are quite brainy.

Köpfe • über die Köpfe hinwegreden
not to get one's message across (coll)
The politicians from England could not get their message across to the Irish public.

kopflos sein
to be at a loss (coll)
When they told us our application had been rejected we were completely at a loss for a moment.

Korb • einen Korb bekommen
to be turned down (coll)
I asked that girl for a dance, but I was turned down.

Korb • jmd einen Korb geben
to turn sbd down (coll)
I asked that girl for a dance, but she turned me down.

Korn • jmd aufs Korn nehmen
to put to the test
The Opposition have decided to put the Prime Minister's reputation for social awareness to the test.

Körper • In einem gesunden Körper wohnt ein gesunder Geist. (prov)
Mens sana in corpore sano. (prov)

Kosten • auf seine Kosten kommen
to get one's money's worth (coll), to be catered for (coll)
As half of us are vegetarians we had better go to an Indian restaurant, and then everyone will get their money's worth.

Kosten • weder Kosten noch Mühen scheuen
to spare neither effort nor expense
She decided to spare neither effort nor expense in making her daughter's wedding a success.

Kostverächter • kein Kostverächter sein
to fancy a bit on the side (coll)
He was a wonderful husband but nevertheless he always fancied a bit on the side.

kotzen • Das ist zum Kotzen!
That is shitty!/Digusting!/It makes you sick!

Kraftmeier • ein Kraftmeier sein
to be a barbarian, to be a ruffian (coll), to be a thug/lout (coll).
The boys in the Fourth Form are all absolute thugs.

Kragen • jmd platzt der Kragen ▷ Höhe: das ist die Höhe!

Kragenweite • Der ist nicht meine Kragenweite!
That's not my cup of tea. (coll)/That's not my idea of fun. (coll)/That's not my bag. (coll)

Krähe • Eine Krähe hackt der anderen kein Auge aus. (prov)
Dog don't eat dog. (prov)

Krämerseele • eine Krämerseele sein
to be small-minded, to be petty
After they had determined to form a team in a spirit of mutual generosity everybody spent at least a year and a half accusing everybody else of being small-minded.

kratzen • Das kratzt mich nicht!
It's no skin off my nose!

Kraut • dagegen ist kein Kraut gewachsen
There's no answer to that./There's no cure for that./You can't do anything about that.

Kraut • wie Kraut und Rüben
higgledy-piggledy
The books in the library were lying around all higgledy-piggledy after the students had prepared for their exams.

Kreide • bei jmd in der Kreide stehen
to be in debt to sbd, to have a slate with sbd (coll)
I am in debt to my father in the sum of about two thousand pounds.

kreidebleich • kreidebleich werden / sein
to turn / to be as pale as chalk / paper, to turn / to be as white as a sheet
He turned as pale as chalk when he heard the news.

Kreis • sich im Kreis drehen
to be going round in circle
We were going round in circle at the meeting and didn't dicuss any of the questions thoroughly.

Kreis • der Kreis schließt sich
the solution is near, one nears a solution
I think we are getting near to a solution.

Kreise • etwas zieht Kreise
to make waves
The scandal about her adulterous affair made waves in the whole village.

Krethi • Krethi und Plethi ▷ Hinz und Kunz

Kreuz • zu Kreuze kriechen ▷ Asche

Kreuz • jmd aufs Kreuz legen ▷ reinlegen

Kreuz • sein Kreuz tragen
to bear / shoulder one's cross (bibl)
The cross I have to bear is the incompetence of my secretary.

Kriegsbeil • das Kriegsbeil begraben
to bury the hatchet (coll)
Those two have been on bad terms for years, but last week they buried the hatchet. I don't know why.

Kriegsfuß • mit jmd auf Kriegsfuß stehen ▷ in den Haaren liegen
<u>mit etwas auf Kriegsfuß stehen:</u> to be hopeless at (coll), to be bad at
My son is hopeless at maths.

Kriegspfad • auf dem Kriegspfad sein
to be on the warpath
Watch out, she's on the warpath again!

Krug • Der Krug geht solange zu Wasser, bis er bricht. (prov)
It's the last straw that breaks the camel's back. (prov)
MIND FF: It's the cracked pitcher that goes longest to the well. (prov)

Küche • von hinten durch die kalte Küche
sneakily (coll)
If he wants to get his revenge on you, he won't be open about it. He'll do it sneakily.

Kuckuck • Scher dich zu Kuckuck!
Go to the devil! / Go to hell!

Kuckuck • Kuckuckskleber
bailiff
If we don't get our money soon, we'll send the bailiffs in to take walking possession.

Kugel • eine ruhige Kugel schieben
not to believe in overstraining oneself (coll), to take it easy (coll)
He takes it fairly easily, doesn't he? I could have done that job in two hours, and it's taken him a week.

kugeln • sich kugeln vor Lachen / sich kringeln vor Lachen
to laugh till one cries (coll), to laugh o.s. to death (coll), to laugh o.s. silly (coll), to split one's sides laughing (coll)
They laughed themselves to death over the news.

Kuh • eine heilige Kuh schlachten
to kill a sacred cow (coll)
In abolishing child benefit, the Government were killing one of the sacred cows of the Socialist party.

Kuh • wie die Kuh vorm neuen Tor stehen
to be completely bewildered
I was completely bewildered by the confusing news.

Kulissen • hinter die Kulissen schauen
to look behind / into the wings, to look backstage
They had no idea how badly things were going in that other office, but I've had a look behind the wings so I know.

Kultur • nicht von der Kultur beleckt sein
to be untouched by civilisation
He is completely untouched by civilisation and couldn't tell Shakespeare from Beethoven.

Kunst • mit seiner Kunst am Ende sein
to have done all one can, to be at the end of one's tether (coll)
Well, I've done all I can. We'll just have to see if it works any better now.

Kurve • die Kurve kriegen
to get through a difficult situation well, to get through a bad / difficult patch (coll)
The Government had a lot of opposition to cope with but it has now got through that difficult patch.

kurz • kurz angebunden sein ▷ angebunden

kurz • zu kurz kommen
to go short, to come off badly (coll), to get a raw deal
I came off badly when we were dividing up my father's estate, but it wasn't worth a quarrel with my sisters.
MIND FF: to fall short: Erwartungen nicht entsprechen

kurz • über kurz oder lang
sooner or later, one of these days
Sooner or later they will have to make up their minds.

Kürze • In der Kürze liegt die Würze. (prov)
Brevity is the soul of wit. (Shakespeare: Hamlet)

kürzer • den kürzeren ziehen
to come off worst (coll), to come off second best (coll)

In the televised debate with the opposition candidate, the Government speaker came off worst.

L

lachen • nichts zu lachen haben
to have nothing to laugh about (coll), not to have much / anything to laugh about (coll)
He'll soon have nothing to laugh about, if the news I've heard is correct.

lachen • Lachen ist gesund. (prov)
Laughter is the best tonic.

lachen • Wer zuletzt lacht, lacht am besten. (prov)
He who laughs last, laughs longest. (prov)
(oft auch: to have the last laugh)
He thought he'd trip me up by putting a banana skin on the path, but I had the last laugh, because I was carrying his Ming Vase at the time.

lachen • Das Lachen wird dir noch vergehen!
sth / sbd will soon wipe that smile off your face (coll)
When the boss finds out he'll wipe that smile off your face.
You'll soon have nothing to laugh about! (coll)

Lacher • die Lacher auf seiner Seite haben
to have the laugh on one (coll)
I had the laugh on me when I knocked my glass of water over in the middle of my speech about water resources.

Laden • den Laden schmeißen
to run the whole show (coll)
That girl runs the whole show on her own – and she has only been with us three weeks.

Ladenhüter • ein Ladenhüter sein
to be a flop, sth won't sell
This range of goods is a complete flop: nobody is buying them.
We can't shift this new tin opener. It won't sell.

Lage • die Lage peilen ▷ Fühler

Laie • ein blutiger Laie sein
to be a complete beginner, to be a tyro (coll), to have no idea (coll)
He has absolutely no idea of music. He probably thinks Schubert was a poet or something.

lammfromm • lammfromm sein
to be as gentle as a lamb
Our dog is as gentle as a lamb, but our neighbours still complain about it.

Lampe • einen auf die Lampe gießen
to have a quick one (coll)
I'm going to the pub for a quick one before I go home. Are you coming too?

Lampenfieber
to have stage fright
Actors, public speakers, lawyers, preachers and teachers all suffer from time to time from stage fright.

Land • das Land, wo Milch und Honig fließen
a land of / flowing with milk and honey (bibl)
Many refugees view the Fantasian Republic as a land flowing with milk and honey.

Land • das gelobte Land
The Promised Land (bibl)
The promised land for the Mormons was the State of Utah.

Land • kein Land sehen
to see no light at the end of the tunnel (coll)
Despite the optimistic reports in the newspapers, I can see no light at the end of the tunnel.

Land • sich etwas an Land ziehen
to land o.s. (coll)
He landed himself a brilliant job on the Foreign Exchange market.

Landei
country bumpkin (coll)
The image of the peasant as a country bumpkin is rather wide of the mark. Many are shrewd businessmen.

Landpomeranze ▷ Landei

Länder • Andere Länder, andere Sitten. (prov)
When in Rome, do as the Romans do. (prov)

Landsknecht • fluchen wie ein Landsknecht ▷ Bierkutscher

lang • etwas lang und breit erzählen
to expatiate on, to hold forth about (coll); to sound off about (coll), to go on and on about (coll)
She started holding forth about knitting and went on and on without pause for breath until six o'clock in the evening.

lang • nicht mehr lange machen
to be on one's last legs (coll)
Our headmaster is on his last legs and it is high time he was put out to grass.

längelang • der längelang hinfallen
to fall full-length, to measure one's length, to fall flat on one's nose
The ship suddenly shook violently, and I measured my length on the ground.

Langfinger ▷ Elster

Lanze • eine Lanze für jmd brechen
to take up the cudgels on sbd's behalf (coll), to break a lance for sbd (dated)
I'm not prepared to take up the cudgels on behalf of that drunken official. If they sack him, so much the better.

Lappen • durch die Lappen gehen
to slip through one's fingers (from one's grasp)
We let the opportunity slip through our fingers and it will never come again.

Lärm • viel Lärm um nichts machen
nach Shakespeare's *Much Ado About Nothing*
to kick up a fuss about nothing (coll), to make a fuss about nothing (coll)
She was very upset when she found out what was going on, and wouldn't believe that we had simply forgotten to tell her beforehand. It took a long time to persuade her that she was making a fuss about nothing.

Latein • mit seinem Latein am Ende sein ▷ Kunst

Lauer • auf der Lauer liegen
to lie in ambush, to lie in wait
The police lay in wait for the robbers.

Lauffeuer • sich wie ein Lauffeuer verbreiten
to spread like wildfire (coll)
The news of the scandal spread through the town like wildfire

Laufpaß • jmd den Laufpaß geben
to jilt sbd (coll), to give sbd the Spanish archer treatment (coll), to dump sbd (coll), to finish with sbd (coll), to send sbd packing (coll), to piss sbd off (vulg)
He found that his girlfriend got on his nerves, so he gave her the Spanish archer treatment.

Laus • sich eine Laus in den Pelz setzen ▷ einbrocken

Laus • jmd ist eine Laus über die Leber gelaufen
to have been hit where it hurts (coll)
He got angry quickly. Something must have hit him where it hurts.

Leben • wie das blühende Leben aussehen
to look / be in the pink (coll), to look as fit as a fiddle (coll), to look the very picture of health
He had never looked the very picture of health, and now he looked dreadful.

Leben • ein gottgefälliges Leben führen
to live one's life with God, to live a life pleasing to God, to live in accordance with God's Word
The wish to live a life pleasing to God should always be reflected in our prayers.

Leben • aus dem Leben gegriffen
taken from real life (coll), based on fact
This film is based on fact.

Leben • etwas für sein Leben gern tun
to be mad on sth (coll), to be mad keen on sth (coll), to be crazy about sth (coll)
She is crazy about Heine, and reads nothing else at the moment.

Leben • das nackte Leben retten
to escape in what one stands up in (coll), to escape in nothing but the clothes (coll)
He had escaped from the prison in nothing but the clothes, and one of his first requirements was a pair of trousers and a shirt.

Leben • sich durchs Leben schlagen
to struggle / fight one's way through life (coll)
He had to fight his way through his whole life – nothing was ever made easy for him.

Leben • jmd das Leben schwer / sauer machen (coll)
to make life difficult for sbd (coll)
They make life difficult for us by refusing to bend any of the rules to save us trouble.

Leben • es geht auf Leben und Tod
It's a matter of life and death.

Leben • jmd das Leben zur Hölle machen
to make life hell for sbd (coll)
They make life hell for us with all their red tape.

leben • leben und leben lassen
to live and let live
I stick to live and let live and have been happy with it all my life.

Lebenslauf • Frühe nieder, frühe auf, ist der beste Lebenslauf. (prov)
Early to bed and early to rise makes a man healthy and wealthy and wise. (prov)

Lebenslicht • jmd das Lebenslicht ausblasen
to deal sbd a death blow
The news of his daughter's third divorce dealt the lonely old man his death blow. He passed away two days later.

Leberwurst • die beleidigte Leberwurst spielen
to be a sulk-pot (coll), to be sulking, to be in a huff (coll), to have got one's back up (coll)
I never meant to insult him, but he got into a huff all the same.

Leckermaul • ein Leckermaul sein
to have a sweet tooth
A young child usually has a sweet tooth.

Leder • jmd ans Leder wollen
to nail sbd for sth (coll)
The police were very eager to nail him for the large burglary, but he was able to prove he had been elsewhere at the time.

Leder • zäh wie Leder sein
to be as tough as leather, as tough as old boots (coll)
This steak is as tough as leather.

Leder • vom Leder ziehen
to pull out all the stops (coll)
The Leader of the Opposition pulled out all the stops, but his speech still failed to convince the MPs.

leer • leer ausgehen
to be left empty-handed, to have nothing to show for one's pains
When Uncle Arthur died, my sisters copped the lot. I never got a penny.
France and Wales carved up the Home Championships between themselves. The England squad had nothing to show for their pains.

Lehrgeld • Lehrgeld zahlen müssen
to have to learn the hard way (coll)
Nobody ever gave me any tips on how to do this – I had to learn the hard way.

Lehrgeld • Laß dir dein Lehrgeld zurückgeben!
You've learnt nothing!

Leib • am eigene Leibe erfahren
to experience sth for o.s., to get a taste of sth for o.s. (coll)
He never worried about not having enough money until he got a taste of being unemployed.

Leib • wie auf den Leib geschrieben sein
the part might have been written for him, to be a natural (coll) (for a part)
This part might have been written for you – it is the right age, the right character and the right type.

Leib • gut bei Leibe sein
to be fat / plump / portly / stout, to have a rubber tyre
The rest of his family are quite slim, but he is quite fat.

Leib • mit Leib und Seele
to put body and soul into sth (coll), to do sth with all one's might
He put body and soul into the new endeavour, and it very nearly succeeded.

leibt • wie er leibt und lebt
to be o.s. all over (coll)
That is him all over – offering to do something, and then letting you down. He's always doing things like that.

Leiche • Nur über meine Leiche!
Over my dead body!

Leiche • eine Leiche im Keller haben
to have a skeleton in the cupboard (coll)
That family has got a lot of skeletons in the cupboard they think nobody knows about.

Leichen • über Leichen gehen
to stick at nothing (coll)
He'll stick at nothing to get his own way – he is quite ruthless.

leichenblaß ▷ kreidebleich

leicht • leichter gesagt als getan
Easier said than done.

Leid • Geteiltes Leid ist halbes Leid. (prov)
A trouble shared is a trouble halved. (prov)

Leiden • wie das Leiden Christi aussehen ▷ ausgeschissen

Leier • Es ist immer dieselbe alte Leier
It's always the same old story.

leihen • Leihen macht Freunde, Wiederfordern Feinde. (prov)
Neither a borrower nor a lender be;/For loan oft loses both itself and friend. (Shakespeare: Hamlet)

Leim • jmd auf den Leim gehen/kriechen
to be conned (coll), to be diddled (coll), to be fooled (coll), to be had (coll)
We were completely had by them, and ended up seven thousand pounds worse off.

Leim • aus dem Leim gehen ▷ Hefekloß

Leine • jmd an der langen Leine halten
to give sbd rope (coll)
We gave him a lot of rope to see what he could do on his own initiative.

Leisetreter • ein Leisetreter sein
smoothie (coll), creep (coll)
He is a creep, who got into the boss's good books by simply agreeing with him.

Leiter • die Leiter des Erfolgs emporsteigen
to climb the ladder (coll)
He climbed the ladder and ended up head of his firm.

Lektion • jmd eine Lektion erteilen
to teach sbd a lesson
He thought he was brilliant at Italian, so I gave him some Dante to translate, unseen. That taught him a lesson.

Lenz • sich einen Lenz machen
to have an easy time of it (coll)
You have an easy time of it in your job, sitting behind a desk all day, talking to people.

lernen • Gelernt ist gelernt.
Once learnt, never forgotten. (prov)

Leseratte • eine Leseratte sein
to be a bookworm (coll)
He is a real bookworm. You never see him without a book in his hand.

letzt • zu guter Letzt
on top of everything else (coll), to cap it all (coll), into the bargain (coll)
I have got three written exams this week and on top of everything else I have to give a lecture on Mesopotamian agriculture to the rest of the geography class.

letzt

letzt • Du bist das Letzte!
You are the flaming limit!

letzt • Den Letzten beißen die Hunde. (prov)
(May the) devil take the hindmost. (prov)

letzt • sein Letztes geben
to give one's all (coll)
He did absolutely all he could. He gave his all.

Leuchte • keine Leuchte sein
to be no great shakes (at sth) (coll)
I am no great shakes at Latin, I'm afraid.

Leute • es ist nicht wie bei armen Leuten
We're not quite broke yet.

Leute • geschiedene Leute
not to be on speaking terms (coll), to have fallen out (coll)
Since we quarrelled during the summer we have not been on speaking terms.

Leute • etwas unter die Leute bringen
to distribute / spread amongst the people
Let's go to town and spread some money amongst the people.

Leviten • jmd die Leviten lesen ▷ abkanzeln

Licht • Licht am Horizont sehen
to see light at the end of the tunnel (coll)
Despite the pessimistic forecasts in the press, I do see light at the end of the tunnel.

Licht • jmd geht ein Licht auf
to dawn on sbd (coll), to tumble to the fact that (coll), the scales fall from sbd's eyes (coll), the penny drops (coll)
"It suddenly dawned on me that we were going to have to invest yet more money in the project." – "And when did the scales fall from your eyes?"

Licht • das Licht der Welt erblicken
to come into the world
Napoleon came into the world in Ajaccio, Corsica.

Licht • jmd hinters Licht führen ▷ anschmieren ▷ reinlegen

Licht • grünes Licht für etwas geben
to give sth the green light (coll), to give sth the go-ahead (coll)
They thought about the suggestion long and hard before they gave the go-ahead, because it was so expensive.

Licht • Licht ins Dunkel bringen
to shed light on sth
I think I can shed light on this mystery, because I know who sent the unsigned letter.

Licht • sich ins rechte Licht setzen
to sing one's own praises, to blow one's own trumpet (coll), to make sure one's efforts are noticed
He blew his own trumpet vociferously about his achievements in office, but nevertheless he was not re-elected.

Licht • Man soll sein Licht nicht unter den Scheffel stellen. (prov)
Do not hide your light under a bushel. (bibl)

Licht • das Licht scheuen / ein lichtscheues Element sein
to be a very suspicious character
He is a very suspicious character, and I don't advise you to have more to do with him than you can help.

Licht • kein großes Licht sein ▷ das Pulver nicht erfunden haben

Lichtblick • ein Lichtblick sein
a ray / gleam of hope / light (coll), a ray / spark of comfort (coll)
There's a ray of hope in the economic forecast for the autumn, in that productivity is on the increase.

Lichte • bei Lichte besehen
on further examination / reflexion / thought(s), when you come to think about it (coll)

It's a very good plan, when you come to think about it – cheap, quick and efficient

Liebe • Liebe geht durch den Magen. (prov)
The way to a man's heart is through his stomach. (prov)

Liebe • Liebe heilt Zeit, und Zeit heilt Liebe. (prov)
Time, the great healer…

Liebe • Eine Liebe ist der anderen wert. (prov)
One good turn deserves another. (prov)

Liebe • Liebe macht blind. (prov)
The eyes of love are blind (prov)

Liebe • Alte Liebe rostet nicht. (prov)
An old flame never dies. (prov)

Liebe • In der Liebe und im Krieg sind alle Mittel recht. (prov)
All's fair in love and war. (prov)

liebedienern
to be sucking up (coll), to be crawling (coll), to be grovelling (coll), to be pandering, to be polishing the apple (coll)
That loathesome girl spent all her time at school sucking up to the teachers.

Lied • Davon kann ich ein Lied singen!
I know a thing or two about that (coll), I could tell you a thing or two about that (coll), I could write a book about that (coll)
I could tell you a thing or two about trying to deal with this firm. For instance, nobody is ever in the office after five pm.

liegen • Damit liegst du richtig!
You're right there. / That's right.

Linie • keine klare Linie vertreten
to chop and change (coll)
He changes his mind every two minutes, and you can't rely on him to keep to his opinion at all, he chops and changes the whole time.

linientreu • linientreu sein
to be faithful to the party line
Obviously a lot of the party members were not faithful to the party line, otherwise a peaceful revolution would not have been possible.

links • jmd links liegen lassen ▷ jmd die kalte Schulter zeigen

links • etwas mit links machen
to find sth a doddle (coll)
Mathematics is very simple. The last exam I did I found a doddle.

Lippen • an jmds Lippen hängen
to hang upon sbd's lips, to hang upon sbd's every word
The students hung upon the lecturer's every word.

List • mit List und Tücke
by low cunning, chicanery
Some of these estate agents' methods are pure chicanery.

Liste • eine schwarze Liste führen
to keep a black list (coll), to black-list sbd (coll)
They keep a black list of firms trading with countries whose governments they disapprove of.
ABC Ltd was blacklisted for exporting goods to Ruritania.

Litanei • eine lange Litanei von etwas
a litany of sth
He recited a litany of woes to me.

Loch • saufen wie ein Loch
to drink like a fish (coll), to be a boozer
He drinks like a fish – you can smell whisky on his breath from eleven o'clock every morning.

Loch • ein Loch aufreißen, um ein anderes zu stopfen
to rob Peter to pay Paul
We urgently need more people for the Alpha project – but we mustn't take them from the Beta project, because that would be robbing Peter to pay Paul.

Loch

Loch • jmd ein Loch in den Bauch fragen
to drive sbd crazy (coll) / dotty (dated) / up the wall (coll) with questions
He drove me crazy with questions about what we wanted to do, and why, and where – all beside the point.

Loch • auf dem letzten Loch pfeifen
to be on one's last legs
My radio is on its last legs. I think I need a new one.

Löcher • Löcher in die Luft starren
to gaze into the pale blue yonder (coll)
That boy does not pay any attention in class. He just sits there looking out of the window, gazing into the pale blue yonder.

Löffel • jmd über den Löffel balbieren ▷ anschmieren

Löffel • (nicht) mit einem goldenen Löffel zur Welt gekommen sein
(not) to have been born with a silver spoon in one's mouth (coll)
That millionaire came from a poor family and worked his way up. He wasn't born with a silver spoon in his mouth.

Lorbeeren • sich auf seinen Lorbeeren ausruhen
to rest on one's laurels
After his first great success, he did not rest on his laurels, but followed it up with two more.

loseisen • jmd loseisen
to prise / drag sbd away (from sth) (coll)
I prised him away from the card table for a few seconds to tell him the news.

loslegen • loslegen mit etwas
to fire away (coll), shoot (coll) (bes. Fragen stellen)
You wanted to tell me about your experience in Russia so fire away.

loswerden • etwas loswerden wollen (von der Seele reden)
to want to unburden o.s., to want to get sth off one's chest (coll)

She could see something was troubling her son, but he didn't seem to want to talk about it. She waited patiently until he was ready to unburden himself.

Lot • wieder ins Lot bringen
to smoothe things over (coll), to patch things up (coll)
I have been trying to smooth things over between those two for years, but I'm afraid they simply want to remain enemies.

Lotto • Du hast wohl im Lotto gewonnen!
You're loaded!
Have you won the pools?

Luchs • wie ein Luchs (aufpassen)
to keep watch like a lynx
The customer kept watch like a lynx to make sure the shop assistant did not overcharge her again.

Lückenbüßer • der Lückenbüßer sein
to be (sbd's) stand-in (coll), to stand in for sbd (coll)
Mr Trundlehumper is on holiday and I have to be standing in for him again.

Luft • dicke Luft
bad atmosphere
When I went round to my sister's family I could tell there was a really bad atmosphere, so I went home again.

Luft • in die Luft gehen ▷ Decke: an die Decke gehen

Luft • an die Luft setzen ▷ achtkantig

Luft • sich in Luft auflösen
to vanish into thin air (coll)
I have looked for it everywhere, but it has vanished into thin air.

Luft • aus der Luft gegriffen sein
to be pure imagination
The ideas propounded in this book are pure imagination, and have nothing to do with the facts.

Luft • von Luft und Liebe leben
to live on nothing (coll)
He has no money at all, as far as I know, but he always looks perfectly well fed and dressed. He must be able to live on nothing.

Luft • in der Luft hängen
to be up in the air (coll)
The plans for the new opera house are still up in the air, as we don't yet know where half of the money is coming from.

Luft • seinen Gefühlen Luft machen
to give vent to one's feelings, to let off steam (coll)
He let off steam for half an hour about the fact that he had not got the promotion he wanted.

Luft • in der Luft liegen
to be in the offing (coll), to be pending
I knew the children were planning some sort of a surprise this afternoon, I could tell there was something in the offing.

Luftschlösser • Luftschlösser bauen
to build a castle / castles in the air (coll), to build a castle / castles in Spain
Without waiting for the results of the competition, they started making plans about what they would do if they won. In the event they turned out to have been building castles in Spain.

lügen • Wer einmal lügt, dem glaubt man nicht, auch wenn er dann die Wahrheit spricht. (prov)
Don't cry wolf. (prov)

lumpen • sich nicht lumpen lassen
to spare no expense
The bride's family spared no expense and organised a splendid wedding.

Lunge • die grüne Lunge
green lung
Central Park is New York's most important green lung.

Lunge • sich die Lunge aus dem Hals schreien
to shout oneself hoarse (coll), to scream one's head off (coll)
The football fans shouted themselves hoarse during the match.

Lunte • Lunte riechen ▷ Braten

Lupe • unter die Lupe nehmen
to scrutinize sbd / sth, to a good look at sbd / sth, to examine closely, to put under the microscope
We examined closely their financial plans and they seemed all right to us.

lupenrein • nicht ganz lupenrein sein ▷ astrein

Lust • mit Lust und Liebe
to do sth with a will, to do sth with relish, to throw oneself into sth (coll), to put one's heart into sth (coll)
The secretary worked with a will, finishing the letters in the morning.

Lust • ganz nach Lust und Laune
as the fancy takes you (coll), just as you like (coll)
You can dine at seven or eight, as the fancy takes you.

M

Mache • alles Mache
all show (coll)
His self-confidence is all show: he's quite shy underneath.

Macht • Macht geht vor Recht. (prov)
Might is Right. (prov)

Machtwort • ein Machtwort sprechen ▷ Faust: mit dem Faust auf dem Tisch hauen

Macke • eine Macke haben ▷ Dachschaden

Mädchen • ein gefallenes Mädchen sein
to be a fallen woman (dated)
The fallen woman of the village, who had a son born out of wedlock, was nevertheless much respected for her needlework.

Mädchen • Mädchen für alles sein
to be a maid-of-all-work, to be a drudge
They have made their poor au pair girl, who thought she'd just have to look after the children into a maid-of-all-work.

Mädchen • ein spätes Mädchen sein
to be an old maid
My ancient aunt, who is an old maid, loves to tell us about how all her boyfriends jilted her in about 1066.

Mädchen • ein leichtes Mädchen sein
an easy lay (coll), to be a girl of loose morals
That girl is an easy lay – she's slept with practically every boy at the school.

Made • wie die Made im Speck leben
to be as happy as a pig in clover (coll), as snug as a bug in a rug (coll)
He is as snug as a bug in a rug in Austria – he has a good job, lots of friends – why should he want to come home to England?

Magen • Das liegt mir im Magen
to be still cross / seething about sth / with sbd (coll)
I am still cross about that!

Magen • der Magen knurrt
My stomach is rumbling.

Magen • jmd dreht sich der Magen um
to turn one's stomach, to make sbd want to throw up (coll) / puke (vulg)
I cannot stand the fellow. The very thought of spending a weekend with him makes me want to throw up.

Magen • Der Magen ist leichter zu füllen als die Augen. (prov)
▷ Augen: die Augen sind größer als der Magen.

Magnet • wie ein Magnet
like a magnet
The pretty woman drew all the young men to her like a magnet.

mahlen • Wer zuerst kommt, mahlt zuerst. (prov)
First come, first served. (prov)

Mahlzeit • Prost Mahlzeit!
I give up!

Mann • der Buh-Mann sein
to be the scapegoat
The Foreign Secretary was the scapegoat for the mistakes of the whole government.

Mann • ein Mann, ein Wort
A gentleman's word is his bond. (prov)

Mann • etwas an den Mann bringen
to find a market for sth, to find a purchaser for sth
We hope to find a purchaser for some of our old stock over the next few weeks.

Mann • mit Mann und Maus (untergehen)
to sink / go down with all hands
H.M.S. Hood sank in the Denmark Strait with the loss of almost all hands.

Mann • ein gemachter Mann sein
to be a made man, to have it made (coll)
After publishing his first best-seller he had it made.

Mann • Mann(s) genug sein
to be man enough (coll)
If her brother is not man enough to help her the poor girl will have to try and cope on her own.

Männchen • Männchen machen
to grovel to sbd for sth
I don't want to have to grovel for what is actually my right.

Manschetten • Manschetten vor etwas / jmd haben
to be scared stiff

Mantel • seinen Mantel nach dem Wind hängen ▷ Fahne

Mantel • den Mantel christlicher Nächstenliebe über etwas breiten
to draw a veil over sth (coll)
He very kindly drew a veil over my blunder.

Märchen • Erzähl keine Märchen!
Don't tell tales! / Don't tell stories! / Pull the other one!

Mark • jmd bis ins Mark treffen
to cut sbd to the quick
When her parents died the whole family was cut to the quick.

Marsch • jmd den Marsch blasen ▷ abkanzeln

Masche • Das ist die neueste Masche.
That is the latest trick. / That is the new ploy.

Maschen • durch die Maschen schlüpfen
to slip through the net (coll)
In spite of an intensive search by the police, the criminal managed to slip through the net.

Maske • jmd die Maske vom Gesicht reißen
<u>norm. passiv:</u> to unmask sbd (coll), to show sbd up (coll)
The new employee was speedily unmasked as a scoundrel.

Masse • die graue Masse
the great unwashed (coll), the hoi polloi
Dickens had a soft spot for the great unwashed.

Maß • mit zweierlei Maß messen
to use double standards, to apply a double standard
The judge tried to take into account the individual circumstances of the accused persons without too obviously applying a double standard.

Maßstab • einen hohen / strengen Maßstab anlegen
to lay down a high standard
English criminal law lays down a high standard of proof for a conviction: proof beyond a reasonable doubt.

Mattscheibe • eine Mattscheibe haben / kriegen
to be unable to think straight (coll), my / your (etc) mind has gone blank.
I'm sorry, could you repeat that? I couldn't follow you: I can't think straight today.

Mätzchen • (keine) Mätzchen machen ▷ Faxen

Mauerblümchen • ein Mauerblümchen sein
wallflower (coll) (dated)
No-one wanted to dance with my sister at the ball – she was left as a wallflower all evening.

Maul • jmd das Maul / den Mund stopfen
to silence sbd, to shut sbd up (coll)
I'll silence him so that he'll never complain about that matter again.

Maul • sich das Maul über etwas zerreißen
to sound off about sth (coll)
He sounded off about the bad bus services for about half an hour.

Maulaffen • Maulaffen feilhalten
to stand around uselessly (coll)
He stood around uselessly all afternoon while the rest of us were working.

maulfaul • maulfaul sein
to be a person of few words, to be taciturn
He is a man of few words and didn't say anything all evening.

Maulkorb • jmd einen Maulkorb verpassen
to muzzle / gag sbd (coll)
The Government managed to muzzle the journalist by threatening to give him no further briefings.

Maus • da beißt die Maus kein' Faden ab
You can't get away from that (coll)!/There's no getting away from that (coll)!/That's flat (coll)!

Mäuse • Mäuse haben (machen) ▷ Kohle haben

Mauseloch • sich ins Mauseloch verkriechen
to want the ground to swallow one up (coll), to want to crawl into a corner and hide, to be able to (could, could have) die from embarrassment.
When I found out that he knew I could have died from embarrassment.

Mäusemelken • Das ist zum Mäusemelken!
It's enough to drive you up the wall.

mausern • sich mausern
to be coming along nicely (coll)
Our new project is coming along nicely – we should be able to publish a report in a few weeks.

mausetot • mausetot sein
to be as dead as a doornail (coll), to be as dead as mutton (coll), to be as dead as a dodo (coll)
The transmitter was as dead as a doornail.

Mäuschen • Mäuschen spielen mögen
to want to be a fly on the wall (coll)
I would love to be a fly on the wall in that meeting and see how the quarrel develops.

Meer • ein Meer von Blumen, ein Menschenmeer
a sea of flowers, a sea of people

Meilen • drei Meilen gegen den Wind stinken
to be able to be smelt a mile off (coll)
There's something wrong with that girl – you can smell it a mile off. She never smiles or laughs.

Meilenstein • ein Meilenstein (in der Geschichte) sein
to be a milestone in history
The fall of Constantinople was a milestone in history.

mein • mein und dein verwechseln ▷ Elster

Meise • eine Meise haben ▷ Dachschaden

Meister • seinen Meister finden
to meet one's match
The champion had an easy time of it in the early rounds of the tournament, but he met his match in the quarter final and was beaten after a long game.

Meister • Es ist noch kein Meister vom Himmel gefallen. (prov)
Practice makes perfect. (prov)

melden • nichts zu melden haben
to have one's view count for nothing, to have no say (coll), to have no influence, to have no pull / clout (coll)
I have no pull with the boss at all.

Menschenseele • keine Menschenseele
not a (living) soul (coll)
In the desert for miles around there was not a living soul.

Messer • unters Messer kommen
to be operated on, to go under the knife (coll)
He had to be operated on last week for appendicitis.

Messer • jmd ans Messer liefern
to send sbd to his doom
Hundreds of thousands were sent to their doom on the Western Front.

Messer • auf Messers Schneide stehen ▷ Kippe

messerscharf • messerscharf schlußfolgern
to reason closely
He made a very closely reasoned speech.

Methusalem • alt wie Methusalem
Leute: to be as old as Methuselah (coll), to be as old as God's grandfather (coll)
He's not going to be a success with the youngsters – he's as old as God's grandfather.

Miene • mit eisiger Miene
icily
He greeted me icily. Clearly he had not forgotten our argument of the previous week.

Miene • gute Miene zu bösem Spiel machen
to make the best of a bad job (coll), to grin and bear it (coll)
We're not going to be able to do this job the way we wanted, because the head office didn't agree. Still, we shall have to grin and bear it and do the best we can.

Miene • keine Miene verziehen
ohne die Gefühle zu verraten: without batting an eyelid (coll)
When the managing director starts to give us his views we have to sit there and just listen to the nonsense without batting an eyelid.
kaltblütig reagieren oder handeln: without turning a hair (coll)
He received the news of his wife's death without turning a hair.

Miete • Das ist schon die halbe Miete!
That is more than half the battle!

Milchgesicht • ein Milchgesicht sein
milksop (coll), wimp (coll)
He is a complete milksop – I don't think he has ever stood up for himself in his life.

Milchmädchenrechnung
a naïve calculation
The plans of the oppositon parties are full of the most naive calculations.

Minna • die grüne Minna
Black Maria (coll)
The police took the prisoners away in a Black Maria.

minus • minus machen
to make a loss, to go into the red (coll)
This company has gone badly into the red.
We have gone badly into the red on this deal.

Minute • in letzter Minute
at the last minute (coll), at the eleventh hour (coll)
We only found out at the last minute and had to react very quickly.

mir • Wie du mir, so ich dir. (prov)
What is sauce for the goose is sauce for the gander. (prov)
An eye for an eye, a tooth for a tooth. (prov)

mir • mir nichts, dir nichts
just like that (coll), as bold as brass (coll), as cool as be damned (coll)
In he came, cool as be damned, and asked if he could take over my office.

Mist • Das ist nicht auf seinem Mist gewachsen.
That can't have been his idea.

Mist • Mist reden ▷ Quatsch

mitgegangen • Mitgegangen, mitgefangen, mitgehangen. (prov)
▷ A: Wer A sagt, muß auch B sagen

mitgehen • etwas mitgehen lassen
to lift (coll), to pinch (coll), to nick (coll), to half inch (coll)
I left my bicycle unlocked outside the shop and somebody nicked it.

mitkommen • (in der Schule) nicht mitkommen
to get left behind (coll)
I keep getting left behind in maths classes.

Mitte • ab durch die Mitte
Off you go!

Mittel • Mittel und Wege finden
to have ways and means (of doing sth)
The security services have ways and means of finding things out.

Mittelweg • der goldene Mittelweg
the golden mean
We must find some sort of golden mean between intolerance and indifference.

Moment • einen lichten Moment haben
to have a brainwave (coll)
He had a brainwave and saw the solution to a problem which had been troubling us for weeks.

Mond • jmd auf den Mond schießen wollen
to wish sbd to the devil (coll)
I was so annoyed by the pair of them I wished them both to the devil.

Mond • hinterm Mond leben / vom Mond kommen ▷ Mustopf

Moral • die Moral von der Geschicht'
the moral of the tale (coll)
The moral of the tale is that one should never trust anyone.

Moralpredigt ▷ Gardinenpredigt

Mord • Mord und Totschlag
blood on the carpet (coll)
There will be blood on the carpet before the end of that meeting.

Mördergrube • aus seinem Herzen keine Mördergrube machen
▷ Herzen

Mordshunger • einen Mordshunger haben
to be mortally hungry (dated), to be famished, to be starving (coll)
I could eat a horse!
The children are always starving when they come home from school.

Mordskerl • ein Mordskerl sein
He's quite a lad. / She's a girl, she is.
He is disgustingly talented: plays the piano, reads Kant for pleasure and he's a good cricketer, too.

Mordsspaß • einen Mordsspaß haben
to go completely mad (coll)
The audience went completely mad with their water pistols and rice at the Rocky Horror Picture Show.

Mores • jmd Mores lehren
to teach sbd manners
I'll teach him manners!

Morgen • Morgen, morgen, nur nicht heute, sagen alle faulen Leute. (prov)
Never put off to tomorrow what should be done today. (prov)
Never put off to tomorrow what you can do today. (prov)

Morgenstund • Morgenstund(e) hat Gold im Mund(e). (prov)
The early bird catches the worms. (prov)

Morpheus • in Morpheus Armen ruhen
to be in the arms of Morpheus, to be in the land of Nod
When we left the house at five o'clock everyone else was still in the arms of Morpheus.

Motten • von etwas angezogen sein, wie die Motten vom Licht
to be attracted by sth like a moth to a candle (coll)
The men are attracted to her like moths to a candle.

Mücke • aus einer Mücke einen Elefanten machen
to make a mountain out of a mole-hill (coll)
It is not so difficult as they all seem to think. They are making mountains out of mole-hills.

Mücke • die Mücke machen
to do a moonlit flit, to make oneself scarce
Make yourself scarce!

mucksmäuschenstill
<u>von Menschen:</u> to be as quiet as a mouse (coll)
We were quiet as mice when we came in, but our parents still woke up.

Mühlrad • wie ein Mühlrad im Kopf herumgehen
to give one no rest / peace, to go round and round in one's head (coll)
The thought of this catastrophe went round and round in my head all night so that I could not sleep.

Mühlstein • wie ein Mühlstein am Halse hängen
to be a millstone round someone's neck, to be more trouble than it's worth
I'm afraid that these reinforcements are so badly trained they are just a millstone round our necks – we'd be better off without them.

Mund • Im Munde Bibel, im Herzen übel. (prov)
The Devil can quote Scripture to his purpose. (prov)

Mund • jmd über den Mund fahren
to interrupt
He interrupted me in the middle of what I was saying.

Mund • sich den Mund fusselig reden
to talk until one is blue in the face (coll)
The diplomats can talk until they're blue in the face but it won't solve anything.

Mund • nicht auf den Mund gefallen sein
to have the gift of the gab (coll)
He has the gift of the gab and persuades people of anything.

Mund • einen großen Mund haben
to be cheeky (coll), to be mouthy (coll)
That child is horribly cheeky to her teachers.

Mund • den Mund halten
to shut up (coll), to shut one's mouth, to shut one's face (coll) / trap (dated), to shut one's hole (vulg), to put a sock in it (coll), to belt up (coll)
He was insulting my mother so I told him to shut his face.

Mund • den Mund nicht aufmachen ▷ maulfaul

Mund • jmd nach dem Mund reden
to repeat what sbd says parrot-fashion (coll)

He never contributed anything himself to the discussion, he just repeated what other people said parrot-fashion.

Mund • in aller Munde sein
to be on everyone's lips
The scandalous news was on everyone's lips as soon as the first reports came out.

Mund • Mund und Nase aufsperren
to be agape, open-mouthed (coll)
He stood there agape with astonishment.

Mund • sich den Mund verbrennen
to burn one's fingers (coll), to get one's fingers burnt (coll), to get into hot water (coll), to come a cropper (coll)
I got into hot water over my critical report and I certainly don't want to tell the truth to these people any more – I'd just get my fingers burnt again.
You came a cropper over that one, didn't you.

Mund • jmd den Mund wässrig machen
to make sbd's mouth water, to whet sbd's appetite (for sth)
We whetted their appetites with a short concerto, and then we played the long symphony.

Mund • den Mund zu voll nehmen
to bite off more than one can chew (coll)
You've bitten off more than you can chew in volunteering to do this job – I don't see how you can possibly get it done in the time.

Munition • seine Munition verschossen haben
to have played all one's shots
We have played all our shots and have no further arguments to put forward.

Münze • etwas für bare Münze nehmen
to take sth at face value (coll)
English are so given to irony that lots that they say shouldn't be taken at face value.

Münze • mit gleicher Münze zurückzahlen
to pay sbd back in their own coin (coll)
He had been scrumping my apples, so I paid him back in his own coin by cutting his roses.

Murmeltier • schlafen wie ein Murmeltier
to sleep like a log / top (coll), to be dead to the world (coll)
Don't wake her if she's still dead to the world.

Muse • von der Muse geküßt werden
to be gifted
She is extremely gifted and has won several competitions for young violinists.

Musik • Hier (Vorn) spielt die Musik!
Pay attention please!

Musik • Das ist Musik in meinen Ohren!
That is music to my ears.

Musik • Musik im Blut haben
to have music in the blood
She is descended from a famous violinist, so she has music in the blood.

Mustopf • aus dem Mustopf kommen
to be (have been) living on another planet (coll)
You must have been living on another planet if you think that idea has the slightest chance.

Müßiggang • Müßiggang ist aller Laster Anfang. (prov)
Idleness breeds vice. (prov)

Mut • mit dem Mut der Verzweiflung
the courage of despair
The surrounded army fought on with the courage of despair.

Mut • den Mut nicht sinken lassen
to keep up one's courage, to keep one's pecker up (coll)
We must keep up our courage in these difficult times.

Mütchen • an jmd sein Mütchen kühlen
to vent one's rage on sbd, to take it out on sbd (coll)
All right, so you failed the exam! You don't have to take it out on me.

mutig • Dem Mutigen gehört die Welt. (prov)
Fortune favours the brave. (prov)

Mutter • Mit der Mutter soll beginnen, wer die Tochter will gewinnen. (prov)
He who shall the daughter win, must with the mother first begin. (prov)

Muttermilch • etwas mit der Muttermilch einsaugen
sth is mother's milk to sbd, to learn sth at one's mother's knee (coll)
I learned to play the violin at my mother's knee.

mutterseelenallein
to be all on one's own, on one's tod (coll), on one's jack (coll)
Head office left him with all that work to do on his jack.

Muttersöhnchen ▷ Milchgesicht

N

nachsagen • Das laß ich mir nicht nachsagen!
I'm not having that said about me.

Nachspiel • Das wird noch ein Nachspiel haben.
I'm sure we haven't heard the last of that.

Nachspiel • ein Nachspiel haben
to have undesirable consequences
The secret meetings between the Government minister and the terrorist organization had undesirable consequences when the press found out about them.

Nacht • schwarz wie die Nacht ▷ pechschwarz

Nacht • eine Nacht der langen Messer
a "Night of the Long Knives" (fast nur in Beziehung auf deutsche NS Geschichte, oder Umgestaltungen des Kabinetts)
It has been a real "Night of the Long Knives" in Whitehall. Almost one-third of the cabinet have been asked to resign.

Nacht • bei Nacht und Nebel
at dead of night, in the middle of the night
Many persons were arrested at dead of night.
Er floh bei…: *He did a moonlight flit.*

Nacht • häßlich wie die Nacht sein
to be as ugly as sin (coll)
Have you seen her sister? She is as ugly as sin – I can't imagine anyone dancing with her.

Nacht • sich die Nacht um die Ohren schlagen
feiern: to go out on the tiles (coll)
nachts studieren: to burn the midnight oil (coll)
Raubbau mit seiner Gesundheit treiben: to burn the candle at both ends (coll)
I have been burning the midnight oil all this week and now I am quite exhausted.

Nacht • eine Nacht über etwas schlafen
to sleep on sth (coll)
I've slept on what you said yesterday, and I think you are right.

Nacht • die Nacht zum Tage machen ▷ die Nacht um die Ohren schlagen

Nachtigall • Nachtigall ick hör dir trapsen!
Aha, I know what's cooking (coll)!

Nackenschläge • Nackenschläge bekommen
to suffer a (a series of) reverse(s)
We have suffered a series of reverses since you were last here. At least three things have gone seriously wrong.

Nagel • etwas an den Nagel hängen
to give up, to pack in (coll)
After four years' practice he gave up the law and turned to journalism.

Nagel • den Nagel auf den Kopf treffen
<u>einen Punkt genau treffen:</u> to hit the nail on the head (coll)
When you say we simply don't have enough people prepared to work for us you have hit the nail on the head. That is precisely the problem.
<u>eine Person mit Kritik treffen:</u> to strike home (coll)
When he said that she was not looking after her husband properly that struck home.

Nagel • der Nagel zum Sarg sein
to be another nail in one's coffin (coll)
If the bank is putting up its overdraft rates that will be another nail in this firm's coffin.

Nägel • Nägel mit Köpfen machen
Let's get down to business.
Let's thrash out the details.

Nägel • etwas brennt auf den Nägeln
sth is a burning issue (coll)
The economic position is the burning issue in this election campaign.

Nähkästchen • aus dem Nähkästchen plaudern
to give things away (coll)
This meeting is private and in confidence and nobody must give anything away afterwards to anybody else.

Nahrung • geistige Nahrung
intellectual nourishment
After spending two weeks mountaineering with a Scout troop he was starved of intellectual nourishment and in a hurry to get back to his studies at the University.
MIND FF: food for thought: Stoff zum Nachdenken

Nähte • aus allen Nähten platzen
to be bursting at the seams (coll)
The lecture halls of most German universities are often bursting at the seams.

Name • Mein Name ist Hase.
Search me! / I'm damned/blowed if I know!

Namen • Namen sind Schall und Rauch. (prov)
What's in a name? (prov)

Namen • sich einen Namen machen
to make a name for oneself
He quickly made a name for himself in journalistic circles as a brilliant wit.

Narr • Ein Narr spricht, der Kluge denkt. (prov)
<u>auch Handlung:</u> *Fools rush in where angels fear to tread. (prov)*

Narren • einen Narren an jmd gefressen haben ▷ Affen

Naschkatze • eine Naschkatze sein ▷ Leckermaul

Nase • jmd etwas an der Nase ansehen ▷ Gesicht: im Gesicht geschrieben sein

Nase • mit der Nase auf etwas gestoßen werden
to have sth shoved in one's face (coll)
I only realised how disagreeable she was when I had the fact shoved in my face.

Nase • jmd etwas auf die Nase binden
to let on to sbd about sth (coll), to spill the beans to sbd (coll)
How did he get to know? Who let on to him about it?

Nase • sich an seine eigene Nase fassen
to put one's own house in order, to remove the plank in one's own eye (bibl)
We have to put our own house in order before we start making daring suggestions to anybody else.

Nase • eine Nase für etwas haben
to have a nose for something (coll)
I have a nose for a good product – and I think this one will sell and sell.

Nase • jmd vor die Nase gesetzt bekommen
to be bypassed for promotion
He had worked for the company for many years but he was bypassed for promotion in favour of a younger man who had just joined.

Nase • jmd auf der Nase herumtanzen
to be able to get away with anything with sbd
That schoolmaster is far too soft. You can get away with anything in his classes.

Nase • die Nase hochtragen ▷ hochnäsig sein

Nase • seine Nase in alles stecken
to stick one's nose into everything (coll)
He sticks his nose into everything that goes on. You can't have any secrets from him – he needs to know everything.

Nase • auf der Nase liegen
to be laid up (coll), to be on one's back (coll)
I was laid up last week with the flu.

Nase • jmd eine lange Nase machen
to cock a snook at sbd (coll)
People rarely cock snooks – nowadays all but the least vulgar raise two fingers.

Nase • jmd etwas unter die Nase reiben ▷ Butterbrot

Nase • die Nase rümpfen
to turn up one's nose at sth (coll)
He turned up his nose at the cheaper dishes and chose the most expensive item on the menu.

Nase • nicht weiter als seine Nase sehen
not to see further than the end of one's nose (coll)
I have tried to show them what would be a better method of doing the work, but it is no good: they can't see further than the end of their noses.

Nase • die Nase voll haben ▷ Hals: zum Halse heraushängen

naselang • alle naselang
time and time again, over and over (again), times beyond count, umpteen times (coll)
I have told them time and time again, but they never listen.

Nasenlängen • um Nasenlängen voraus sein
to be in front by a nose
Our competitors are in front by a nose and make it difficult for us to sell our product.

nasführen • jmd nasführen ▷ Arm: jmd auf den Arm nehmen

nehmen • Woher nehmen und nicht stehlen?
Do you think they grow on trees?

Neid • gelb vor Neid sein
to be green with envy (coll)
When I saw his new car I went green with envy.

Neid • Das muß der Neid ihm lassen!
You must grant him that.
You must give the devil his due.

Neid • vor Neid platzen
to burst with envy (coll)
When I saw his new car I almost burst with envy.

Neige • bis zur bitteren Neige
to the bitter end
You will have to go on to the bitter end now you've started.

Nenner • etwas auf einen Nenner bringen
to agree on a form of words
In the end the diplomats were able to agree on a form of words which satisfied everybody.

Nerven • die Nerven verlieren / durchgehen
to lose patience, to go mad (coll), to do a wobbly (coll), to crack up (coll)
MIND FF: to lose one's nerve: den Mut verlieren

After her daughter had pestered her all day for expensive toys she lost her patience and hit her.

Nerven • Nerven wie Drahtseile haben
to have nerves of steel
He has nerves of steel – the terrorists may try to shoot him any day, but he seems to be quite unconcerned

Nervensäge • eine Nervensäge sein
to be a strain on the nerves, to get on sbd's nerves (coll)
That secretary is a strain on the nerves – she hums all the time.

Nesseln • sich in die Nesseln setzen
to be on a sticky wicket
If you tell him the truth, you could find yourself on a sticky wicket.

neugeboren • sich wie neugeboren fühlen
to feel on top of the world (coll), to feel on cloud nine (coll), to feel like a new man / woman / person
After arriving in Paris for my holiday I felt on top of the world.

Neunmalklug ▷ Klugscheißer

nichts • für nichts und wieder nichts
for no reason at all
He attacked his neighbour for no reason at all.

nichts • aus dem Nichts auftauchen
to pop up from nowhere (coll)
He popped up from nowhere and in less than no time he was boss of the firm.

nichts • nach nichts aussehen
to look very ordinary, to be bog-standard (coll), to not look anything special
It is a very ordinary looking car, but it is more powerful than it appears.

nichts • Von nichts kommt nichts.
Nothing ventured, nothing gained.

nichts • vor dem Nichts stehen
to stand on the edge of the abyss, to be faced with ruin, to have ruin stare one in the face, to teeter on the brink (coll)
This business is teetering on the brink of collapse.

nichts • Nichts für ungut!
No offence meant! / No harm intended!

Nichtsnutz
she's / he's useless, to be a useless person, drip (coll), wanker (vulg)
She is a useless person – it took her a week to discover that the files are in date order.

Nickerchen • ein Nickerchen machen
to take a nap

nie • Man soll niemals nie sagen.
Never say never again.

Nieren • etwas geht jmd an die Nieren
to shake sbd's composure
The bad news shook his composure, and it was a few moments before he was his usual confident self again.

niet • alles, was nicht niet-und nagelfest ist
everything that is not nailed down (coll)
The burglars took everything that was not nailed down.

Niete • eine Niete sein
to be a loser (coll)
The man's a loser, of course, but that doesn't mean we should not feel sorry for him.

Nimmerleinstag • am Sankt Nimmerleinstag
the Greek kalends, the sweet bye-and-bye (coll)
We should adjourn the rest of this discussion to the Greek kalends – it is not getting us anywhere.

Nimmersatt • ein Nimmersatt sein ▷ Freßsack

Nimmerwiedersehen • auf Nimmerwiedersehen verschwinden
to disappear for good (coll)
I had a quarrel with my girlfriend and shortly after she disappeared for good out of my life.

Not • wenn Not am Mann ist
if push comes to shove (coll), if the worst comes to the worst (coll)
If push comes to shove we shall have to work through the night to get this finished on time.

Not • mit jmd / etwas seine liebe Not haben ▷ Hände voll zu tun haben

Not • aus der Not eine Tugend machen
to make a virtue of necessity
If we have to work through the night we can make a virtue out of necessity and take advantage of the peace and quiet in the office.

Not • in der Not frißt der Teufel Fliegen
Beggars cannot be choosers.

Not • Not bricht Eisen (prov)
Necessity knows no law. (prov)

Not • Not macht erfinderisch. (prov)
Necessity is the mother of invention. (prov)

Notgroschen • einen Notgroschen haben
to have a spare bob or two (coll)
Have you got a spare bob or two? I need to borrow some money.

Notiz • von etwas keine Notiz nehmen
to take no cognizance / notice of sth
I took no cognizance of his complaints, putting them down to sheer ill-humour.

Null • eine Null sein
to be a nonentity
He picked a team of colourless nonentities so that his own talents would shine more brightly.

Nullpunkt • auf dem Nullpunkt angekommen sein
to have touched bottom (coll)
Relations between the two men touched bottom at this point, and for years afterwards they were not on speaking terms.

Nummer • auf Nummer Sicher gehen
just to be on the safe side …
I'll ring him and ask, just to be on the safe side.

O

ob • Und ob!
And how! (U.S.); Not half!
"Did you enjoy yourself at the party?" – "And how!"

ob • Ob im Osten, ob im Westen, in der Heimat ist's am besten. (prov)
East, West, home's best. (prov)

oben • Mir steht es bis oben.
I am sick and tired of it. (coll)
I am fed up (to the back teeth) with it. (coll)

oben • jmd von oben herab behandeln
to look down one's nose at sbd (coll), to treat sbd in a condescending manner, to treat sbd in a superior way, to be superior, to be patronizing
The senior official looked down his nose at the younger employees.
"Don't be so superior – I'm not a complete fool!"

oben • das Oberste zuunterst kehren
to turn sth upside down (coll)
I turned the whole house upside down looking for my glasses.
The new manager has turned the whole organisation upside down and now nobody knows what they are supposed to be doing.

obenauf • obenauf sein ▷ Oberwasser kriegen

Oberhand • die Oberhand gewinnen
endgültig gewinnen: to come out on top (coll)
After a long and confused struggle the English came out on top.
im Begriff sein zu gewinnen: to gain (get) the upper hand, to get the better of sbd
In the long and confusing struggle the English are gaining the upper hand/are getting the better of their opponents.

Oberstübchen • nicht richtig im Oberstübchen sein ▷ Dachschaden

Oberwasser • Oberwasser kriegen (haben)
to reach (be in) calmer waters, to be on even heel (coll), to get a grip on things (coll)
After making a lot of silly mistakes in his work he finally had a string of good successes and has now reached calmer waters.

Ochse • wie der Ochs vorm Scheunentor stehen ▷ Kuh: wie die Kuh vorm neuen Tor stehen

Ochse • Man kann vom Ochsen nur Rindfleisch erwarten. (prov)
You can't make a silk purse out of a sow's ear. (prov)
Brass is brass and muck is muck. (prov)

ochsen ▷ pauken

Ofen • ein heißer Ofen
normalerweise: ein aufgemotzter Wagen: a hot rod (U.S.) (coll) (dated), a smart (set of) wheels (coll), a mega (set of) wheels (coll), bike.
The fifties and sixties were the age of Presley and of the 'hot rod'.
"That's a pretty smart set of wheels you've got there."

Ofen • der Ofen ist aus
to be through with sth or sbd (coll); to throw over (coll) (dated), to finish with (coll), to chuck (a boyfriend, girlfriend) (coll)
ABC Limited delivered late again – that is the third time this month, and I'm through with them. I shall use XYZ Limited instead.
Paul was late for our date again, so I chucked him. I'm going out with Simon now.

Ofen • sich nicht hinterm Ofen vorlocken lassen
It doesn't grab me. / It doesn't sound very tempting to me.
<u>ironisch:</u> *Yes, sounds great!*

offen • offen und ehrlich
quite frankly, to be quite frank
To be quite frank, I'm not interested.
Quite frankly, I'm not interested.

Ohr • ein feines Ohr haben
to have a good ear
He has a very good ear and realised immediately that the piano was slightly out of tune.

Ohr • jmd übers Ohr hauen ▷ anschmieren

Ohr • sich aufs Ohr legen
to have a snooze (coll), to have a kip (coll), to snooze (coll), to kip (coll), to crash out (coll), to have forty winks (coll), to have (take) a nap
We drank so much beer at lunchtime we all crashed out in the afternoon.

Ohr • jmd sein Ohr leihen
to lend sbd one's ear (<u>oft</u> "a sympathetic ear")
The managing director lent a sympathetic ear to the complaints of the export department and granted an increased budget.

Ohr • noch grün hinter den Ohren sein
to be wet behind the ears (coll), to be completely green (coll)
You mustn't use Simon. He only qualified last week; he is still wet behind the ears.

Ohr • ganz Ohr sein
to be all ears (coll)
"Go ahead and tell me about it; I'm all ears."

Ohr • auf diesem Ohr taub sein
to turn a deaf ear (to)
He turned a deaf ear to all his brother's requests for money.
His brother repeatedly asked him for money but he turned a deaf ear.

Ohren • Mir klingen die Ohren.
My ears are burning.

Ohren • viel um die Ohren haben
to be up to one's eyes in work (coll), to be up to one's eyes in things. (coll), to be up to one's eyes in it (coll), to have a lot on one's plate (coll)
"I can't possibly come round tomorrow: I'm up to my ears in work."

Ohren • es faustdick hinter den Ohren haben
to be a cunning devil (coll)
That child is a cunning devil, he can twist grown-ups round his little finger.

Ohren • jmd etwas um die Ohren hauen
to scold sbd about sth, to take sbd to task for sth, to lay into sbd about sth (coll), to haul sbd over the coals because of (about) (for) sth (dated)
She laid into the kid about his careless work.

Ohren • zu Ohren kommen
to come to one's ears
"It has come to my ears that you have been telephoning your young man on company time. This must stop."

Ohren • jmd die Ohren langziehen ▷ abkanzeln

Ohren • jmd mit etwas in den Ohren liegen
to nag at sbd about sth (for sth), to pester sbd about sth (for sth)
My daughter pestered me for more pocket money and finally I gave in.
My mother kept nagging at me about starting a family.

Ohren • die Ohren offen halten
to keep one's ear to the ground, to keep one's ears open (coll), to keep one's ears pinned (coll), to keep an ear open (coll)
I haven't heard that the company has any jobs going which could interest you, but I'll keep my ear to the ground and let you know if I hear of anything.

Ohren • tauben Ohren predigen
it's like talking to a brick wall, to talk to the wall (coll), to preach to deaf ears

"I have told you to buy a new coat over and over again but I might just as well talk to the wall – you never take any notice."

Ohren • mit den Ohren schlackern
to stand there gaping (coll), sbd's mouth fell open
When they told me the price of the car I just stood there gaping.

Ohren • die Ohren spitzen
to prick up one's ears (coll)
Whenever we start talking about Christmas the children prick up their ears.

Ohren • Halt die Ohren steif!
"Keep your pecker up!" / "Chin up!"

Ohren • auf offene Ohren stoßen
to push at an open door
We thought we would have to argue for ages to get them to agree, but we were pushing at an open door and they offered us more money at once.

Ohren • auf taube Ohren stoßen ▷ tauben Ohren predigen

Ohren • seinen Ohren nicht trauen
not to be able to believe one's ears
When I heard the news about her death I could hardly believe my ears.

Ohren • sich über beide Ohren verlieben
to fall head over heels in love with sbd, to fall for sbd (coll)
Romeo and Juliet fell head over heels in love with each other the first time they met.
Teenage boys and girls are always falling for each other but it doesn't often last long.

Ohrenschmaus
a feast for the ears
The new production of Aida is a feast for the ears.

Ohrfeige • jmd eine Ohrfeige geben
a box on the ear, to box sbd's ears (a child), to slap sbd's face (adult)

"If you don't stop that, you'll get a box on the ears."
She boxed his ears because he was cheeky.
When he tried to kiss her she slapped his face.

Ohrwurm
a catchy tune, I (you, etc.) can't get that song out of my (your etc.) head
The audience leaves the theatre humming the catchy tunes.

Öl • Öl ins Feuer gießen
to fan the flames, to pour water on burning oil, it just adds grist to the millstone
If children try to keep the peace between quarrelling parents they usually just fan the flames.

Ölgötze • wie ein Ölgötze dasitzen
to sit (stand) there like a stuffed dummy (dated), like Pippy on a rock bun (used in and around Manchester)
The chairman sat there throughout the argument like a stuffed dummy, contributing nothing.

Opfer • jmd / etwas zum Opfer fallen
to fall victim to sbd / sth, to fall prey to sbd / sth
European manufacturers are increasingly falling victim to their Japanese competitors.

Orakel • in Orakeln sprechen
to talk like an oracle, to make oracular utterances
The Minister of Education always preferred giving vague general directions in the form of oracular utterances to giving precise guidance on specific points.

Ordnung • Ordnung ist das halbe Leben. (prov)
You should use your brain to save your legs. (prov)
A tidy house, a tidy mind.

Orgel • wie die Orgelpfeifen
straight as ninepins
The children were all standing up straight as ninepins waiting for their presents.

Ort • an Ort und Stelle
<u>bezogen auf Gesprächsort und -zeit:</u> "here and now"
<u>bezogen auf Ort und Zeit:</u> on the spot
It is usual at antiques fairs to pay in cash on the spot.
So I said to him: "You've got to pay here and now," but he didn't have any cash.

Örtchen • aufs stille Örtchen gehen
to powder one's nose, to be excused, to excuse oneself, to go to the toilet, to go to the lavatory, to go to the loo (coll), to go to the can (U.S.) (vulg), to go the bog (vulg)
He asked them if he could go to the lavatory.

Oskar • frech wie Oskar sein
to have a cheek (coll), to have the cheek of the devil, to be a cheeky, saucy fellow, to get fresh (US) (coll)
You've got a cheek !
The girls didn't like it when he got fresh with them.

Otto • den flotten Otto haben ▷ Durchmarsch

Otto • Otto Normalverbraucher
the average consumer, the man (woman) in the street
Most advertizing campaigns are necessarily directed at the average consumer of a particular product.

P

Paar • ein ungleiches Paar sein
a mis-matched couple, an unlikely couple, a poorly matched couple
John and Claire are a mis-matched couple. I don't know what they see in each other.

paar • Du kriegst ein paar!
I'll land you one! (coll)
I'll bash you one in a minute if you're not careful. (coll)

Pack • Pack schlägt sich, Pack verträgt sich.
Rabble like that are at each other's throat one minute and friends again the next.

Päckchen • sein Päckchen zu tragen haben
to bear one's cross (bibl.) (burden)
"I have to share an office with Jane; she smokes all the time." – "We all have our crosses to bear; Sarah talks non-stop."

packen • Ich pack' das nie.
<u>nicht können:</u> *I'll never get the hang of it. (coll)*
<u>nicht verstehen:</u> *I'll never get it (coll)*
<u>nicht schaffen:</u> *I'll never manage it. (coll)*

packen • Pack dich!
Clear off! (coll) / Beat it! (coll) / Sod off! (vulg) / Piss off! (very vulg) / Fuck off! (very vulg)

Packesel
to be a beast of burden, "I'm not your carthorse!"
"Why do I always have to carry everything? You shouldn't treat me as a beast of burden."

Palme • jmd auf die Palme bringen
to make sbd see red (coll), to make sbd's blood boil (coll)
The article in today's newspaper made me really see red! I've written a letter to the editor to protest.

Pantoffel • unterm Pantoffel stehen
to be under sbd's thumb (coll)
If he marries her, he'll be under her thumb for the rest of his life.

Pantoffelheld
henpecked husband
He is a typical henpecked husband; his wife never leaves him alone.

Pantoffelkino
telly (coll), the (idiot) box (coll)
What's on the box tonight?

Panzer • stur wie ein Panzer sein
to be as obstinate (stubborn) as a mule
It's no use arguing with him, he is as obstinate (stubborn) as a mule.

Papier • die Papiere bekommen
to get one's cards (coll), to be sacked (coll), to get the sack (coll), to be fired (coll), to be dismissed
Peter was always late for work, so he got the sack.

Papier • Papier ist geduldig.
You can say what you like on paper.

Papierkrieg
<u>vorhandene Unterlagen bearbeiten:</u> paperwork
Poor Simon has to do his accounts, and he hates paperwork.

Papiertiger
paper tiger

Pappenheimer • Ich kenne meine Pappenheimer.
I know you lot (coll)
"It's no use asking any of you to phone back, you'll only forget. I know you lot."

Pappenstiel • etwas für einen Pappenstiel kaufen
to get (buy) sth for a song, (sth) to be going for a song, buy sth for next to nothing
I got it for a song from a friend who didn't need it any more. It was going for a song.

Papst • päpstlicher als der Papst sein
to be more royalist than the king
Over-enthusiastic supporters can be embarrassing to a practical leader. They can be more royalist than the king.

Parade • jmd in die Parade fahren
to counter
The employers countered the argument of the trade unions by pointing out that higher wages would increase unemployment.

Pardon • kein Pardon kennen
to be ruthless, merciless
Deserters were ruthlessly dealt with, and anyone found away from his unit was shot.

Parkett • sich auf internationalem Parkett bewegen
to move in diplomatic circles (polit)
The new Secretary of State has long moved in diplomatic circles.

Partie • eine gute Partie machen
to marry (into) money (coll), to make a good catch (coll)
He married money: all he has now came from his wife's family.
You've made a good catch there.

Partie • mit von der Partie sein
to be in on it (plan, conspiracy)
If White knew about this fraud, then his wife must have been in on it too.
to count sbd in (as active participant) (coll)
"We're going to play football: do you want to come?" – "Count me in."

passen • wie angegossen passen
to fit like a glove, to fit to a T
That dress fits you like a glove (fits you to a T).

passen • Das paßt mir nicht!
That doesn't suit me at all.
I don't like that idea.

Pate • bei etwas Pate gestanden haben
to be the inspiration for sth
The Pantheon in Rome has been the inspiration for many domed buildings.

Patentlösung
instant recipe
There's no instant recipe for curing unemployment.

Patsche • in der Patsche sitzen ▷ in der Klemme sein

patschnaß
soaking wet, dripping wet; to be looking like a drowned rat, soaked to the skin (only animals or people)
Then it came on to rain and we were soon soaked to the skin. When we finally got back even our underclothes were dripping wet.

Pauke • auf die Pauke hauen
to paint the town red (coll), to make whoopee (coll) (dated), to really go for it, to let one's hair down, to rave it up (<u>feiern</u>)
It was Saturday night and the girls decided to really go for it, so they painted the town red from end to end and came back smashed at three o'clock in the morning.

Pauke • auf die Pauke hauen
<u>angeben:</u> to show off
He was showing off all evening – talking about the famous people he's met.

Pauke • mit Pauken und Trompeten durchfallen
to fail miserably, to fail resoundingly, to botch up (the exam) (sl)
She didn't prepare for the exam and failed miserably.

Pauker/in
teacher, schoolmaster, schoolmistress, beak (coll) (dated)

pauken
to swot
She won't come, she's swotting for her A Levels.

pechschwarz • Die Nacht war pechschwarz.
pitch dark, pitch black, pitchy (coll)
It was pitch dark in the cellar; you could not see your hand in front of your face.

Pech!
bad luck, tough (coll) luck, rough (coll) luck, hard luck, hard lines (coll) (dated), hard cheese (coll) (dated)
She caught a cold just before her exams which was tough luck.

Pech • So ein Pech
What bad luck!
What rotten (coll) luck!
Just my (our) luck!

Pech • wie Pech und Schwefel zusammenhalten
to be as thick as thieves
They were at school together and remained as thick as thieves all their lives.

Pechsträhne • eine Pechsträhne haben
to have a run (streak) of bad luck, to strike a bad (rough) patch (coll)
I've had a run of bad luck at cards: could you lend me $100?

Pechvogel
tollpatschig sein: walking disaster area (coll)
to be an unlucky devil (coll);
bei weibl. Person auch: Calamity Jane (coll)
He broke all the glasses washing up and then spilt wine down his trousers: he's a walking disaster area.

Pelle • jmd nicht von der Pelle gehen
to pester (coll) sbd
They won't stop pestering me for my tax return.

Pelle • jmd auf der Pelle sitzen
to have got sbd on one's back (coll)
"Why haven't you done it yet?" – "For God's sake get off my back! I'm doing it as quick as I can."

Pelle • jmd auf die Pelle rücken
to invade someone's space (auch Zimmer, geteilter Schrank usw.)
Would you mind moving away a bit? You're invading my space.

Pelz • Wasch mir den Pelz, aber mach mich nicht naß.
You can't have your cake and eat it.

per • per pedes
to slog it (sl), on shank's pony (hum) (dated), on shank's mare (hum) (dated)

Perle • Da wird dir keine Perle aus der Krone fallen!
It won't kill you.
Try and mend your shirts yourself – it won't kill you.

Perle • eine Perle sein
to be a real gem / jewel / pearl / treasure
Have you met Mrs Brown's German au pair? She's a real gem, she does all the washing and ironing as well as looking after the baby.

Perle • Perlen vor die Säue werfen. (bibl)
to cast pearls before swine (bibl)
Teaching the Fourth Form about Shakespeare is a waste of time, it's casting pearls before swine.

Person • die Pünktlichkeit in Person sein
to be punctuality itself
He's always on time, he is punctuality itself.

Pest • jmd die Pest an den Hals wünschen
to wish sbd would drop dead (coll)
I wish he'd just drop dead – he does nothing but criticise.

Pest • jmd / etwas wie die Pest hassen
to loathe sbd / sth, to hate sbd's guts (coll)
I'm certainly not going to waste my time asking favours of her, she hates my guts and always has.

Pest • jmd wie die Pest meiden
to avoid sbd like the plague (coll)
We had a disastrous love affair two years ago and we still avoid each other like the plague.

Pest • stinken wie die Pest
to stink to high heaven (coll), to stink like hell (coll)
The lavatory stinks like hell – why don't you disinfect it?

Petersilie • Dir hat es wohl die Petersilie verhagelt?
You look as though the bottom had dropped out of your life.

Pfad • auf dem Pfad der Tugend wandeln
to keep (to stick) to the straight and narrow (path) (bibl.)
She stuck (kept) to the straight and narrow (path) all her life, avoiding pubs, drugs and men.

Pfanne • jmd in die Pfanne haun
to do the dirty on sbd (coll)
He did the dirty on her by criticising her work in front of the boss.

Pfau • eitel wie ein Pfau sein
to be as proud as a peacock (coll), as vain as a peacock (coll), to be puffed up with pride, to plume oneself, to give oneself airs
She was as proud as a peacock after she won the competition.

Pfeffer • hingehen (bleiben) wo der Pfeffer wächst
to go to hell (coll), sbd can take a running jump (coll), to get knotted (coll), to get lost (coll), piss off (vulg), fuck off (vulg), get fucked (very strong)
They started demanding almost twice as much for the same amount of work so I told them to get knotted (to go to hell, etc.).

Pfeffer • Pfeffer (im Hintern) haben
to have spirit, pep (coll)
She danced with such spirit that she exhausted three partners.

Pfeffer • gepfefferte Preise
jacked-up prices
The stores have jacked all the prices up for Christmas.
This shop isn't exactly cheap, is it?

Pfeife • nach jmds Pfeife tanzen
to dance to sbd's tune
The Chancellor's ministers were required to dance to his tune, and individual initiative was often rewarded with dismissal.

pfeifen • auf etwas pfeifen
(I) couldn't care less
I told them that they were damaging my property but they couldn't have cared less – they carried right on.

Pfeil • wie ein Pfeil
to be off like a shot (coll)
After class, once you tell the children they can go they are always off like a shot.

Pfennig • Wer den Pfennig nicht ehrt, ist den Taler nicht wert. (prov)
If you look after the pennies, the pounds will look after themselves. (prov)

Pfennig • auf den Pfennig sehen
to count the pennies (coll)
Since the recession started to bite everyone in the country has had to start counting the pennies.

Pfennig • jeden Pfennig umdrehen müssen
to think twice about every penny one spends
Since they have bought that big car they've had to think twice about every penny they spend.

Pfennigfuchser
to be a miser, skinflint (coll), Scrooge (coll) (ref: Scrooge, a character in Charles Dickens's "A Christmas Carol")
to be tight fisted, to be tight (coll), to be as tight as a limpet (coll), to be as tight as a greyhound's arse (vulg), to have short arms (and deep pockets) (coll), to be a tight-wad (coll)
It's no good expecting him to pay, he's got such short arms, the tight-fisted bastard (vulg).

Pferd • das Pferd beim Schwanze aufzäumen
to put the cart before the horse (coll)
They started designing the house before they bought the land – they didn't even know how much space there would be. It was really putting the cart before the horse.

Pferd • Das hält kein Pferd aus.
It's more than flesh and blood can stand.

Pferd • aufs falsche Pferd gesetzt haben
to have backed the wrong horse (coll)
Companies investing in electric typewriters soon found that they had backed the wrong horse when word processors came in.

Pferd • das beste Pferd im Stall sein
to be the pick of the bunch (coll)
Our team are all good, but the goalkeeper is the pick of the bunch – he's never let anything past him.

Pferd • wie ein Pferd schuften
to work like a horse (dated), to work like a Trojan (dated), to work like a black (<u>rassistisch</u>), to work like a nigger (<u>rassistisch und vulg</u>)
The peasants worked like Trojans to get the harvest in before the rains.

Pferde • Immer langsam mit den jungen Pferden!
Easy does it! (coll) / Hold your horses! (coll)

Pferde • Da bringen mich keine zehn Pferde hin.
Wild horses wouldn't drag me there.

Pferde • nicht die Pferde scheu machen
Easy does it! / Keep cool!

Pferde • mit jmd Pferde stehlen können
to be a great guy (coll), to be a great bloke (coll), to be a good (real) sport (coll) (dated)
He's a great bloke, you can always rely on him to help out.

Pferdefuß • einen Pferdefuß haben
there is a catch in it, it's got a snag (coll)

So where's the catch? There have got to be some snags; it's far too cheap otherwise.

Pferdefuß • den Pferdefuß zeigen
to show the cloven hoof (coll)
"All aunts are the same. Sooner or later, out pops the cloven hoof." (P.G. Wodehouse)

Pfifferling • keinen Pfifferling wert sein
to be not worth a farthing, to be not worth tuppence, to be not worth a thing, to be not worth a rap, to be not worth a tinker's cuss (coll) (dated), to be not worth a monkey's (vulg)
This ring isn't gold, it's brass – not worth a rap.

Pfingstochse • herausgeputzt wie ein Pfingstochse
to be dressed (done) (dolled) up to the nines (coll) (dated), to be dressed to kill
Jane went to the disco dressed to kill and came back with a broad assortment of possible boyfriends.

Pflaster • ein heißes Pflaster
a notorious crime spot
Tottenham is full of notorious crime spots.

Pflaster • ein teures Pflaster
an expensive part of town
Mayfair is a really expensive part of town.

Pflege • in gute Pflege abzugeben
"Kitten needs good home." (advertisement in newspaper)

Pflege • Wie die Pflege, so die Erträge. (prov) ▷ Fleiß

Pflicht • Das ist deine verdammte Pflicht und Schuldigkeit.
You damn well (jolly well) ought to do it. (coll)

Pflock • einen Pflock zurückstecken
to back-pedal a bit (coll)
First of all they said they wouldn't pay anything, but then they back-pedalled a bit and offered to cover our expenses.

Pfoten • sich die Pfoten verbrennen
to burn one's fingers (coll)
He burnt his fingers investing in real estate.

Pfund • mit seinen Pfunden wuchern
to make the most of one's opportunities (chances, talents)
He joined as a Midshipman, had a bit of luck, made the most of his chances and ended up an Admiral.

Pfundskerl ▷ mit jmd Pferde stehlen können

Phantom • einem Phantom nachjagen
to tilt at windmills (episode in Cervantes's "Don Quixote")
He thinks that they are going to put that product on the market and is wondering how we'll compete. He's tilting at windmills; they'll never put it on the market.

Phrase • leere (hohle) Phrasen dreschen
hot air (coll) (hum), empty words
The Prime Minister made a speech – all hot air as usual.

Piep • einen Piep haben
to be off one's head (coll), to have a screw loose (coll), to be a few bricks short of a load (coll), to be a few sandwiches short of a picnic (coll), not to have all one's marbles (coll) (dated), to be round the bend (coll) (dated), to be bonkers (coll) (dated), to be balmy (coll) (dated), to be off one's rocker (coll) (dated)
The result of modern selection procedures is usually a single successful candidate who often proves to be off his head.

Piep • keinen Piep sagen
not a peep out of sbd (coll)
"And didn't he protest?" – "Not a peep."
"I don't want another peep out of you tonight, children!"

piep • nicht piep sagen
not to say boo to a goose (coll)
The board is full of people who wouldn't say boo to a goose and the Chairman always gets what he wants without any argument.

Piesack • Einen Piesack muß der Mensch haben.
We all have our weaknesses.

Pike • eine Pike auf jmd haben
to have a grudge against sbd, to have a down on sbd (coll)
My boss has had a down on me ever since I forgot her birthday.

Pike • etwas von der Pike auf lernen
to learn sth (to start sth) from scratch (coll)
He's really learnt his craft from scratch.

piekfein
posh (coll) (abbr. for 'Port out, starboard home' annotation on cabin tickets for the most expensive cabins on certain ships)
"Those glasses look posh." – "Yes, we only use them on special occasions."

Pille • eine bittere Pille
a bitter pill
The election outcome was a bitter pill for the Popular Conservative Party to swallow.

Pilz • wie Pilze aus dem Boden schießen
to spring up like mushrooms (coll)
Real estate prices are so low here that estate agents' offices are springing up like mushrooms.

Pinkel • ein feiner Pinkel
a swell (coll) (dated)
I felt quite lost amongst all those swells in white ties and tailcoats.

Pistole • jmd die Pistole auf die Brust setzen
(fig) to hold a pistol (gun) to sbd's head
The suppliers were holding a pistol (gun) to our heads – we had to pay the new price or shut the factory down.

Pistole • wie aus der Pistole geschossen
like a shot (coll)
The witness answered like a shot without hesitating an instant.

Plan • auf den Plan treten
to appear on the scene (coll), to turn up (coll), to show up, to show (coll) (U.S.)
I waited for him for hours at the airport, but he never showed (up).

Plappermaul
chatterbox
That child is such a chatterbox: she talks all day long.

plastisch • sich etwas plastisch vorstellen können
in one's mind's eye, to see it all before one
I want to live in a house in the Swiss Alps – I can see it all before me now.

platt • platt sein (verblüfft)
to be flabbergasted (coll), to be able to be knocked down with a feather (coll) (oft beide zusammen)
I was absolutely flabbergasted, you could have knocked me down with a feather.

Platze • die Platze kriegen / sich die Platze an den Hals ärgern
to drive sbd up the wall (coll)
The noise from next door is driving me up the wall.

platzen (vor Lachen)
to split one's sides laughing, to split one's sides with laughter
I split my sides laughing.

platzen (vor Neid)
to almost burst with envy, to be bursting with envy, to be (go) green with envy
When our neighbours saw our new car they almost went green with envy.

platzen (vor Ungeduld)
to almost burst with impatience, to be bursting with impatience
I was almost bursting with impatience to see her new lover.

platzen (vor Wut)
to hit the roof (coll), to almost burst with rage, to explode with rage
When she threw away my trousers I almost burst with rage, because my only other pair was at the cleaner's.

Pleitegeier • **der Pleitegeier sitzt auf dem Dach.**
to be heading for bankruptcy, to be in Queer Street, to be up to one's eyes in debt (coll), to be in debt (up) to the hilt
He has mortgaged his house to the hilt and is up to his eyes in debt.

Polizei • **dümmer sein als die Polizei erlaubt**
to be criminally stupid
To lend him more money at this stage would be criminally stupid.

Pontius • **von Pontius zu Pilatus laufen / geschickt werden**
to go / to be sent from pillar to post (coll)
I was sent from pillar to post trying to find out what form I was supposed to fill in.

Portion • **es gehört eine ganze Portion Glück dazu**
to need a good slice of luck (coll), to need a healthy dose of luck (coll)
You need a good slice of luck to get a job in the theatre these days.

Portion • **eine halbe Portion sein**
to be a half-pint (coll)
His sister is an absolute half-pint. She's much tinier than other girls her age.

Porzellan • **viel Porzellan zerschlagen**
to leave blood on the carpet (coll)
After the argument with the boss there was a lot of blood left on the carpet – lots of people were very upset.

Positur • **sich in Positur werfen**
to spread oneself (coll)
He spread himself at the graduation ceremony.

Posten • **(nicht) auf dem Posten sein**
to be a bit off colour (coll), (not) to be in (on) good form (coll), (not) to be in (on) top form (coll), (not) to feel a hundred per cent (fit) (coll), (not) to be in fine fettle (dated)
He is not in very good form at the moment, he spent too long in the pub last night.

Posten • auf verlorenem Posten stehen
to fight a losing battle (coll)
I know people who still won't use computers, but they are fighting a losing battle.

Prag • Prager Frühling
the Prague Spring

Präsentierteller • wie auf dem Präsentierteller sitzen
to feel one is being watched by everybody, to feel as if one were under a microscope (in a spotlight) (coll)
I hated sitting out there in front of everybody; I felt as if I were under a microscope.

Preis • um jeden Preis
at all costs
Sport should not be ruled by the desire to win at all costs.

Preis • Alles hat seinen Preis.
Everything has its price.

Presse • eine gute Presse haben / kriegen
to have / to get a good press
Like all opposition leaders he had a good press until he found himself in Government.

Presse • eine schlechte Presse haben / kriegen
to have / to get a bad press, to get the thumbs-down from the press (coll)

Pressezar
press king, press baron

Preußen • So schnell schießen die Preußen nicht! ▷ Pferde: Immer langsam mit den jungen Pferden.

Primel • eingehen wie eine Primel
to wither (pine) away (and die)
If I had to live in that damp and dirty flat, I would just wither away (and die).

Prinzipien • Prinzipien haben
To be (high-) principled, to be a person of principle
She is a woman of principle, and wouldn't dream of making a false tax return.

Prinzipienreiterei
bloody-mindedness (coll), to be bloody-minded (coll), pedantry
Out of sheer bloody-mindedness the bus driver refused to say what the fare was. That, he said, was the conductor's job.

Probe • Unsere Geduld wurde auf eine harte Probe gestellt.
Our patience was sorely tried.

probieren • Probieren geht über Studieren. (prov)
The proof of the pudding is in the eating. (prov)

Prophet • Der Prophet gilt nichts im eigenen Land. (bibl)
A prophet is without honour in his own country. (bibl)
No man is a prophet in his own country. (bibl)

Prozeß • mit jmd kurzen Prozeß machen
to make short work of sbd (coll), to give sbd short shrift
When they got hold of the rapist they made short work of him (gave him short shrift).

prüfen • Drum prüfe, wer sich ewig bindet. (prov)
Marry in haste, repent at leisure. (prov)

prüfen • (vom Schicksal) hart geprüft werden
to be sorely tried (by fate, providence, destiny)
He lost his wife and nephew to assassins, his brother to revolutionaries, his son by suicide and wondered why he was so sorely tried.

Prügelknabe
to be the whipping boy
Parents make very convenient whipping boys for teachers having difficulties with the youngsters in their care.

Pudel • wie ein begossener Pudel dastehen
to look small (coll)
His girlfriend told him off in front of everyone at the party and then went home and left him standing there looking small.

Pudel • des Pudels Kern
to be the heart of the matter, the long and the short of it (coll)
He says he wants to do it for the job satisfaction, but really he's after the money. That's the long and the short of it.

pudelwohl • sich pudelwohl fühlen
to feel as fit as a fiddle (health) (coll) (dated), to feel like a million dollars (coll) (dated), to be full of beans (coll) (dated), to be on top of the world
He's just come back from a skiing holiday and now he feels as fit as a fiddle.
He's just fallen in love again, so naturally he feels on top of the world.

Pulver • Der hat das Pulver nicht erfunden.
He'll never set the Thames on fire.

Pulver • sein Pulver verschossen haben
to have shot one's bolt
Manchester United managed to equalise before half time, but when Nottingham scored again in the second half it was clear that United had shot their bolt and they hardly threatened the Nottingham goal again.

Pulver • Geld verpulvern
to be a spendthrift, to be a big spender (coll), to splash out (money) (on) (coll)
At university he kept splashing out money on women and drink.

Pulverfaß • einem Pulverfaß gleichen
to be like a powder keg
The Fantasian army is split between the Nationalists and the Communists and the whole country is like a powder keg – it could go up any time.

Pulverfaß • wie auf einem Pulverfaß sitzen
to be sitting on (top of) a volcano
For the duration of the cold war the nations of the world were sitting on top of a volcano.

Pump • auf Pump kaufen
to buy sth on the never-never (coll)
She bought all her kitchen fitments on the never-never and fell behind with her interest payments.

Pump • auf Pump leben
to live on credit
More and more people live on credit nowadays.

Punkt • Nun mach aber mal einen Punkt!
Come off it! (coll)/Give over! (coll)/Come on! (coll)/Tell that to the marines! (dated) (coll)

Punkt • ein dunkler Punkt
a dark chapter
Nazism is a dark chapter in German history.

Punkt • der springende Punkt
the crucial point, the vital point, the crux of the matter
That's the crucial point.
That's the crux of the matter.

Punkt • ein wunder Punkt
to touch a sore spot (coll), a sore point (coll), to touch sbd on the raw
If you talk to him about his ex-wife, you really touch a sore point.
Don't talk to him about his ex-wife: it's a sore point with him.
She talked to him about his ex-wife – that touched him on the raw.

Punkt • den Punkt aufs i setzen
to give sth the finishing touch
To give the party a finishing touch, he booked a live band.

Punkt • ohne Punkt und Komma reden
to talk non-stop, to talk nineteen to the dozen (coll)
The teacher talked non-stop the whole lesson and his pupils never got a chance to ask questions.

Pünktlichkeit • Pünktlichkeit ist die Höflichkeit der Könige. (prov)
Punctuality is the politeness of princes (kings). (prov)

Punktum
And that's flat.
"You're not going out to the disco tonight and that's flat."

Puppe • bis in die Puppen schlafen
to sleep to all hours (coll)
My son sleeps to all hours at weekends and spoils all our plans.

Puppe • die Puppen tanzen lassen ▷ auf die Pauke hauen

Pustekuchen
No chance. Not a chance. You can forget that for a start. No way!
I tried to get tickets for "Cats" – but no chance, they sold out weeks ago.

Putz • auf den Putz hauen (angeben) ▷ auf die Pauke hauen

Pyrrhussieg
Pyrrhic victory

Q

Quadratlatschen
barges (dated), beetle-crushers (dated), great clompers (coll)
He trod on my foot with his great clompers and really hurt me.

Qual • die Qual der Wahl
to be spoilt for choice (coll)
In recent years one has been spoilt for choice in the wine section of English supermarkets. Bulgarian and South American products are widely available.

Quark • Quark reden
to talk rubbish (coll), to talk nonsense, to talk drivel (coll), to drivel (on) (coll), to blether (on) (coll), to blather (coll), to bullshit (vulg)
Politicians much prefer to drivel about peace and the environment than to do anything practical. Practical things cost votes.

Quasselstrippe
chatterbox
My daughter is a frightful chatterbox – from the minute she comes home from school to when she goes to bed she doesn't stop talking.

Quatsch • Quatsch mit Soße
rubbish, nonsense, drivel (coll), bosh (coll), tosh (coll) (dated) bunk (coll) (dated), bunkum (coll) (dated), balderdash (dated), bollocks (vulg), balls (vulg), bullshit (vulg)
The Prime Minister's speech was a load of absolute bosh from beginning to end.

Quecksilber • ein Quecksilber sein / Quecksilber im Leibe haben
to have the fidgets (coll), to be a fidget (coll), to be unable to sit still
That boy is such a fidget! He can never sit still for two minutes together.

Quelle • aus gutunterrichteter Quelle
<u>Auskunft von einem Beteiligtem oder Augenzeugen:</u> straight from the horse's mouth (coll), reliable (trustworthy) sources
"Simon and Jane are getting married! I have it straight from the horse's mouth." – "Really? Which of them told you?"
Reliable sources close to the Government have emphasised that there is no intention of increasing interest rates in the near future.

Quere • jmd in die Quere kommen
to get in sbd's way
My little son always likes to help in the kitchen, but he just gets in my way.
We have been trying to meet for lunch for months but something always gets in the way.

Querkopf
difficult person, difficult customer (coll), awkward customer (coll), cross-grained personality
He is a difficult, cross-grained man. He always wants his own way and is quite unable to see when he is upsetting people.

quietschvergnügt
bright and cheerful, relaxed and carefree, to be pleased as Punch
The students went to the pub, relaxed and carefree after their last exam.

Quirl
<u>Mensch:</u> live wire
She is such a live wire, she was down the stairs and into the car almost before we had decided where we were going to go.

quitt • mit jmd quitt sein
to be quits with sbd (coll), to call it quits (coll)
He broke my hi-fi and now I've damaged his video, so we're quits.
I owed him 10 Marks and he owed me six dollars. There is practically no difference, so we decided to call it quits.

Quittung • die Quittung für etwas bekommen
pay the penalty (price) for sth
He paid the price for his laziness when exam time came.

R

Rabe • stehlen wie ein Rabe
to thieve like a magpie, to be a thieving magpie, to have nimble fingers
"The people round here thieve like magpies, and if you don't watch your bag, it'll walk."

Rabe • ein weißer Rabe sein
to be a rare bird (coll)
He's a rare bird, a German living in Scotland.

Racker • ein Racker sein
to be a real handful (coll)
She is only three but she is getting to be a real handful. She dug up all the rose bushes last week.

Rache • Rache ist süß. (prov)
Revenge is sweet. (prov)

Rachen • jmd etwas in den Rachen werfen
to shove sth down sbd's throat (coll)
In this profession you are always having to thrust your personality down other people's throats and expect them to enjoy it.

Rachen • den Rachen nicht voll kriegen
can't get enough, to be grabby (coll)
He's really grabby. He can't get enough to satisfy him.

Rad • ein Rad ab haben, (nicht rund laufen) ▷ einen Piep haben

Rad • das fünfte Rad am Wagen sein
to be de trop, to be the odd man out (coll), to feel (to be) out of place, <u>bei Paaren:</u> to play gooseberry (coll)
I went out with my brother and his girl-friend last night. Never again! I hate playing gooseberry.

Rad • Das Rad der Geschichte läßt sich nicht zurückdrehen.
You can't turn the clock back.

Rädchen • ein Rädchen im Getriebe sein
to be only a cog in the works (coll)
He never wanted to be a mere cog in the works with neither power nor influence, but the need for a regular income became more important to him than his ambition.

Räder • unter die Räder kommen
to go to the dogs (coll), to go off the rails (coll), to come to grief
He did well at school but at university he went right off the rails: too much drink, too many girls.

Radaubruder
hooligan, yobbo (coll), yob (coll)
The football pitch was invaded by hooligans from M.

Radfahrer • ein Radfahrer sein
to be an arselicking bully (vulg)
He is one of those arselicking bullies who gets on well with the boss by bawling out subordinates.

Rahm • den Rahm abschöpfen
to skim the cream
Old established firms managed to skim the cream off the Government contracts, leaving newer and smaller businesses with the leftovers.

Rahmen • aus dem Rahmen fallen
to be way out (coll), to be far out (coll)
<u>nur Gegenstände:</u> to be something else (coll)
Simon's girlfriend is really way out – she appeared at the dinner party with green hair and a ring in her nose.

rammdösig • rammdösig werden
to get all fuddled (coll)
I work in the Social Service offices, and in the afternoon I always get all fuddled in the overheated rooms with all the people asking for advice.

Rand • am Rande der Verzweiflung sein
to be on the verge of despair (madness)
After I had explained fractions to my daughter for about a hundred times without success, I was really on the verge of despair.

Rand • zu Rande kommen mit jmd / etwas
to get to grips with sth (coll), to be able to handle sth (coll), to cope with sbd / sth (coll), to get on top of sth (coll), to get the measure of sbd
She can't cope with the new situation.

Rand • außer Rand und Band sein
to go wild (coll), there is no holding sbd (coll)
There was no holding the children when we got to the ice cream parlour – they were so hungry and hot they just went wild.

Rang • jmd den Rang ablaufen
to outstrip sbd
Japan has long since outstrippped the United States as an exporter of motor cars.

Rang • Rang und Namen haben
the wealth and beauty (of the town, land)
All the wealth and beauty of the town could be seen at the Opera Ball.

rangieren • bei etwas ganz vorn rangieren
to rank in the forefront, to rank at the top
Paris ranks at the top of our possible holiday destinations.

ranhalten
<u>beeilen</u>: to be pretty fast work (coll), to get a move on (coll)
"She's only seventeen and she's had two children already? That's getting a move on, isn't it?"
<u>beim Essen</u>: to tuck in (coll)
The Headmaster said Grace and the children all tucked in ferociously.

Ränke • Ränke schmieden
to hatch a plot, to work up a conspiracy
She's always hatching plots to secure her divide-and-rule control of the office.

ranklotzen
to get stuck in (coll) and finish sth quickly
They got stuck in and finished the work in a couple of weeks. I had thought it would take months.

Rappel • einen Rappel haben
to be in a foul mood (coll), to be in a temper
My husband has been in a foul mood ever since he got home from work. Something went wrong at the office today.

rar • sich rar machen
to be out of circulation (coll)
Christine has been out of circulation for weeks, working for her exams. None of her friends have seen her.

rasten • Wer rastet, der rostet. (prov)
One shouldn't let the grass grow under one's feet.
A rolling stone gathers no moss. (prov)

Räson • jmd zur Räson bringen
to make sbd listen to reason, to make sbd see sense (coll)
The hapless mayor was quite unable to make the enraged mob listen to reason.

Rast • ohne Rast und Ruh
without cease, without rest, without halt, without letting up (coll), without pause for rest, to keep one's nose to the grindstone (coll)
The search parties searched for survivors without pause for rest.
The lawyer received the papers in the case so late he had to keep his nose to the grindstone all night.

Rat • Da ist guter Rat teuer.
That's a good question. / That's a poser. / You've bowled me a difficult one there.

Rat • jmd mit Rat und Tat zur Seite stehen
to give sbd moral and practical support, to lend a helping hand
My parents always gave me moral and practical support in my efforts to become an opera singer.
He's a real friend, always ready to lend a helping hand.

raten • Dreimal darfst du raten!
I'll give you three guesses…

raten • Wem nicht zu raten ist, dem ist auch nicht zu helfen. (prov)
A bit of advice never hurt anybody.
A lawyer who represents himself has a fool for a client.

Rätsel • vor einem Rätsel stehen
to be faced with a riddle, to be baffled (coll), to be defeated (coll)
When we saw the new figures we were completely baffled but then the accountant explained it all.
Why they have to introduce a new system of book-keeping now utterly defeats me.

Rätsel • Das ist des Rätsels Lösung!
That's the answer.

Ratte • Die Ratten verlassen das sinkende Schiff.
The rats are leaving the sinking ship.
Rats always desert a sinking ship.

Ratz • schlafen wie ein Ratz
to sleep like a log
When he got back from America he was so jet-lagged he slept like a log for ten hours.

ratzekahl • alles ratzekahl aufessen
to eat the cupboard bare, to polish off the lot (coll)
The children always get so hungry after games that they eat the cupboard bare.

Raubbau • (mit seiner Gesundheit) Raubbau treiben
<u>normalerweise gleichzeitig fleißig arbeiten und zu viel Spaß haben;</u>
to burn the candle at both ends
She is working at least twelve hours a day and then she goes out nightclubbing in the evenings. If she goes on burning the candle at both ends like this she'll make herself ill.

räubern • (den Kühlschrank) räubern
to raid the fridge (coll)
The boys have raided the fridge again: the ice-cream is all gone.

Räuberzivil
to be dressed all anyhow (coll)
He turned up dressed all anyhow as usual; he never makes any attempt to look nice.

Rauch • sich in Rauch auflösen
to vanish into thin air (coll)
I can't find my wallet; it's vanished into thin air.

Rauch • Kein Rauch ohne Feuer. (prov)
There's no smoke without fire. (prov)

Raufbold
ruffian, roughneck (coll) (dated), thug (coll)
He looks like a real thug: unshaven, dirty and strong.

rauh • eine rauhe Schale haben: Hinter einer rauhen Schale verbirgt sich oft ein weicher Kern.
Under a rough exterior you may find a heart of gold.

Raum • die Frage steht im Raum
The question is open. / It's an open question. / It's a moot point.

Rausch • einen Rausch haben ▷ auch Affe: einen Affen haben
to be tipsy, to have had a few (coll), to be pleasantly buzzed (coll), to be half-seas over (coll), to be slightly oiled (coll), to be mildly lubricated (coll)
After dinner he was mildly oiled and said at least two things he regretted next day.

rauschen • rauschende Feste, eine rauschende Ballnacht
glittering parties, a glittering ball
The summer term at Cambridge University culminates in a series of glittering parties known as " May Balls".

rauspauken • jmd rauspauken
to get sbd off (coll)
The lawyer managed to get his client off the more serious of the two charges.

Rechenschaft • jmd zur Rechenschaft ziehen
to be called to account
I called him to account because of the complaints I had been receiving about the inefficiency of his department.

Rechnung • eine alte Rechnung begleichen
to pay off old scores
Some murders are acts of revenge; the long-planned, deliberate paying off of old scores.

Rechnung • Da hast du die Rechnung ohne den Wirt gemacht!
If you think that, you've got another think coming.

Recht • Das ist mein gutes Recht!
That's only fair.

Recht • Recht muß Recht bleiben.
Fair is fair. / The law is the law.

Recht • das Recht mit Füßen treten
to trample justice underfoot
Whenever convenient, the secret police trampled justice underfoot. For them no legal limits applied.

Recht • an den Rechten geraten
to meet one's match, to meet one's Waterloo
He thought he could beat any of us at tennis but he met his Waterloo when he played Paul. Paul beat him 6-2, 6-0.

Recht • nach dem Rechten sehen
to keep an eye on things (coll), to see that everything's OK (coll), to check that everything is all right (coll)
The teachers had the gloomy task of checking that everything was all right at the children's party.

Recht • Was dem einen recht ist, ist dem anderen billig. (prov)
What's sauce for the goose is sauce for the gander. (prov)

recht • Alles was recht ist!
Oh, for crying out loud! (coll)

recht • nur recht und billig
to be fair and just, it's only right and proper
It's only right and proper that the best applicant should get the job.

Rede • Langer Rede kurzer Sinn
to put it in a nutshell…, the long and the short of it is…, keeping it short and sweet (coll)…

Rede • große Reden führen (schwingen)
to talk big (coll), to open one's mouth too wide (coll)

The Opposition promised full employment, low taxes and better state pensions: they were talking really big – until they won the election.

Rede • Reden ist Silber, Schweigen ist Gold. (prov)
Speech is silver but silence is gold(en). (prov)

Rede • jmd zur Rede stellen
to take sbd to task
The managing director took him to task for the failure of his department.

Rede • jmd Rede und Antwort stehen
to justify oneself to sbd, to face the music
She faced the music at the meeting and convinced the audience that she had been acting in good faith.

Rede • für etwas Rede und Antwort stehen
to account for sth
He accounted for the decline in turnover, saying it was all due to the general economic condition of the country.

reden • Du hast gut reden!
"It's all very well for you to talk." / "You can talk!"

Redeschwall • Ein Redeschwall prasselte auf sie nieder.
A torrent (flood) of words overwhelmed the orator's listeners.

Redner • kein großer Redner sein
to be unaccustomed to public speaking
"Unaccustomed as I am to public speaking I feel I must nevertheless say a few words in gratitude to my colleagues…"

Regel • nach allen Regeln der Kunst
thoroughly, to use every trick in the book (coll)
She used every trick in the book to seduce him.

Regel • Keine Regel ohne Ausnahme. (prov)
It is the exception that proves the rule.

Regen • ein warmer Regen
a windfall
I had a windfall the other day. My uncle died and left me a fortune.

Regen

Regen • vom Regen in die Traufe kommen
to jump out of the frying pan into the fire (coll)
When I switched jobs I was just jumping out of the frying pan into the fire.

Regenschirm • gespannt sein wie ein Regenschirm
to be on tenterhooks (coll), to be all keyed up (coll), to be all agog (coll)
I'm on tenterhooks to know what happens next.

Regiment • das Regiment führen
to rule the roost
Grandma rules the roost in our house and nobody dares to disobey her.

Regionen • in höheren Regionen schweben
to have one's head in the clouds (coll), to be in another world (coll)
It's no good expecting anything practical from him, he's always got his head in the clouds.

Register • alle Register ziehen
to pull out all the stops (coll)
The showmaster pulled out all the stops to make the evening a memorable one.

Reibach • einen Reibach machen
to make a killing (coll)
He invested in copper at the right time and made a killing.

reichen • Jetzt reicht's!
Enough is enough! / That's enough!

reif • im reiferen Alter, die reifere Jugend
those past the first flush of youth (people in their 40s), at the ripe old age (people in their 80s), those of mellower years (people in their 60s), those who have passed the prime of life (coll)
Those past the first flush of youth shouldn't go to discos and the like.

reifen • Was schnell reift, fällt bald ab. (prov)
Soon ripe, soon rotten. (prov)

Reigen • den Reigen eröffnen
to set (start) the ball rolling (coll), to start things off (coll)
Amanda started the ball rolling at the children's party by explaining the matchbox on nose passing game.

Reihe • Die Reihen lichten sich.
the ranks are thinning out (are getting thin)
At the beginning of the term we had 30 students on the course and now we have only 18. The ranks are thinning out.

Reihe • aus der Reihe tanzen
to step out of line, to stray from the fold, to go off on a frolic of one's own (coll)
The whole family were Communists, but the daughter went off on a frolic on her own and became a Catholic.

Reihe • in Reih und Glied
to line up, to come into line (coll)
The other nations of the European Community waited patiently for Britain to come into line with them on the question of a single European currency.

Reihe • Nichts ist schwerer zu ertragen als eine Reihe von guten Tagen. (prov)
Nothing is worse than Christmas every day.

Reiher • kotzen wie ein Reiher
to throw up (coll), to puke (up) (vulg), to puke up one's guts (vulg)
He drank a bottle of whisky and then puked up all over the carpet.

Reim • Ich kann mir meinen Reim darauf machen.
I can put two and two together (as well as the next man).

Reim • Ich kann mir keinen Reim darauf machen.
I can't make (neither) head (n)or tail of it.

rein • Dem Reinen ist alles rein.
To the pure all things are pure.

rein • etwas ins reine bringen
to straighten sth out (coll), to clear sth up (coll), to sort sth out (coll)

The whole matter was straightened out as soon as we realised we had left the advertizing budget out of our calculations.

rein • mit sich selbst ins reine kommen
to sort oneself out (coll)
He left university without any idea of what he wanted to do in life, so he spent a year travelling to sort himself out.

rein • mit sich selbst nicht im reinen sein
to be odds with oneself
He liked his wife and children well enough, but he went and fell in love with another woman. He couldn't make up his mind what to do but was pulled both ways and was completely at odds with himself.

reinkriechen • jmd hinten reinkriechen
to suck up to sbd (coll), to crawl up someone's backside (vulg), to lick someone's bum (vulg), to lick someone's arse (vulg)
He licked the boss's arse to get his promotion and now he wants all of us to lick his.

reinlegen • jmd reinlegen
to do the dirty on sbd (coll)
He was promoted deputy manager after he had done the dirty on all his competitors.

reinwaschen • sich reinwaschen (wollen)
to put oneself in the clear, to clear oneself, to wash one's hands of sth
The police wanted to charge him with murder, but he produced an alibi and to put himself completely in the clear.

Reise • Wenn einer eine Reise tut, dann kann er 'was erzählen. (prov)
Strange things happen when you are abroad.

Reiselust • jmd packt die Reiselust
sbd has got itchy feet (coll), the travel bug (coll)
Every summer I get itchy feet and want to go off to Greece or Morocco or somewhere.

reißen • hin und hergerissen sein
to be torn, to be pulled both ways
He was pulled both ways between his wife and children and his secretary, who he had come to love passionately.

Reiz • nicht mit Reizen geizen
to display (reveal) one's charms, to show what one has got (coll)
She always shows so much of what she's got, I sometimes wonder why she bothers to wear any clothes at all.

Reklamerummel
ballyhoo (coll), hoo-ha
The ballyhoo of American Presidential campaigns comes near to exhausting the public as much as the politicians.

Religion • Religion sehr gut, Kopfrechnen schwach.
Virtuous but stupid.

Remmidemmi • Remmidemmi machen
to make a row (coll), to kick up a row (coll)
The youngsters gave a wild party and they and their friends were kicking up a row dancing to rock music until three a.m.

Rennen • das Rennen machen
to make the running (coll), to set the pace, to lead the field
The Liberal Democrats have made all the running in the campaign so far.

Reserve • jmd aus der Reserve locken
to draw someone out
I wish I could draw her out a bit during the classes, she always sits there and says nothing.

Respekt • jmd Respekt einflößen
to command (inspire) respect in sbd
The chairman commands a lot of respect in the committee, but even he could not persuade them to adopt the proposal.

Rest • der letzte Rest vom Schützenfest
the last little bit, the remains

Rest • Das gibt mir den Rest
That finishes me off! That cooks my goose! That does for me! That's the last straw!
So he lost his job, his wife left him and then the last straw was that his daughter was killed in a car crash. He shot himself the next day.

Rest • sich den Rest holen
to make oneself really ill
He already had a bad cold, and then he went out into the snow and made himself really ill.

Retourkutsche
tit-for-tat answer, a repartee, a come-back (coll)
Churchill was a master of the instant repartee as well as of the set speech.

Retter • Retter in der Not
like a knight in shining armour (coll)
We were really short of money but then Simon arrived like a knight in shining armour and lent us some.

retten • nicht mehr zu retten sein
to be beyond redemption, to be past saving (helping), to be out of one's mind (coll), have gone completely round the bend (coll)
She has fallen in love with this awful man and she is past saving. She won't listen to anybody. She's gone completely round the bend about him.

Reue • Reu und guter Rat sind unnütz nach der Tat. (prov)
It's no use crying over spilt milk.

richtig • Du kommst gerade richtig.
You are just what I need.
You are just the man I'm looking for.

richtig • Höre ich richtig?
Am I hearing things?/Did I hear you right?

richtig • mit etwas richtigliegen
to have a point (coll)
You have a point when arguing for more jobs, but hardly when you say that these should be offered at higher wages.

riechen • Das kann ich doch nicht riechen!
How am I to know, I'm not psychic!
I'm not clairvoyant!

riechen • jmd nicht riechen können
not to be able to stand (bear) sbd (coll), to hate sbd's guts (coll)
You will never be able to get those two to work together. They can't stand each other.

Riecher • den richtigen Riecher für etwas haben
to have a nose for sth (coll)
I knew the play would fail. I have a nose for such things.

Riegel • einer Sache einen Riegel vorschieben
to put a stop to sth
The two children were fighting all the time until their mothers put a stop to it.

Riemen • den Riemen enger schnallen
to tighten one's belt (coll), to cut one's coat according to one's cloth (coll)
We shall have to tighten our belts, the bank is not prepared to give us another loan.

Riemen • sich am Riemen reißen
to get a grip on oneself (coll)
When he saw the exam paper he panicked for a moment, as it seemed to be so hard. But then he got a grip on himself, set to work and in the end did quite well.

Rindvieh
blockhead (dated), dolt (dated), bonehead (coll) (dated), donkey (dated), numbskull (dated), chump (coll) (dated), twerp (coll) (dated),

twit (coll) (dated), ass (coll), idiot, fool, dimwit (coll), fathead (coll) (dated), jackass (coll) (dated), cunt (vulg)
He forgot his passport and missed the plane, the chump.

Rippen • nichts auf den Rippen haben
to be nothing but skin and bones
By the time help arrived the prisoners were nothing but skin and bones.

Rippen • Ich kann es mir doch nicht aus den Rippen schneiden.
"I can't produce it from nowhere!"
"And where am I to get it?!"

Rippen • bei jmd die Rippen zählen können
You could play a tune on his ribs.

Riesenspaß
to get a kick out of sth (coll)
I get a real kick out of a good football match.

Riesenwirbel • einen Riesenwirbel machen
to raise Cain
"They've sent the wrong papers again. I'm going down to their office to raise Cain."

Ritt • auf einen Ritt
in / at one go
She sent off thirty postcards in one go.

Rock • bei jmd am Rockzipfel hängen
to cling to (one's) mother's apron-strings (coll)
It's time he took a few risks in life – he'll never achieve anything if he always stays at home and clings to mother's apron-strings.

Röhre • in die Röhre gucken
to be left out (coll)
He came along hoping to play football, but as they already had eleven for the team he was left out.

Rohrspatz • schimpfen wie ein Rohrspatz
to swear like a trooper (coll)

When the traffic warden gave him a parking-ticket he began to swear at her like a trooper, and a passing policeman arrested him for insulting behaviour.

Rolle • aus der Rolle fallen
to act out of character
<u>immer negativ:</u> to forget oneself, to kick over the traces
When he offered me the money I was very surprised. It was so out of character.
When I heard the news I'm afraid I forgot myself completely and started telling my father exactly what I thought of him.

Rolle • sich in die Rolle von jmd versetzen
to put oneself in sbd else's place
I put myself in his place and tried to work out what was the best thing for him to do.

Rom • Viele Wege führen nach Rom. (prov)
All roads lead to Rome. (prov)

Rom • wie im alten Rom
It's medieval.

Rom • Rom ist auch nicht an einem Tag erbaut worden. (prov)
Rome wasn't built in a day. (prov)

rosa • etwas rosarot malen
to paint a rosy picture of sth
The government painted too rosy a picture of the country's future and disappointed everybody in the end.

rosa • durch die rosarote Brille sehen
to see through rose-coloured (rose-tinted) glasses, to view sth through rose-tinted spectacles
After falling in love with her of course he viewed everything she did through rose-tinted spectacles.

Rose • nicht auf Rosen gebettet sein
Life isn't a bed of roses. (prov)

Rose • Keine Rosen ohne Dornen.
No rose without a thorn.

Rosinen • Rosinen im Kopf haben
to have high-flown ideas in one's head, to be full of high-falutin' ideas, to have big ideas
He had high-falutin' ideas about teaching the Third Form Hungarian, but he was soon cured of that.

Roß • hoch zu Roß
on horseback

Roß • auf dem hohen Roß sitzen
to get on one's high horse (coll)
As soon as we tried to point out his failings he got on his high horse and refused to listen.

Roßkur • eine Roßkur machen
to follow a drastic cure, to take drastic action, to take drastic measures
He followed a drastic cure so as to recover as soon as possible.

Rostlaube
junk-heap (coll), old banger (coll), old wreck (coll), jalopy (coll)
Old Andrew turned up again in that heap of junk he calls his car. I don't know how that thing keeps going.

rot • rot sehen ▷ Palme

Rotz • der ganze Rotz
the whole caboodle (coll); lock, stock and barrel (coll)
I bought the whole caboodle and it cost me a fortune.

Rotz • jmd Rotz auf die Backe schmieren
to suck up to sbd (coll)
"Catherine in our class is always sucking up to Miss Peterson."

Rotz • Rotz und Wasser heulen
to blubber (coll)
The little boy started to blubber because his mother refused him chocolate.

Rotzjunge
snotty-nosed kid (coll), snotty-nosed brat (coll)
The snotty-nosed brat pulled faces at me while I was changing my tyre.

Rübe • jmd die Rübe abhacken
to have sbd's guts for garters (coll)
If you don't have that worked out in time, I'll have your guts for garters!

Rubel • Der Rubel rollt.
to be coining it (coll), to be raking it in (coll)
Since we invested in Japan, we have been coining it.

Ruck • sich einen Ruck geben
to give oneself a kick up the backside (coll), to take the plunge (coll), to take the bit between one's teeth (coll)
He took the bit between his teeth and did the washing up.

ruck • das geht ruck, zuck
It won't take a sec. / Just like that.

Rücken • jmd in den Rücken fallen
to stab sbd in the back
I was counting on his support in the committee but he stabbed me in the back and voted for the other side.

Rücken • jmd / etwas den Rücken kehren
to turn one's back on sbd/sth, to give sbd/sth the go-by (coll) (dated)
He turned his back on his home and his family to start a new life abroad.

Rücken • jmd den Rücken stärken
to give sbd encouragement (a boost), to back sbd up (coll)
I could do with sbd to back me up because my position in the firm isn't a very strong one.

Rückgrat • kein Rückgrat haben
to have got no backbone (coll)
As soon as the boss started to object, she abandoned the whole scheme – she's got no backbone.

Rücksicht • ohne Rücksicht auf Verluste
regardless of the consequences
Lots of enterprises are reducing expenditure, regardless of the consequences to the staff.

Rückzieher
to withdraw, to climb down (coll)
After hours of argument he climbed down and withdrew his demands.

Ruder • das Ruder fest in der Hand haben
to be in control of the situation
He always appears to be in full control of the situation.

Ruder • das Ruder herumwerfen
to change course (track)
After months of inflationary policies the Governmment took fright at the rate at which prices were rising and abruptly changed course.

Ruder • ans Ruder kommen
to take over (at) the helm, to take the reins, to take the wheel, to take over the ship, to come to power
Newly elected American Presidents do not take over the reins until the January after the election.

Rüffel • einen Rüffel bekommen
to get a dressing-down (coll)
The boy got a monumental dressing down by his father because he was late for dinner.

Ruhe • Das läßt mir keine Ruhe.
I can't stop thinking about it.
I can't stop worrying about it.

Ruhe • immer mit der Ruhe
Don't panic!

Ruhe • jmd zur letzten Ruhe betten
to lay sbd to rest
He was laid to rest in the country churchyard.

Ruhe • jmd in Ruhe lassen
to leave sbd in peace (alone)
The best thing is to leave him in peace for the afternoon, and give him time to recover on his own.

Ruhe • die Ruhe selbst sein
to be calmness itself
Despite a series of disasters he remained calmness itself.

Ruhe • sich zur Ruhe setzen
to retire
It's time he retired.

Ruhe • in Ruhe und Frieden leben
live in peace
The only thing I want is to live in peace in my own home.

Ruhe • Ruhe vor den Sturm
the calm before the storm
The inactivity on the Western Front in the winter of 1939-40 was the calm before the storm.

ruhen • ruhe sanft
"rest in peace" / "R.I.P."

Ruhm • Er hat sich nicht mit Ruhm bekleckert.
He didn't exactly cover himself with glory.

Ruhm • mit etwas keinen Ruhm ernten können
to win no medals for sth (coll)
The judge won no medals for leniency at the end of the trial. The shortest sentence he gave any of the defendants was four years imprisonment.

Ruhm • sich in seinem Ruhm sonnen
to rest on one's laurels
After winning the championship in 1986, he rested on his laurels for two years before returning to the sport.

rühren • nicht daran rühren wollen
to prefer not to dwell on sth

We would prefer not to dwell on the reasons for our parents' divorce. Let sleeping dogs lie. (prov)

Rummel • einen großen Rummel um jmd / etwas machen
to make a great to-do about sbd / sth (coll)
She made a great to-do about how successful her son was.

rund • Jetzt geht's rund!
Now we are off!

rund • Auf der Party ging es ganz schön rund.
The party went with a swing.

rund • nicht rund laufen ▷ einen Piep haben

Runde • die Runde machen
to do the rounds (coll), to circulate
At British parties one circulates, drink in hand, for a series of polite conversations, each lasting ten minutes, with a succession of perfect strangers.

rundweg • etwas rundweg ablehnen
to turn sth / sbd down point-blank, to turn sth / sbd down flat (coll), to reject sth out of hand
I turned her idea down flat, because breaking into a bank wasn't the way I wanted to solve our money problems.

Runden • über die Runden kommen
<u>Gesundheit:</u> to pull through (coll)
He had a long and serious bout of influenza, but he pulled through in the end.
<u>Geld:</u> to make (both) ends meet
What with the children, the mortgage and the car they found they were having increasing difficulty in making ends meet.

Rute • mit eiserner Rute regieren
to rule with a rod of iron
Bismarck ruled his ambassadors with a rod of iron and discouraged displays of initiative.

S

Saat • Ohne Saat keine Ernte. (prov) ▷ Fleiß
MIND FF: As you sow, so you shall reap. (bibl): Wer Wind sät, …

Säbel • mit dem Säbel rasseln
to sabre-rattle (<u>normalerweise Gerundium</u>)
The formerly favourable diplomatic outlook has been clouded by Fantasian sabre-rattling.

Sache • Das tut nichts zur Sache!
That is beside the point!

Sache • Das ist meine Sache!
That's my business! / That's none of your business!

Sache • Das ist nicht jedermanns Sache.
It's a matter of taste, I suppose.
That is not everyone's cup of tea. (coll)

Sache • seine Sache gut machen
to make a good job of sth (coll), to make a success of sth, to get on all right with sth, to make a good fist of sth (coll)
He had never done a job like that before, but he made a pretty good fist of it.

Sache • zur Sache kommen
to get down to brass tacks (coll), to get down to the nitty-gritty (coll)
The chairman of the meeting wasted no time on formalities but got down to brass tacks at once.

Sache • Sachen gibt's, die gibt's gar nicht
Would you believe it! / Would you credit it!

Sache • nicht bei der Sache sein
sbd's mind is elsewhere / not on sth (coll), to be woolgathering (coll), to be daydreaming
I tried to explain to him about deponent verbs, but he was woolgathering the whole time and took none of it in.

Sack • fauler Sack
lazy / idle bugger (vulg), lazy / idle bastard (vulg), lazy / idle sod (vulg), lazy / idle so-and-so (coll)
Get up and do some work for a change, you lazy sod!

Sack • in Sack und Asche ▷ sich Asche aufs Haupt streuen

Sack • jmd in den Sack stecken
to put sbd in the shade (coll), to show the others up, to put the others in the shade, to outshine the others
He put the other members of the class in the shade through his splendid work.

Sack • mit Sack und Pack
bag and baggage
The invaders were driven out of the country bag and baggage.

Sack • schlimmer als einen Sack voller Flöhe hüten
to be as soon hanged (coll)
I'd as soon be hanged as look after her children. They are full of beans, aren't they?

Sack • Du hast wohl zu Hause einen Sack vor der Tür?
Were you born in a barn?

Sackgasse • in eine Sackgasse geraten sein
to be have gone up a blind alley (coll), to be on the wrong track
The scientists found that they had gone up a blind alley in their research.

Saft • im eigenen Saft schmoren
to stew in one's own juice
He absolutely refuses our help however much he needs it, so we have had to leave him to stew in his own juice.

Saft • ohne Saft und Kraft
wishy-washy (coll), namby-pamby (coll)
We were all hoping he was going to order some decisive action, but the Prime Minister's speech was hopelessly wishy-washy.

sagen • unter uns gesagt
between you and me (and the gatepost (coll)), just between ourselves (coll), within these four walls (coll)
She told me, but it was just between ourselves, that she was in love with your husband.

sagen • nichts zu sagen haben
to have no say in a matter (coll)
I can't influence what the appointments committee does – I have no say in its decisions at all.

sagen • sage und schreibe ...
believe it or not ...
<u>with numbers:</u> no less than

Saite • andere Saiten aufziehen
to get tough (coll)
After spending the whole morning in fruitless negotiation, the lawyer decided to get tough and threatened to take the whole issue to court.

Salat • Da hast du den Salat!
Now you are in a fine mess! (coll) / Now you're in a jam! (coll) / Now you're in the shit! (vulg) / That's what comes of ...

Salon • nicht salonfähig
<u>Witz:</u> rude / naughty (coll), objectionable, doubtful, dirty (coll), risqué
He spent the whole afternoon telling risqué jokes to my daughter – I'm not inviting him here again.

Salz • das Salz in der Suppe
that's what makes life / sth interesting (coll), that's what adds spice to life / sth
Of course my job is a little bit dangerous – but that's what makes my life interesting.

sammeln
<u>Kräfte:</u> gather one's strength
The expedition stopped for two days at the 8.000 metre mark to gather strength for the assault on the summit.

seine Gedanken: to collect one's thoughts
He paused for moment to collect his thoughts before replying.

samt • samt und sonders ▷ Bausch

Samt • jmd mit Samthandschuhen anfassen
to handle / treat sbd with kid gloves
He is a very sensitive person and you have to treat him with kid gloves.

Sand • wie Sand am Meer
there are heaps of them (coll), they are ten a penny (coll); to have them in spades (coll), to be lousy with them (coll)
positiv: galore
You think there are a lot of cars here? London is worse. London is lousy with them.
There'll be toffee apples galore at the fair.

Sand • auf Sand gebaut haben
to have built on sand (normalerweise passiv)
The financing of the whole project is built on sand.

Sand • jmd Sand in die Augen streuen
to pull the wool over sbd's eyes (coll)
The Nationalists succeeded in pulling the wool over the electorate's eyes and did not reveal their true intentions until it was too late.

Sand • Sand ins Getriebe streuen
to put a spanner in the works (coll), to upset the applecart (coll)
She put a spanner in the works by refusing to get the advertising department to help.

Sand • (Geld) in den Sand setzen
to throw money away (coll), to waste money on sth
I'm not throwing away money on cars for my children.

Sand • im Sand verlaufen
to recede into the dim and distant past, to fall into oblivion, to come to nothing
The depression had receded into the dim and distant past by 1941.

sang- und klanglos
im allgemeinen: without any more ado (coll), without any fuss (coll)
The class did the difficult exercises without any more fuss.
verschwinden: to vanish into space (coll), to vanish into thin air (coll)
I heard no sound of his going, but when I turned round I found that he had vanished into thin air.

Sargnagel
Zigarette: cancer stick (coll), fag (coll)
He asked me if I could spare him a fag, so of course I gave him one.

Satansbraten
young devil (coll), demon (coll), monster (coll)
Have you met his loathsome monster of a little brother yet? He causes as much trouble as six normally naughty children.

satt • etwas / jmd satt haben
to be fed up (to the back teeth) with sth / sbd (coll), to be sick of sth, to have had sth / sbd up to here (oft mit Geste) (coll)
I have been going to his lectures since the start of term and I've had them up to here. I can never understand a single word he says.

Sattel • fest im Sattel sitzen
to be in full control, to have sth under one's thumb
He is already in full control of the department although he has only been there for one week.

sattelfest • sattelfest sein
to know one's stuff (coll), know one's onions (coll), not to be able to fault sbd on sth
In the Greek history exam he had to show that he really knew his stuff.
You can't fault him on Ancient history.

Sau • unter aller Sau
lousy (coll), crap (vulg), crappy (vulg), shit (vulg), dire (coll), awful
I thought his latest book was complete crap.

Sau • wie eine gesengte Sau
like a maniac
He drove down the high street like a maniac.

Sau • jmd zur Sau machen ▷ abkanzeln

Sau • die Sau rauslassen ▷ Pauke: auf die Pauke hauen

sauber • Bleib sauber!
Keep your nose clean! / Mind your ps and qs! / Look after yourself!

sauer • sauer sein
to be (hopping) mad at sbd (coll), to be cross with sbd about sth, to be angry with sbd about sth, to be vexed with sbd about sth (dated), to be in a strop (coll)
Don't get mad at me – it's not my fault.

Sauregurkenzeit
silly season (coll)
This story would never have seen the front page if it were not the silly season.

Saus • in Saus und Braus leben
to live in the lap of luxury, to live high on the hog (coll)
He lived in the lap of luxury for several years on the proceeds from the sale of his book.

Schach • jmd in Schach halten
to keep sbd neutralized
Some of the police kept the armed gangsters neutralized while the rest of them freed the hostages.

Schach • jmd schachmatt setzen
to stymie sbd (coll) (<u>norm. passiv oder als Adjektiv</u>)
Unless we can get help from somewhere they have got us absolutely stymied.

Schachtel • eine alte Schachtel
to be an old bag (coll)
The school cleaners were all unfriendly old bags.

Schädel • jmd brummt der Schädel
sbd's head is going round and round (coll)
Whenever he tries to explain his job to me my head starts to go round and round.

Schaden • aus Schaden klug werden
to learn by (from) one's mistakes
We lost a lot of money at first, but we learnt from our mistakes and now things are going well.

Schaden • Wer den Schaden hat, braucht für den Spott nicht zu sorgen. (prov)
Don't mock the afflicted.

Schaf • das schwarze Schaf sein
to be the black sheep
He's always been the black sheep of the family, wasting all his money on women and drink.

Schaf • Ein räudiges Schaf steckt die ganze Herde an. (prov)
One rotten apple spoils the whole barrel.

Schäfchen • sein Schäfchen ins trockene bringen
to feather one's nest (coll)
Roman tax collectors were often more concerned with feathering their own nests than with sending money back to the Imperial exchequer.

Schale • sich in Schale werfen
to dress up

Schalk • den Schalk im Nacken haben
to have the devil in one (coll), to be an imp (coll)
That child is a real imp – he has painted the bath in stripes.

schalten • schnell / langsam schalten
to be quick / slow on the uptake (coll)
You will have to explain simultaneous equations very slowly with that class – they are not at all quick on the uptake.

schalten • frei schalten und walten können
to have a free hand

I can only make anything of the department if you give me a free hand – I won't have time to refer back to you for approval every five minutes.

Scham • Ich wollte vor Scham in den Erdboden versinken.
I wanted the earth to swallow me up.

Schande • Mach mir keine Schande!
Don't let the side down! / Don't disgrace me!

Schandmaul
malicious tongue
No amount of virtue can save one from the malicious tongues of the envious.

Schandtat • zu jeder Schandtat bereit sein
to be always ready for a lark (coll) / for mischief, to be game (for anything)
I'm game!
Sailors on shore leave are always ready for a lark.

scharf • jmd scharf ansehen
to look sharply at sbd
The judge looked sharply at the witness – obviously he did not believe what he had just heard.

scharf • scharf nachdenken
to think long and hard (coll)
It is an interesting idea, but we shall have to think long and hard about it.

Scharte • eine Scharte auswetzen
to make amends, to patch things up (coll)
They patched up their friendship as best they could after their quarrel.

Schatten • nur noch ein Schatten seiner selbst sein
to be only the shadow of one's former self
When Oscar Wilde emerged from Reading Gaol he was only the shadow of his former self.

Schatten • nicht über seinen eigenen Schatten springen können
▷ nicht aus seiner Haut können

Schatten • alles in den Schatten stellen
to put everything else in the shade (coll), to be streets ahead (of the field)
His competition entry was so good it put all the others in the shade.

Schatten • Große Ereignisse werfen ihre Schatten voraus.
Events cast their shadow before.

Schattenseite • die Schattenseite des Lebens
the gloomy side of life (coll)
He is a complete pessimist, always expecting things to go wrong, always looking on the gloomy side of life.

Schatz • Du bist ein Schatz!
You are a real treasure!

Schatz • nicht für alle Schätze der Welt
not for all the tea in China (coll)
I wouldn't do your job for all the tea in China.

Schau • jmd die Schau stehlen
to steal the show (from sbd) (coll)
One competitor played a short piece by Chopin very prettily, but then someone played a tremendous concerto by Brahms and stole the show from him completely.

Schaumschläger
bullshitter (vulg), all hot air
The Minister of Finance is an absolute bullshitter – he talks for hours and never says anything at all.

Scheibe • Da kannst du dir eine Scheibe abschneiden.
you could take a leaf out of sbd's book
You could take a leaf out of your brother's book and get down to your homework a bit earlier – then you could watch T.V. in the evening like him.

scheiden • Scheiden tut weh
Parting is such sweet sorrow. (Shakespeare: Romeo and Juliet)

Schein • mehr Schein als Sein
It's all show.

Scheiß • Red keinen Scheiß!
Don't talk crap!

Scheiße • Scheiße bauen
to make a balls-up (vulg), to balls-up (vulg), to bugger up (vulg), to bog up (good and proper) (vulg)
Well, he ballsed that up good and proper!

Scheiße • in der Scheiße sitzen ▷ Klemme

Scheißer
bugger (vulg), bastard (vulg), shit (vulg)
That bastard is always causing trouble.

Scheißeritis ▷ Durchmarsch

scheißfreundlich
to be as nice as pie (coll / not necessarily false), to be as nice as ninepence (coll), to be a smoothy, to be all smarmy
Her daughter is all smarmy, but we still know she really hates us.

scheitern • zum Scheitern verurteilt sein
to be doomed to failure
The whole enterprise was doomed to failure from the very beginning because of lack of cash.

Schelm • Ein Schelm, der Arges dabei denkt. (prov)
Evil to him who evil thinks. (prov)

Schema • nach Schema F vorgehen
to go off pat (coll), to go off like a dream (coll), to go like clockwork (coll)
The first two performances went off pat, but then the players got overconfident.

schenken • Das ist geschenkt!
That's no great shakes. / Forget it.

schenken • einer Sache / jmd keinen Glauben schenken
to give no credence to sth / sbd
I give no credence to his tale of having found the bracelet in the street.

scheren • sich nicht um etwas / jmd scheren
etwas ist jmd egal: not to care about sth / sbd, not to give a damn (coll) / fuck (vulg)
He made his ex-girlfriend very unhappy, but obviously did not give a damn.
jmd macht sich keine Sorgen um etwas: not to worry about sth, not to be bothered about sth (coll)
The engine may make a funny noise from time to time, but don't be bothered about that.

Scherflein • sein Scherflein zu etwas beitragen
to chip in (coll)
I chipped in twenty pounds to the boss's retirement present.

Scheuklappen • Scheuklappen vor den Augen haben
to be blinkered (coll), to have tunnel vision (coll)
You can't really expect them to pull their weight in the new project – they have got such tunnel vision they won't be able to see the value of it.

Schicksal • vom Schicksal gestraft sein
to be cursed by fate, fate (has) dealt a cruel blow to sbd by sth
The people of X-Land have been cursed by fate to live in an indefensible land surrounded by more powerful neighbours.

Schicksal • dem Schicksal in die Speichen greifen
to try to halt the wheel of history
It is no use trying to prevent the collapse of Western civilisation – you can't halt the wheel of history.

schieflachen ▷ totlachen

Schiff • klar Schiff machen
to clear the decks for action (coll)
After making preparations on paper for months, after delays and hesitations, we finally cleared the decks for action.

Schikane • mit allen Schikanen ▷ Drum und Dran

Schild • etwas (nichts Gutes) im Schilde führen
to be up to no good (coll), to be up to sth
Those two boys over in the gymnasium are up to no good, I'll bet.

Schimmer • keinen blassen Schimmer von etwas haben
not to have the slightest / faintest / remotest / foggiest idea / notion / clue (coll) about sth
My son asked me to help me with his maths homework, but unfortunately I haven't got the remotest clue about differential calculus.

Schimpf • mit Schimpf und Schande
in disgrace
He was sacked from the job in disgrace after being discovered stealing.

Schindluder • (mit seiner Gesundheit) Schindluder treiben
▷ Raubbau

Schinken • ein alter Schinken (Film, Buch)
a film / book with a hackneyed plot (coll)
The plot of this new movie is very hackneyed.

Schippe • eine Schippe machen (ziehen)
to pout (fast nur Frauen und Kinder)
"I thought you said you weren't going to touch my toys," she said pouting.

Schippe • jmd auf die Schippe nehmen ▷ Arm: jmd auf den Arm nehmen

Schiß • Schiß haben
to be shit scared of sth / sbd (vulg)
All of them are shit scared of their boss and do what she wants.

Schlaf • den Schlaf der Gerechten schlafen
to sleep the sleep of the just
After a hard day's work he went to bed and slept the sleep of the just.

Schlaf • etwas im Schlaf können
to be able to do sth in one's sleep (coll)
He had worked in the factory for so long he could have done the job in his sleep.

Schlafmütze
to be a sleepy-head (coll)
He is such a sleepy-head – I don't think I have ever seen him fully awake, except at meal-time.

Schlag • zum entscheidenden Schlag ausholen
to deliver the decisive blow, to deliver the coup-de-grace (Fr.)
The increase in American interest rates delivered the decisive blow to our plans of opening a new factory in the United States.

Schlag • ein Schlag ins Gesicht
a slap in the face (coll)
We asked the bank for a further loan and their firm refusal was like a slap in the face.

Schlag • Schlag bei jmd haben
to have a way with sbd (coll)
I can calm him down, if he's in a rage. I have a way with him.

Schlag • ein Schlag ins Kontor
a nasty shock (coll), a bit of a blow (coll), a nasty blow (coll), a hard knock (coll)
The news of the rise in American interest rates was a bit of a blow.

Schlag • vom gleichen Schlage sein ▷ Kaliber

Schlag • ein Schlag ins Wasser
a wash-out (coll), a let-down (coll), a flop (coll)
We invited a rock band to come and play in the school, but they forgot half their equipment and the whole thing was a wash-out.

Schlag • Schlag unter der Gürtellinie
a blow below the belt (coll)
Making nasty remarks about his retarded son was a blow below the belt.

schlagen • Ehe ich mich schlagen lasse …
Yes, I don't mind if I do.

Schlamassel • Das ist vielleicht ein Schlamassel.
That's a fine mess!

Schlange • eine falsche Schlange sein
to be a snake in the grass (coll)
We soon realised that someone was betraying us, but it took a while before we worked out who the snake in the grass was.

Schlaraffenland
Cockaigne, the land of milk and honey, El Dorado
Many country folk thought of London as the land of Cockaigne.

schlau • aus etwas nicht schlau werden
I can't make head or tail of it (coll), to be none the wiser for sth, it's a bit above me (coll)
I can't make head or tail of this diagram. Do you understand it?

Schlauberger
clever-dick (coll), cleverboots (coll), clever clogs (coll), smart alec (coll), smart arse (vulg) (U:S: smart ass (vulg))
The new assistant manager is a real smart arse – he makes clever remarks the whole day long.
<u>als Adjektiv:</u> smart-arse (vulg), smart-arsed (vulg)
The new assistant manager makes smart-arsed remarks the whole day long.

schlecht • jmd/etwas schlechtmachen
to bitch about sbd (coll), to badmouth sbd (coll), to run sth/sbd down
I won't tell you who it was, and I don't want to discuss it either. I don't like bitching about people behind their backs.

Schleier • der Schleier des Vergessens
the veil of oblivion
We will draw a veil of oblivion over the rest of that scene.

Schliff • etwas den letzten Schliff geben
to put the finishing touches to sth
He is just putting the finishing touches to his new advertising strategy.

schlimm • Halb so schlimm!
That doesn't matter./That's O.K.

schlimm • das Schlimmste überstanden haben
to be over the worst (coll), to be over the hill
He was very ill for about a week, but he is over the worst now.

Schlinge • den Kopf aus der Schlinge ziehen
to get out of a tight spot (coll), to get oneself out of a hole (coll), to get oneself out of the shit (vulg)
The accused got himself out of the shit with a couple of very shrewd replies to the lawyers' questions.

Schlips • sich auf den Schlips getreten fühlen
to feel put out (coll), to be miffed (coll)
He's a bit miffed that you put that suggestion forward without consulting him beforehand.

Schlips • in Schlips und Kragen
in jacket and tie
Most London office workers go to work in jacket and tie.

Schlitten • mit jmd schlittenfahren ▷ abkanzeln

Schlitzohr
sly fox (coll)
He is a sly fox, that lawyer. He doesn't miss a trick.

Schloß • jmd hinter Schloß und Riegel bringen
to get sbd banged up (coll)
They denounced him to the police and got him banged up for six months.

Schlot • rauchen wie ein Schlot
to smoke like a chimney
He smokes like a chimney and gets through at least four packets a day.

Schmiere • Schmiere stehen
to be a / the look-out (coll), to make sure that the coast is clear
Whilst her boyfriend robbed the bank, the young girl was the look-out outside.

schmieren • wie geschmiert
like clockwork (coll), off pat (coll)
The whole thing went like clockwork

Schmutz • jmd in den Schmutz ziehen
to drag sbd's name through the dirt (coll), to fling / throw dirt at sbd (coll), to sling mud at somebody (coll), to indulge in muck-raking
The politicians started slinging mud at each other at the very beginning of the election campaign.

Schnäppchen • ein Schnäppchen machen
to get / pick up a bargain
I got a good bargain in the January sales this year.

Schnapsfahne • eine Schnapsfahne haben
to have a reek of booze, to be able to smell the drink / booze (coll) on sbd
He has started drinking whisky first thing in the morning and you can smell the drink on him when he arrives in the office.

Schnauze • eine große Schnauze haben
to be a big-mouth (coll), to talk big (coll)
He came over here with various ideas about setting us all to rights – he's such a big-mouth, he never listened to anything that we had to say.

Schnauze • die Schnauze halten
to shut one's face (coll)
I told him to shut his face because he was being rude about my sister.

schneeweiß • schneeweiß (vor Entsetzen) werden ▷ kreidebleich

Schneider • frieren wie ein Schneider
to be / get frozen to the marrow
We stood in the snow at the bus stop and got frozen to the marrow.

Schnelle • auf die Schnelle
to do sth in a rush (coll)
There are lots of mistakes in this exercise because I did it in a rush.

Schnippchen • jmd ein Schnippchen schlagen
to steal a march on sbd (coll)
They stole a march on us by getting their product on the market first.

schnuppe • Das ist mir schnuppe!
I couldn't care less.

schön • zu schön, um wahr zu sein
too good to be true
I looked at the job offer carefully because it seemed too good to be true.

schön • schön und gut
That's all well and good. / That's all very well. / That's all very fine (and large).

Schornstein • etwas in den Schornstein schreiben können
to write sth off (coll), to ditch sth
We had to write off that whole project as a dead loss.

Schoß • Es fällt mir nichts in den Schoß.
Nothing is handed to me on a plate.

Schoß • im Schoße der Familie
in the bosom of one's family
I always like to spend Christmas in the bosom of my family.

Schraube • eine alte Schraube ▷ Schachtel

Schraube • eine Schraube locker haben
to have got a screw loose (coll)
I listened to his plan, but it was just plain crazy. I think he has got a screw loose.

schrauben • geschraubt sprechen
to talk in stilted English
Queen Victoria talked in slightly stilted English.

Schreck • mit dem Schrecken davonkommen
to get off (escape) with no more than a fright (coll), to be saved by the bell
He fell asleep at the wheel of his car, but his passenger woke him and they both got off with no more than a nasty fright.

Schreck • der Schreck fuhr jmd in die Knochen
sbd's knees turned to jelly
His knees turned to jelly as he waited for the jury's verdict.

Schreck • Der Schreck sitzt mir in den Knochen.
My knees are like jelly.

Schritt • gemessenen Schrittes
at a measured pace
The king entered the throne room at a measured pace.

Schritt • den zweiten vor dem ersten Schritt tun wollen
to try to run before you can walk (coll)
Don't try to run before you can walk.

Schritt • auf Schritt und Tritt
wherever you go
He follows me wherever I go.

Schubladendenken
to think in rigid categories, to think in stereotypes, to put things in pigeonholes
The scientific mind thinks in categories – once a problem has been analysed, reduced to its elements and put in a category the task is completed. Solving a problem is not considered important.

Schuh • Wo drückt denn der Schuh?
What's the trouble?/What's up (coll)?/What's wrong?/What's the problem?/What's bugging/eating you?

Schuh • Umgekehrt wird ein Schuh draus!
Quite the reverse is true./On the contrary.

Schuhe • jmd etwas in die Schuhe schieben
to lay the blame for sth at sbd's door, to pass the buck to sbd
Don't you try to lay the blame for that at my door – I had nothing to do with it.

Schulden • mehr Schulden als Haare auf dem Kopf haben
to be up to one's ears in debt (coll)
You won't get any money out of him – he is up to his ears in debt.

schuldig • jmd nichts schuldig bleiben
to give as good as one gets (coll)
In the course of the argument with the landlord the tenant gave as good as he got.

Schule • Schule machen
to become an accepted thing, to catch on
It has become an accepted thing to allow children a great deal of freedom at school.

Schule • aus der Schule plaudern
to tell tales out of school (coll)
That secret was supposed to be kept to our group only – somebody must have been telling tales out of school.

Schulgeld • Du kannst dir dein Schulgeld wiedergeben lassen.
School didn't do you much good.

Schulter • etwas auf die leichte Schulter nehmen
to take sth lightly (coll), to brush sth off (coll)
I heard his threat, but I didn't take it seriously – I just brushed it off.

Schulter • jmd die kalte Schulter zeigen ▷ abblitzen

Schürzenband • noch an Mutter's Schürzenband hängen
to be still tied to one's mother's apron strings (coll)
He is twenty-seven and still tied to his mother's apron-strings. She sews on his buttons and he won't do anything unless she has approved of it first.

Schuß • ein Schuß ins Schwarze
Bull's eye (coll/exclamation), to hit the mark, to be right on (coll)
That speech was right on. It got the crowd completely on our side.

Schuster • Schuster, bleib bei deinen Leisten! (prov)
Cobbler, stick to your last. (prov)

Schutt • in Schutt und Asche legen
to reduce sth to rubble
Enemy air attacks reduced the town to rubble, but the defenders still fought on.

Schutt • Schutt und Asche sein
to be in ruins
At the end of the war many of Germany's cities were in ruins.

schwach • Mach mich nicht schwach!
Don't say that!

Schwachheit • Schwachheit, dein Name ist Weib.
Frailty, thy name is woman! (Shakespeare: Hamlet)

Schwalbe • Eine Schwalbe macht noch keinen Sommer. (prov)
One swallow does not make a summer. (prov)

Schwamm • Schwamm drüber!
Why don't we forget it? / Shall I forget it?

schwarz • schwarz fahren
<u>nur als Substantiv:</u> fare dodging
Fare-dodging is a much more serious offence in England than in Germany.

schwarz • schwarz für jmd / etwas sehen
to take a gloomy view of sbd's / sth's future (coll)
I take a gloomy view of Europe's future as a base for manufacturing industry.

schwarz • ins Schwarze treffen ▷ Schuß: ein Schuß ins Schwarze

schwarz • etwas schwarz-weiß malen
to paint a very black and white picture of …
In that novel the author paints a black-and-white picture with no room for shades of grey.

schwarz • Da kannst du warten, bis du schwarz wirst!
You can wait there until the cows come home.

schweigen • sich in Schweigen hüllen
to take refuge in silence
When asked about the fate of the Polish officers the Russian government took refuge in silence.

Schweigen • Schweigen ist auch eine Antwort.
Silence gives consent. (prov) / Silence came the stern reply.

Schwein • sich benehmen wie ein Schwein
to behave like a pig (coll)
The children behaved like pigs at the tea party – I don't believe they will be invited anywhere ever again.

Schwein • Schwein gehabt!
That was a stroke of luck!

Schwein • Schwein haben
to be lucky, to be in luck, my luck's in
I was really lucky at cards today – I had all four aces twice.

Schweiß • im Schweiße meines Angesichts
by the sweat of my brow (coll)
I did it all by the sweat of my brow. There were no easy short cuts.

Schwelle • die Schwelle eines Hauses nicht betreten
not to set foot in sbd's house, not to set foot over the threshold

For as long as the objectionable cousin is there I decline to set foot over the threshold.

Schwelle • Er darf meine Schwelle nicht mehr betreten.
He may not darken my door again.

Schwips • einen Schwips haben ▷ Affe: einen Affen haben

Schwulitäten • jmd in Schwulitäten bringen
to put sbd in a hole (coll), to make things awkward for sbd
They really put us in a hole, letting us down like that. I don't know how we can get out of this mess.

Seele • etwas liegt mir auf der Seele
sth weighs heavily on my mind
My friend's illness weighs heavily on my mind.

Seele • sich etwas von der Seele reden
to get sth off one's chest (coll)
I could tell something was troubling him so I told him to get it of his chest. Then he told me the whole story.

Seele • Dann hat die liebe Seele Ruh.
That'll put an end to the matter.
That'll put us out of our misery. (MIND: "to put sbd out of the misery" can also be "to kill sbd")

Seele • jmd aus der Seele sprechen
to express exactly what sbd feels
When he said that after a bereavement one sees the whole world in black and white he expressed exactly what we were all feeling.

Seele • jmd in tiefster Seele verletzen
to cut sbd to the quick (<u>oft passiv</u>)
When she left her husband he was cut to the quick.

Seele • Zwei Seelen wohnen – ach – in meiner Brust.
I'm torn. / I am a torn soul.
I'm torn between the devil and the deep blue sea.

Seelenruhe • in aller Seelenruhe
as cool as you please (coll), as cool as be damned (coll), as cool as a cucumber
He came in here, cool as be damned, and said he had borrowed two hundred dollars from my desk.

Segen • seinen Segen zu etwas geben
to give one's blessing to sth
After thinking long and hard they decided to give their blessing to their daughter's marriage.

sehen • Da kann man mal sehen!
That just goes to show.

sehen • Das kann sich sehen lassen.
to be certainly sth to be proud of
Did you see his examination result? Certainly something to be proud of.

sehen • Jeder muß sehen, wo er bleibt.
It's every man for himself.

Seifenblase • platzen wie eine Seifenblase
to burst like a balloon, to go up in smoke
The chimera of a successful financial recovery burst like a balloon when the stock market collapsed.

Seiltanz • einen Seiltanz vollführen
to walk the tightrope, to do a tightrope act (coll), to do a highwire act (coll), to do a balancing act (coll)
The government is doing a tightrope act, trying to keep all members of the coalition happy.

Sein • Sein oder Nichtsein …
To be or not to be … (Shakespeare: Hamlet)

Seite • Alles hat zwei Seiten
There are two sides to everything.
There are always two sides to the coin.

Seite • sich von seiner besten Seite zeigen
to put on one's best side, to be on one's best behaviour
The Ambassador put on his best side when his guests for the dinner party arrived.

Seitensprung • einen Seitensprung machen
to have a bit on the side (coll)
He has a bit on the side which his wife doesn't know about.

selbst • Das versteht sich von selbst.
That goes without saying.

Semester • ein älteres Semester sein
to be getting on in years (coll)
He is getting on in years now, and no longer comes to the football matches.

Semmel • weggehen wie warme Semmeln
sth sells like hot cakes (coll)
All his books sell like hot cakes. He is one of the most popular authors writing today.

Senf • seinen Senf dazugeben
to shove one's oar in (coll)
He could never hear a discussion of any sort going on without shoving his oar in somehow, and giving his opinion.

Senkrechtstarter
whizz kid (coll)
He was promoted so fast he was on the Board in three months – a real whizz-kid.

Sense • Nun ist aber Sense!
That's the end./That'll be enough of that!

Sesam • Sesam öffne dich!
Open, Sesame!

sicher • so gut wie sicher
to be practically in the bag (coll)
We practically have the trophy in the bag – our team is so much better than theirs.

Sicherheit • sich in Sicherheit wiegen
to lull oneself into a false sense of security
The series of reassuring letters lulled him into a false sense of security, so that when the bad news finally came he was quite unprepared.

Sicht • auf lange Sicht
in the long run
In the long run we will all be dead.

Siebensachen • seine Siebensachen packen
to gather up one's traps (coll), to gather up one's klatsch (coll), to collect one's bits and pieces
He gathered up his klatsch and left the room for good.

Sieg • den Sieg davontragen
to carry (win) the day (coll)
At the Colloquy the arguments of the Professor from Whitchester carried the day.

Siegel • unter dem Siegel der Verschwiegenheit
to swear sbd to secrecy, in the strictest confidence
I swore him to secrecy, but it was all over the college a day later.

siegen • er kam, sah und siegte.
<u>nur in der 1. Person:</u> *Veni, vidi, vici (Lat. Julius Caesar)*
I came, I saw, I conquered.

Silber • ein Silberstreif am Horizont
a silver cloud on the horizon, light at the end of the tunnel (coll)
"As an economy measure the light at the end of the tunnel has been turned off until further notice."(Londoner Witz während der wirtschaftlichen Talfahrt 1992)

singen • Das kann ich schon singen.
I know it backwards.

Sinn • Das will mir einfach nicht in den Sinn!
I just can't understand it.

Sinn • Bist du noch bei Sinnen?
Have you taken leave of your senses?

Sinn • den sechsten Sinn haben
to have a sixth sense (coll)
Most experienced soldiers have a sixth sense for danger.

Sinn • seine fünf Sinne zusammennehmen
to gather one's wits (coll)
The boy sat there cluelessly, so I told him to gather his wits and try to answer the question.

Sisyphusarbeit
It's like the ball of Sisyphus.

sitzen • jmd sitzen lassen
to walk out on sbd (coll), to leave sbd
His wife walked out on him after fifteen years of marriage.

sitzen • (eine Beleidigung) nicht auf sich sitzen lassen
not to stand for sth (coll), not to take sth lying down (coll), not to let sbd get away with sth
I hope you're not going to take those remarks lying down.

Sitzfleisch • kein Sitzfleisch haben
not to be able to sit still, to be a fidget, to have ants in one's pants (U.S., coll)
One of the problems with this class is that half the youngsters simply cannot sit still for more than twenty minutes.

Socke • eine rote Socke sein
to be a commie (coll), to be a Red (coll), to be one of the Comrades (coll)
All the people living on that housing estate are Reds.

Socken • sich auf die Socken machen
to get going (coll), to make a move
Come on, we'd better get going, or we'll miss the plane.

Socken • von den Socken sein ▷ baff sein

sondersgleichen • (mit einer Frechheit) sondersgleichen
with unparalleled / unprecedented cheek
When I asked what he was doing with my money, he told me with unparalleled cheek that I should mind my own business.

Sonne • Die Sonne bringt es an den Tag.
Truth will out. (prov)

spanisch • Das kommt mir spanisch vor.
That seems (a bit) odd to me.

sparen • Spare in der Zeit, so hast du in der Not. (prov)
to put sth by, to save (for a rainy day)
You should always save for a rainy day.

Späne • Wo gehobelt wird, fallen Späne. (prov)
You can't make an omelette without breaking eggs. (prov)

Sparflamme • eine Beziehung auf Sparflamme halten
to put sbd on the back burner (coll)
I have put my boyfriend on the back burner for a few weeks – he was getting too possessive.

Sparschwein • sein Sparschwein schlachten
to break into one's piggy bank (coll)
He will have to break into his piggy bank to buy that car.

Spaß • ein teurer Spaß
an expensive business
Playing golf is an expensive business.

Spaß • Spaß muß sein.
There's no harm in a joke. / Look at the funny side of it.

Spaß • keinen Spaß verstehen
He doesn't stand for any nonsense. / She is a strict person. / They can't take a joke.

spät • Besser spät als nie. (prov)
Better late than never. (prov)

Spatz • Besser einen Spatz in der Hand als eine Taube auf dem Dach. (prov)
A bird in the hand is worth two in the bush. (prov)

Spatz • Das pfeifen die Spatzen von den Dächern
It's the talk of the town. / It's on everyone's lips.

Speck • Ran an den Speck
Let's get stuck in.

Speck • Mit Speck fängt man Mäuse. (prov)
You have to throw a sprat to catch a mackerel. (prov)

Speise • Vielen Dank für Speis und Trank.
Many thanks for the meal.

Spendierhosen • seine Spendierhosen anhaben
to be in a generous mood, to be feeling generous
He was in a generous mood and stood us all a round of drinks.

Sperrfeuer • ins Sperrfeuer der Kritik geraten
to run into a barrage of criticism (coll)
He ran into a barrage of criticism for suggesting that the workforce be cut.

Spesen • Außer Spesen nichts gewesen …
hardly profitable but enjoyable …

spicken • jmd spicken
to bribe sbd, to grease sbd's palm
You have to bribe half the government to get a country like that to buy anything at all.

Gelder, die von einer Firma zum Bestechen betimmt sind: slush fund (coll)
XYZ Ltd needed a big slush fund to get the contract for the African dam.

spicken • eine Rede mit Zitaten spicken
to lard / litter a speech with quotations
In a speech larded with quotations the Leader of the Liberal Nationalist Party tried to arouse the party faithful.

Spiegel • sich etwas hinter den Spiegel stecken können
Put that in your pipe and smoke it!

Spiel • etwas ins Spiel bringen
to bring in (up) sth, to bring sth into play
We brought the resources of local advertising agencies into play in order to try to influence opinion.

Spiel • etwas / jmd aus dem Spiel lassen
to leave / keep sth / sbd out of it (coll)
Although the two problems are linked we left the difficulty with the lease out of the discussion.

Spiel • leichtes Spiel mit etwas / jmd haben
to have an easy time of it (coll)
You will have an easy time of it getting him to help. He is half persuaded already.

Spiel • Spiel mit dem Feuer
to play with fire
He will be playing with fire if he tries to get that woman sacked. She is the shop-steward's wife.

Spiel • sein Spiel mit jmd treiben
to play games with sbd (coll), to mess sbd about (coll)
Stop playing games with me! Will you lend me the thousand pounds or not?

Spiel • etwas aufs Spiel setzen
to put sth at stake / risk, to put sth on the line (coll)
The Prime Minister put all his credibility on the line in promising zero inflation within two years.

Spieß • den Spieß umdrehen
to turn the tables
I turned the tables on them by asking them what they would have done in my place. They hadn't a clue, so they stopped criticising.

Spießruten • Spießruten laufen
to run the gauntlet
He ran the gauntlet of criticism from his father, his sister and his wife. Only his daughter thought he had done the right thing.

spinnefeind • einander spinnefeind sein
to be deadly enemies, to have one's knives into each other (coll)
Those two have had their knives into each other ever since one of them nicked the other's girlfriend.

Spitzbart
goatee

Spitzbube
villain, rogue, scamp (coll), shyster (coll)
Some shyster's nicked my bike!

Spitze • einer Sache die Spitze abbrechen / nehmen
to take the sting out of sth (coll)
Although the bill was larger than we expected he took the sting out of the situation by giving us extra time to pay.

Spitze • etwas auf die Spitze treiben
to carry sth too far (to extremes)
He carried his argument to extremes by saying that we should not rely on our senses but upon reason alone.

Sporen • sich seine ersten Sporen verdienen
to win one's spurs

The young lawyer won his spurs successfully defending shoplifters in magistrates' courts.

Spott • Spott und Hohn ernten
to earn scorn and derision, to be laughed out of court, people pour scorn on ...
Your suggestion will be laughed out of court unless you can think of a better way of presenting it.

spotten • das spottet jeder Beschreibung
that simply defies description
The smell of the lavatories simply defies description.

spottbillig ▷ Apfel: für 'nen Appel und 'n Ei

Sprache • Heraus mit der Sprache!
Come on, out with it!

Sprache • jmd verschlägt es die Sprache
it takes your breath away, to be speechless
When you first see Niagara it takes your breath away.

Sprache • etwas zur Sprache bringen
to bring sth up officially, to discuss
The question of bullying at school was first brought up officially at the last meeting of the PTA.

Sprache • etwas spricht eine deutliche Sprache
that speaks volumes
His behaviour when he was on probation speaks volumes.

sprechen • Das spricht für dich.
That says sth for you. / That's a point in your favour. / That does you credit. / That's very much to your credit.

Spreu • die Spreu vom Weizen trennen
to separate the wheat from the chaff (bibl), to sort the sheep from the goats
The oral examination sorted the sheep from the goats in that class.

springen • etwas springen lassen
to fork out for sth (coll), to stand sth (coll)
I forked out for a round of drinks for the rugby team.

Spritztour • eine Spritztour machen ▷ blau: eine Fahrt ins Blaue machen

Spruch • Sprüche klopfen
to talk fancy / pretty (coll), <u>auch:</u> fancy talk (coll) (<u>Substantiv</u>)
The candidate talked pretty and promised nothing.
The candidate gave them a lot of fancy talk, but was careful to promise nothing.

Spruch • Weise Sprüche, kluge Lehren soll man tun und nicht bloß hören.
Be doers of the word and not hearers only. (bibl.)

Sprung • den Sprung ins Ungewisse wagen
to take the plunge (coll)
He hesitated a long time before he finally took the plunge and handed in his notice to his firm.

Sprung • jmd auf die Sprünge helfen
to give sbd a hand (coll)
I gave my son a hand with his Latin homework which he was finding difficult.

Sprung • jmd auf die Sprünge kommen
to catch on to sbd (coll), to be on to (coll)
The Inland Revenue are onto him. They know he is fiddling his tax return.

Spucke • Da bleibt einem ja die Spucke weg! ▷ baff

Spürnase • eine Spürnase für etwas haben
to have a (good) nose for sth
I have a good nose for a scoundrel. I knew he couldn't be trusted as soon as he walked in the door.

Stab • den Stab über jmd brechen
to condemn sbd

We must not condemn him unheard. Perhaps he has a good explanation for what he did.

Stachel • ein Stachel im Fleisch
a thorn in the flesh / side
I wish I could sack my secretary – she has been a thorn in my flesh for years.

Stamm • vom Stamme Nimm sein
to be a great one for accepting gifts (coll)
She's a great one for accepting gifts – but she hardly ever gives anyone anything.

Stand • einen schweren Stand haben
to have a hard time of it (coll)
He had a hard time of it trying to persuade other party members to support the new policy.

Standpauke • jmd eine Standpauke halten ▷ abkanzeln

Stange • eine Stange angeben
to show off like crazy (coll)
He has been showing off like crazy all afternoon, playing impossible things on his violin.

Stange • eine Stange Geld
a tidy sum (coll), a good round sum (coll), a packet (coll)
His new car cost him a tidy sum.

Stange • jmd die Stange halten
to stick up for sbd (coll), to stand up for sbd (coll)
I tried to stick up for my friend, but everyone else was against him.

Stange • jmd bei der Stange halten
to hold onto sbd (coll)
The party won't be able to hold onto all its members unless it changes policy soon.

Stange • etwas von der Stange kaufen
to buy sth off the peg
She bought all her clothes off the peg in a large department store. She could not afford made-to-measure things.

Starallüren • Starallüren haben
to give oneself airs and graces (coll)
The new King endeared himself to his people by refusing to give himself any airs and graces.

Start • einen guten / schlechten Start haben
to get off to a good / bad start (coll)
The new shop got off to a good start and made a big profit in its first week.

Station • Station machen
to stop off (coll)
On our way to Scotland we decided to stop off with friends in York.

Staub • Staub aufwirbeln
<u>positiv:</u> to make a splash (coll)
The head boy came to Cambridge hoping to make a big splash at the University.
<u>negativ:</u> to stir up trouble (coll)
The Government think that investigative journalists are trying to stir up trouble.

Staub • vor jmd im Staube kriechen
to grovel before/to sbd / at sbd's feet
He decided to improve his chances by grovelling to the police.

Staub • sich aus dem Staube machen ▷ dünn: sich dünnmachen

Stecknadel • eine Stecknadel fallen hören können
to be able to hear a pin drop
It was so quiet in the room you could have heard a pin drop.

Stecknadel • eine Stecknadel im Heuhaufen suchen
to look for a needle in a hay-stack (coll)
Trying to find a particular person in a town the size of Berlin is like looking for a needle in a haystack.

Stegreif • etwas aus dem Stegreif tun ▷ aus dem Ärmel schütteln

Stehaufmännchen • ein Stehaufmännchen sein
You can't keep a good man down. (prov)
to bounce back
Whatever blows destiny blows him, he always seems to bounce back.

stehen • So wahr ich hier stehe…
As sure as I am standing here…
They won't agree to it, as sure as I am standing here.

stehen • etwas steht und fällt mit …
it depends on
It all depends on your mother, and whether or not she agrees.

stehen • sich mit jmd gut / schlecht stehen
to be well in with sbd (coll), to be in sbd's bad books (coll), to be on good / bad terms with sbd
He is so well in with the boss that he is practically allowed to do anything.
He is in the principal's bad books, and isn't allowed to do anything on his own.

steigen • Wer hoch steigt, fällt tief. (prov)
The higher they climb, the harder they fall. (prov)

Stein • da blieb kein Stein auf dem anderen
everything was smashed to pieces, everything lay in ruins, the destruction had been total
After the explosion everything in the surrounding area was smashed to pieces.

Stein • den ersten Stein auf jmd werfen
to cast the first stone at sbd (bibl)
Nobody felt able to cast the first stone, as they all had done the same thing themselves.

Stein • **der Stein des Anstoßes**
a cause of offence, a bone of contention
The advertisements in our magazine that are aimed at children are a cause of offence to some of our readers.
MIND FF: a stumbling block: Stolperstein, Hindernis

Stein • **zum Steinerweichen**
That would move the hardest heart to pity.

Stein • **bei jmd einen Stein im Brett haben**
He/She's taken a shine to you.

Stein • **Stein und Bein schwören**
to swear blind (coll)
He swore blind that he hadn't seen her, although I couldn't see how he could have avoided it.

Stein • **Mir fällt ein Stein vom Herzen.**
That's a load off my mind.

Stelle • **Rühr dich nicht von der Stelle.**
Don't move! / Stay there! / Don't budge!
She refused to budge.

Stelle • **auf der Stelle treten**
not to get anywhere (coll)
We worked solidly for months without getting anywhere.

stellen • **auf sich selbst gestellt sein**
to have to fend for oneself (coll)
Once you are in enemy-held territory you will have to fend for yourself – we won't be able to help you.

Stempel • **etwas seinen Stempel aufdrücken**
to make one's mark on/in sth
He made his mark in our circle. None of us was ever quite the same after he left.

Stengel • **Ich fiel fast vom Stengel.**
I almost fell over backwards.

sterben • und wenn sie nicht gestorben sind, so leben sie noch heute …
and they lived happily ever after…

Sterben • zum Sterben gelangweilt sein
to be bored to death (coll), to be bored stiff (coll), to be bored to tears (coll)
The youngsters were all bored to tears during the lecture.

Sterben • zum Sterben langweilig
deadly boring
The lecture was deadly boring.

Sterben • kein Sterbenswörtchen
not to breathe a word (coll)
Don't breathe a word to anybody – this is strictly secret.

Stern • etwas steht (noch) in den Sternen
it's in the lap of the gods (coll)
The doctors have done all they can – whether or not he survives is now in the lap of the gods.

Stern • unter einem guten Stern geboren sein
to be born under a lucky star
Everything he does turns out right, though he is quite stupid. He must have been born under a lucky star or something.

Stern • Es steht in den Sternen geschrieben.
It is written in the stars.

Stern • unter keinem guten Stern stehen
to be ill-starred / ill-fated
The government invested heavily in the ill-starred High Speed Shuttle scheme.

Stern • für jmd die Sterne vom Himmel holen
to go to the ends of the earth (and back again) for sbd (coll)
I would go to the ends of the earth for that girl after all she has done for me.

sternhagelvoll ▷ einen Affen haben

Stich • einen Stich haben
bei Person: ▷ Dachschaden
Lebensmittel: to have gone off (coll), to have gone bad
The meat will go off if you leave it in the sun.
Milch: to be (to have gone) sour, to be (to have gone) off (coll)
The milk will go sour if you leave it in the sun.

Stich • jmd im Stich lassen
to leave sbd in the lurch (coll), to let sbd down (coll), to leave sbd high and dry (coll), to leave sbd holding the baby (coll)
They offered lots of help and then left us holding the baby.

Stichtag
deadline
The deadline for new copy for the autumn issue of the magazine is already past.

Stiefel • seinen alten Stiefel so weitermachen
to carry on as usual
The policy of shops damaged by bombs in London was that they would carry on as usual; their slogan, painted outside, was "Business as usual".

Stiefel • einen Stiefel vertragen
to be able to hold one's liquor, to be able to take it / the stuff (coll)
She drank three pints of strong beer in the pub and then beat me at darts – she is really able to take the stuff.

stiefmütterlich • jmd stiefmütterlich behandeln
to pay little attention to sbd / sth, to put sbd / sth in second place
They pay very little attention to him – he cuts very little ice with them.

Stielaugen • Stielaugen machen
sbd's eyes nearly popped out of his head (coll)
His eyes nearly popped out of his head with astonishment.

Stielaugen • etwas mit Stielaugen ansehen
to gape (coll) / gawp (coll) / goggle (coll) at sth
The tourists stood and gawped at Niagara.

Stier • (wütend) wie ein Stier
to be beside oneself with rage/fury
I was beside myself with rage when I found that my secretary had yet again mislaid the paperclips.

Stier • den Stier bei den Hörnern packen
to take the bull by the horns (coll)
We have to take the bull by the horns and try – otherwise we shall never know if it will work or not.

stiftengehen ▷ dünn: sich dünnmachen

Stil • Das ist nicht mein Stil.
That's not my style./That isn't how I do things.

Stil • im großen Stil
in a big way (coll)
He went in for 18th century portraits in a big way and now he has a very fine collection.

Stille • in aller Stille
quietly (and calmly)
He went to his office every day, but all the time he was plotting quietly to assassinate the prime minister.

Stillschweigen • Stillschweigen bewahren
to observe (maintain) silence about sth, to keep quiet about sth (coll), to keep mum about sth (coll)
I kept quiet about the new project and didn't tell anybody. My lips were sealed.

stillschweigend • etwas stillschweigend übergehen
to pass over sth in silence
We passed over the errors of his youth in silence.

Stimme • die Stimme der Vernunft
the voice of reason
After the enthusiasm had died away the voice of reason made itself heard in the form of a plaintive question as to how much it was all going to cost.

Stimme • einer inneren Stimme folgend …
something told me / them to …, following some inner voice …
Following some inner voice he retired from his job and went to India, to live among the poor.

Stimme • die Stimmen mehren sich, daß …
There is a growing body of opinion that …

Stimme • der Stimme seines Herzens folgen
to follow the leanings / dictates of one's heart
Edward VIII followed the dictates of his heart and decided to marry Mrs Simpson.

Stimmung • Stimmung gegen / für jmd / etwas machen
to stir up (public) opinion against / in favour of sbd / sth
Right wing radicals stirred up opinion against the left by setting fire to their own party offices.

stinken • Mir stinkt's.
I'm fed up to the back teeth. / I'm sick to death of it.

stinken • vor Faulheit stinken
to be bone-idle (coll)
Your son is bone-idle. He hasn't done any homework all term.

stinken • nach Geld stinken
to be stinking rich (coll)
He is stinking rich. Why does he spend time collecting for charity – he could give the money and save the time.

stinken • nach Verrat stinken
that smells of treachery
The news of some party members being seen deep in conversation with their opponents smelt of treachery.

Stinklaune
stinking / foul mood
She has been in an absolutely foul mood since this afternoon because she burnt the cakes.

stinkvornehm • stinkvornehm sein
to be a posh git (coll), to be toffee-nosed (coll), to be a toff (coll)
Some posh git came along and looked at us as if we were the scum of the earth.

Stirn • jmd etwas von der Stirn ablesen
to tell sth by/from sbd's face
I could tell by her face that she had failed the exam.

Stirn • jmd/etwas die Stirn bieten
to stand up to sbd/sth, to defy sbd/sth
We have to stand up to them – if we give way now, we shall always be giving way in the future.

Stirn • jmd steht etwas auf der Stirn geschrieben
it is written in/all over sbd's face
It was written all over her face that she had failed the exam.

Stirn • die Stirn haben, etwas zu tun
to have the nerve/gall/cheek to do sth (coll)
I don't know how you have the nerve to criticise him like that after all he has done for you.

Stock • Da gehst du am Stock!
You'll be flabbergasted!

Stock • als ob man einen Stock verschluckt hat
to stand there as stiff as a poker, to stand there as if one has swallowed a ruler (coll)
The guard of honour stood stiff as pokers on the parade ground.

stockbetrunken ▷ einen Affen haben

stocknüchtern sein
to be as sober as a judge (coll)
He can't have drunk all that much – he seemed as sober as a judge to me.

stocksauer • stocksauer auf jmd wegen etwas sein
to be livid with sbd about sth
I am livid with my son about his school report – he never does any work at all.

stolz • stolz wie ein Pfau
to be as proud as a peacock (coll)
She was as proud as a peacock because she had passed the exam.

stopfen • jmd den Mund stopfen
to silence sbd
She wanted to interrupt, but he silenced her with a look and continued to talk.

Storch • vom Storch ins Bein gebissen worden sein ▷ guter Hoffnung sein

Störenfried
trouble-maker
That boy is a trouble-maker – if you are not careful he will disrupt the work of the entire class.

Strafe • Die Strafe folgte auf dem Fuße.
to be swift (on the heels) of sth
Punishment was swift to come.

strafen • mit etwas gestraft sein
to be cursed with sth, to be a real trial to sbd (coll)
Her relatives are a real trial to her.
Kaiser William II was cursed with a whithered arm.

strahlen • vor Freude strahlen
to be beaming all over one's face, to beam with joy
The teenagers came out of the rock concert beaming all over their faces because the music had been so good.

Straße • Das Geld liegt auf der Straße.
It's raining soup (coll).
<u>nur auf einen Ort bezogen:</u> The streets are paved with gold.
The streets of Berlin are paved with gold if you are in the building business.

Straße • für etwas auf die Straße gehen
to take sth onto the streets
The workers took their struggle for higher wages onto the streets.

Straße • auf die Straße gesetzt werden
to be turned out onto the streets
His landlady turned him out onto the streets because he could not pay the rent.

Streber • ein Streber sein
to be a swot (coll)
Those three girls are such swots they will have learnt the whole syllabus by half term. Then what do we do with them?

Strecke • auf der Strecke bleiben
to fall by the wayside
Half the class fell by the wayside when we got to deponent verbs.

Strecke • (einen Verbrecher) zur Strecke bringen
to hunt sbd down (coll)
The police finally hunted him down in a flat belonging to a former girlfriend.

Streit • einen Streit vom Zaun brechen
to start a quarrel
He is incredibly argumentative – you can put him in any company you like and in five minutes he has started a quarrel.

streiten • Wenn zwei sich streiten, freut sich der dritte. (prov)
The enemy of my enemy is my friend. (prov)

Streithammel
squabbler (coll), quarrelsome person, trouble-maker, to be always spoiling for a fight
He is very quarrelsome and always contradicts everyone in the hope of an argument.

Strich • Das geht mir gegen den Strich.
That goes against the grain.

Strich • jmd einen Strich durch die Rechnung machen
to thwart sbd's plan
They thwarted our plans by creating difficulties at every turn.

Strich • auf den Strich gehen
to walk the streets, to go on the game (coll)
Some unfortunate girls find they are practically forced to go on the game.

Strich • nur ein Strich (in der Landschaft) sein
to be as thin as a rake
He is as thin as a rake – he always looks as if he could do with a square meal.

Strich • jmd nach Strich und Faden versohlen
to give sbd a good (thorough) hiding, to do sbd over (coll), to duff sbd up (coll), to beat sbd up (coll)
The police duffed up the demonstrators.

Strick • Dann kann ich mir einen Strick nehmen.
I may as well pack it all in.

Strick • wenn alle Stricke reißen …
If the worst comes to the worst, …

Stroh • leeres Stroh dreschen ▷ Phrasen dreschen

Stroh • nur Stroh im Kopf haben
to have nothing between one's ears (coll), to have nothing up there (coll), to be solid wood from the neck up (coll), to be as thick as two short planks (coll)
My brother doesn't understand differential calculus. He's as thick as two short planks.

Strohfeuer
to be a passing fancy
I thought I'd like to go to Germany for my holidays, but it was only a passing fancy. I really prefer France.

Strohhalm • nach dem rettenden Strohhalm greifen
to clutch at a straw, at straws

He is in such a desperate position financially he is clutching at straws. His cousin will never be able to help him.

Strohmann
to be a catspaw, lackey
He has got too many ideas of his own to accept being a mere catspaw.

Strom • mit dem / gegen den Strom schwimmen
to swim with / against the tide
As a politician he swam against the tide all his life.

Stube • Herein in die gute Stube!
Come right in.

Stube • in der Stube hocken
to sit / hang around indoors
Even in the finest weather Londoners prefer to sit around indoors watching TV.

Stück • Das ist ein starkes Stück!
That's a bit thick!

Stück • Das ist mein bestes Stück
That is my pride and joy.

Stück • aus freien Stücken
off one's own bat (coll), of one's own free will
Nobody asked me to do it, I did it off my own bat.

Stück • jmd / etwas in Stücke reißen
to tear sbd / sth to pieces (coll)
He tore our plans to pieces with a few well-considered objections.

Stück • sich für jmd in Stücke reißen ▷ die Sterne vom Himmel holen

Stufe • sich (nicht) mit jmd auf gleiche Stufe stellen wollen
(not) to put oneself on a level with sbd
Don't descent to that level!
Doctors sometimes find they have to put themselves on a level with God and decide who is to live and who is to die.

Stuhl • Da bin ich fast vom Stuhl gefallen.
I nearly fell off my chair.

Stuhl • jmd den Stuhl vor die Tür setzen
to kick sbd out (coll), to turf sbd out (coll), to boot sbd out (coll)
His landlady kicked him out because he could not pay the rent.
<u>im Sinne von "entlassen"</u> ▷ jmd einen Tritt geben

Stuhl • zwischen zwei Stühlen sitzen
to fall between two stools
We cannot hesitate any more about which holiday to book. We must choose one or the other, otherwise both will be booked up and we shall fall between two stools.

Stumpf • etwas mit Stumpf und Stiel ausrotten
to get rid of something root and branch
It is no use trying to reform the old system – we must get rid of it root and branch and start afresh.

Stunde • meine schwerste Stunde
my darkest hour
My darkest hour was when I had to bury my wife.

Stunde • von Stund an
henceforth
Henceforth we shall not make this mistake again.

Stunde • wissen, was die Stunde geschlagen hat
<u>in Bezug auf das, was passiert ist:</u> to know what's happened, to know what happened
I know what happened at the meeting last Thursday.
<u>in Bezug auf das, was passiert:</u> to know what's cooking (coll), to know what's going on (coll)
I would like to know what's cooking – lots of people are having mysterious conversations.
<u>in Bezug auf das, was passieren wird:</u> to know what's cooking (coll), to know which way the wind is blowing (coll)
I know which way the wind is blowing as far as his job is concerned – he will have got the sack by Friday.

Stunde • seine Stunde kommen / nahen fühlen
to know one's last hour has come
The condemned men knew that their last hour had come when their gaolers came to fetch them from their cells.

Stündlein • sein letztes Stündlein hat geschlagen
his last hour has come, he has had it (coll)
When the bomb went off in the next street I thought my last hour had come.

Stunk • Stunk machen
to kick up a stink (coll)
When I discovered how incompetently the job was being done I kicked up as big a stink as I could, but nobody took any notice.

Sturm • gegen etwas Sturm laufen
to be up in arms against / about sth (coll)
She was up in arms about how incompetently the job was being done, but nobody took any notice.

Sturm • ein Sturm im Wasserglas
a storm in a teacup (coll)
I thought they had had a serious argument, but as they were clearly still good friends the next day I decided it must have been a storm in a teacup.

Sturmschritt
at the double
The squad marched across the parade ground at the double.

Sündenbock ▷ Mann: Buh-Mann

Suppe • Die Suppe die man sich einbrockt, muß man auch wieder auslöffeln. (prov) ▷ betten

Suppe • jmd die Suppe versalzen
to put a spoke in sbd's wheel (coll), to queer sbd's pitch (coll)
She queered our pitch completely by suddenly giving away all our secrets to a rival firm.

Süßholz • Süßholz raspeln
to whisper sweet nothings (coll)
He sat in the corner of the pub, his arm round the girl, whispering sweet nothings in her ear.

Szene • jmd eine Szene machen
to make a scene
His wife made a tremendous scene when he forgot her birthday, and threatened to leave him.

T

Tablett • jmd etwas auf dem silbernen Tablett servieren
to hand sbd sth on a plate (coll)
He had his new position handed to him on a plate – he didn't have to fight for it at all.

Tabula • Tabula rasa machen
to make a clean sweep (coll)
We were so unimpressed with the staff working in that office that we decided to make a clean sweep and sack them all.

Tacheles • mit jmd Tacheles reden
<u>offen reden</u> ▷ deutsch: auf gut deutsch gesagt
<u>konkrete Angebote machen:</u> to talk turkey (coll)
We are ready to talk turkey. We will offer you thirty thousand pounds if you will give us possession of the house.

Tag • bis auf den heutigen Tag
to this (very) day
To this day I don't understand how to do simultaneous equations.

Tag • ein schwarzer Tag
a black day
The day my wife left me was a black day in my life.

Tag • am hellichten Tage
in broad daylight
The thieves broke into the house in broad daylight.

Tag • noch ist nicht aller Tage Abend
Don't count your chickens before they're hatched. (prov)
<u>negatives Ergebnis erwartet:</u> *We have not heard the end of it.*
<u>man hofft noch auf ein positives Ergebnis:</u> *The position is not yet final. / You never know. / Never say die!*

Tag • etwas an den Tag bringen
to bring sth to light, to reveal
The escape of the convicts brought to light the inadequacy of prison security.

Tag • auf den Tag genau
to the day
My marriage lasted sixteen years to the day.

Tag • seine Tage sind gezählt
sbd's days are numbered
If he doesn't improve his standard of work his days in that job are numbered.

Tag • einen guten / schlechten Tag haben
to have one of one's good days (coll), to have one of one's bad / off days
I've made a lot of silly mistakes today – it is one of my off days.
<u>nur schlecht:</u> *It's just one of those days! / It's not my day!*

Tag • in den Tag hineinleben
to live for today (coll)
He lives for today, and doesn't bother his head about what he'll be doing the year after next.

Tag • den lieben, langen Tag lang
all day long
He practises the piano all day long so as to be ready for the exam.

Tag • viel reden, wenn der Tag lang ist
<u>viel reden:</u> to talk one's head off (coll), to talk nineteen to the dozen (coll), to talk till the cows come home
The girls didn't notice. They were talking their heads off at the other end of the room.
<u>Unsinn reden</u> ▷ Quatsch

Tag • Man soll den Tag nicht vor dem Abend loben. (prov)
Do not count your chickens before they are hatched. (prov)

Tag • Es ist nicht alle Tage Sonntag. (prov)
Christmas comes but once a year. (prov)

Talfahrt • (die Wirtschaft ist) auf Talfahrt
The economy is in recession.

Tamtam • ein großes Tamtam machen
to make a big fuss (coll)
He made a big fuss about what suit he should wear for his daughter's wedding.

Tanne • schlank wie eine Tanne
to be as slender as a reed
She was a delicate girl, soft-spoken and slender as a reed.

Tantalusqualen
<u>jmd bereiten:</u> to tantalize sbd
She tantalized her younger brother with an offer of chocolate "tomorrow" – but tomorrow never came.
<u>erleiden:</u> to find sth tantalizing
I find these negotiations very tantalizing – are they going to agree in the end or not?

Tante • Tante-Emma-Laden
corner shop
The corner shops are being driven out of business by the supermarkets.

Tanz • einen Tanz um jmd aufführen (machen)
to make a fuss of sbd (coll)
When he brought his new girlfriend home we all made a fuss of her – but she didn't seem to appreciate it.

Tapet • etwas aufs Tapet bringen
to bring sth up, to broach the subject of
I decided to broach the subject of the summer holiday while she was in a good mood.

tapfer • sich tapfer schlagen
to make a good fist of something (coll), to do a great / grand job of sth
My son made a really good fist of it when I asked him to break in the horse.

Tarantel • wie von der Tarantel gestochen
as if stung by a bee (coll), as if bitten by a snake (coll)
He jumped, as if stung by a bee. "That's it!" he cried.

Tasche • jmd auf der Tasche liegen
to live off (at) sbd's expense
He is still living off his parents' expense at the age of thirty.

Tasche • jmd in die Tasche stecken
to run rings around sbd (coll)
The young king was clever enough to run rings round most of the people in his entourage.

Tasse • Hoch die Tassen!
Bottoms up!

Tasse • eine trübe Tasse sein
to be a wet blanket (coll)
He is as gloomy as can be – a complete wet blanket.

Tasse • nicht alle Tassen im Schrank haben ▷ Dachstübchen: nicht richtig im Dachstübchen sein

Tat • jmd auf frischer Tat ertappen
to catch sbd red-handed (coll), to catch sbd in the act (of doing sth)

They caught the burglars red-handed as they were breaking into the house.

Tat • zur Tat schreiten
to get down to business, to proceed to action, to get on with it (coll)
He likes to plan everything down to the last detail before he proceeds to action.

Tatsache • nackte Tatsachen
the hard fact(s), the plain fact, the plain truth of the matter
The hard fact is that we have no money to pay.

Tatsache • jmd vor vollendete Tatsachen stellen
to present sbd with a fait accompli (Fr.)
As he was so slow to agree in advance we decided to go ahead without him and present him with a fait accompli.

Tattergreis
old dodderer (coll)
It seemed to take the old dodderer half an hour to get his things together and leave the train.

taub • Keiner ist so taub wie derjenige, der nicht hören will. (prov)
There are none so blind as those who will not see. (prov)

Taube • Die gebratenen Tauben fliegen einem hier nicht in den Mund.
This isn't exactly the land of milk and honey.

Taubenschlag • Es geht hier zu wie im Taubenschlag.
It's like Piccadilly Circus here.

Taufe • etwas aus der Taufe heben
to launch sth, to bring sth on to the market
He launched his new project just in time for it to be included in the Company's annual report.

Tee • Abwarten und Tee trinken.
Just wait and see.

Teil • sich seinen Teil denken
to keep one's own counsel
I kept my own counsel at that meeting – there was no point in saying anything because I completely disagreed with everyone else there.

Telephon • die Telephonitis haben
to be a telephone addict
He is a telephone addict, and makes dozens of unnecessary calls every day.

Teller • nicht über den eigenen Tellerrand blicken können
to be unable to see beyond the end of one's nose (coll)
The managers of the various shops can't see beyond the ends of their noses to the broader interests of the shopping centre as a whole.

Teppich • den roten Teppich ausrollen für jmd
to unroll (roll out) the red carpet for sbd (coll), to give sbd the red carpet treatment (coll)
The University gave the Duke the red carpet treatment when he came to receive an honorary degree.

Teppich • Nun bleib mal auf dem Teppich!
Be realistic!/Be reasonable!/Don't get carried away!

Teppich • etwas unter den Teppich fegen
to sweep sth under the carpet (coll)
There was a good deal of friction between the various government ministers, but they managed to sweep it all under the carpet in order to win the election.

Terrain • sich auf unsicheres Terrain begeben
to be on shaky ground (coll), to be skating on thin ice (coll)
You are on shaky ground if you are counting on getting money from that source. They are very unlikely to help.

teuer • Das wird dir teuer zu stehen kommen!
That will cost you dear.

Teufel • jmd zum Teufel jagen
to send sbd packing (coll)
He came round here asking for money, but I sent him packing.

Teufel • den Teufel im Leibe haben
to have got the devil in one (coll)
He has the devil in him – I don't know why he always stirs up trouble.

Teufel • ein armer Teufel sein
poor devil (coll)
One of the students sitting in the exam looked very ill, poor devil.

Teufel • Wenn man vom Teufel spricht …
Talk of the devil!

Teufel • Mich muß der Teufel geritten haben!
I don't know what got into me!

Teufel • auf Teufel komm raus
like crazy (coll), hand over fist (coll)
On holiday we spent money hand over fist.

Teufel • in Tcufels Küche kommen
sbd will be in one hell of a mess (coll)
If he doesn't manage to raise some money soon he will be in one hell of a mess.

Teufel • Den Teufel werde ich tun!
I'll be dammned if I will.

Text • am Text kleben
to stick to the printed text, not to ad lib (Lat)
The orator stuck to his printed text and did not say anything unexpected.

Theater • Das ist doch nur Theater!
It's all just play-acting.

Theater • Theater machen
to make a big fuss about sth (coll), to make a scene about sth (coll), to make a song and dance about sth (coll)
He made a big fuss about his flute exam, but it was quite easy really.

Theater • jmd ein Theater vorspielen
to put on an act for sbd's benefit
He seemed cheerful, I know, but he was just putting on an act for our benefit.

Thema • Für mich ist das Thema erledigt.
As far as I am concerned, the matter is closed.

Thema • Thema Nr. 1
sex, the other thing (coll)
That guy has only two interests – money and the other thing.

ticken • Du tickst wohl nicht richtig!
You are off your rocker (coll)! / You are out of your head (coll)! / You are right off the wall (coll)!

tief • Das läßt tief blicken!
That reveals all. / What more is there to be said?

tief • tief gesunken sein
to have come down in the world
He has come down in the world and nowadays only offers his guests non-vintage champagne.

Tiefe • aus der Tiefe seines Herzens
from the depths / bottom of one's heart
He uttered words of anguish from the depths of his heart.

Tiefschlag • jmd einen Tiefschlag versetzen
to hit sbd below the belt (coll)
When he dragged my wife's illness into the argument I thought that was really hitting below the belt.

Tier • ein hohes (großes) Tier sein
to be a big shot (coll), to be no small potato (coll)
That man over there is a real big shot – he's the managing director.

Tier • Jedem Tierchen sein Pläsierchen. (prov)
Each to his own. (prov)

Tisch • reinen Tisch machen
to clear the air (coll)
I didn't agree with one of my colleagues about the way we should teach the course, so I had a discussion with him to clear the air.

Tisch • vom Tisch sein
to be dealt with
I managed to find a girl from my school who was willing to be an au pair for them, so that was that problem dealt with.

Tisch • jmd unter den Tisch trinken
to drink sbd under the table (coll)
He had been used to alcohol for many years so it was easy for him to drink the young girl under the table.

Tisch • getrennt von Tisch und Bett ...
to be separated, to be living apart
<u>wenn noch im selben Haushalt, dann:</u> to be living separate lives
He and his wife have been living apart for many years.

Tobak • Das ist starker Tobak!
That's a bit thick! / I'm not just talking that!

Tod • der Tod als Schnitter
the Grim Reaper / the old man with the scythe / Father Time

Tod • vom Tode gezeichnet sein
to be marked for death
As I walked through the hospital I could see which patients were marked for death.

Tod • Des einen Tod ist des anderen Brot. (prov)
It's an ill wind that blows nobody any good. (prov)

Tod • sich den Tod holen
to catch one's death (coll)
If you don't put on a coat you will catch your death of cold.

Tod • sich zu Tode langweilen
to be bored to death (coll)
The students were all bored to death by the lecture.

Tod • jmd / etwas auf den Tod nicht ausstehen (leiden) können
to be unable to abide (stand) sbd / sth
I cannot stand my geography teacher – her lessons are so boring.

Tod • Weder Tod und Teufel können mich davon abhalten.
I'll do it, come hell or high water.

Tod • über Tod und Teufel reden
to talk about everything under the sun (coll)
When old friends meet after a long separation they either talk about everything under the sun or they find it hard to talk at all.

Tomate • Du treulose Tomate!
You are a fine friend!

Tomate • rot wie eine Tomate werden
to go red as a beetroot (coll)
He went red as a beetroot with embarrassment.

Ton • der gute Ton
good form
I feel he should have discussed the matter with us beforehand for the sake of good form, even if the rules don't absolutely require him to.

Ton • Hat man da Töne!
Did you ever! / Would you believe it!

Ton • den Ton angeben
to call the tune
The Headmaster calls the tune in this school. The parents have no say in things at all.

Ton • andere Töne anschlagen ▷ Saiten

Ton • (nicht) den richtigen Ton finden
(not) to strike the right note
In his speech the Prime Minister struck the right note of quiet confidence.

Ton • jmd / etw in den höchsten Tönen loben
to praise sbd / sth to the skies
The critics praised the new play to the skies.

Ton • Der Ton macht die Musik.
It's not what you say but the way you say it.

Ton • keinen Ton sagen
not to make a sound
The children sat there and didn't make a sound while their parents argued.

Ton • große Töne spucken
to talk big (coll)
He talked big about his plans for a factory in Poland, but I could not see where the money was going to come from.

Topf • Alles in einen Topf werfen.
to mix everything up, to make no distinction, to generalise
It is wrong to make no distinction between people who actively support criminals and people who simply don't do anything against them.

Topf • Gesprungene Töpfe halten am längsten.
It is the cracked pitcher that goes longest to the well. (prov)

Toresschluß • kurz vor Toresschluß
in the nick of time (coll)
I got there in the nick of time, just before it would have been too late.

tot • mehr tot als lebendig
more dead than alive (coll)
He was picked up out of the water more dead than alive.

tot • sich totlachen wollen (können)
to crack one's sides laughing, to laugh till one cries (coll), to laugh oneself to death (coll), to rock with laughter, to hold one's sides with laughter, to laugh like a drain (coll)
They laughed themselves to death when they saw that their trick had succeeded.

Tour • in einer Tour
incessantly, the whole time, non-stop
The children talked non-stop throughout the geography lesson.

Tour • krumme Touren machen
to cut corners (coll)
I think he cut a few corners in his dealings with the tax man.

Tour • etwas auf die sanfte Tour versuchen
to try to get sth with a bit of soft soap (coll)
He tried to get our support with a bit of soft soap, but we could see what he was up to.

Touren • auf vollen Touren (laufen)
to be in full swing (coll)
The pop concert was already in full swing by the time we arrived.

Trab • jmd auf Trab bringen
to make sbd get a move on (coll)
I tried to make him get a move on, but he still had a lot left to do at seven pm when I left the office.

Trab • jmd in Trab halten
to keep sbd on the go (coll)
They kept their poor au pair girl on the go all day, washing and cooking and shopping and looking after the baby.

Tracht • jmd eine Tracht Prügel verabreichen
to give sbd a (sound) beating (thrashing)
When I found out how he had treated my sister I wanted to go out and give him a sound thrashing – but unfortunately we don't live in the nineteenth century any more.

Träne • keine Träne wegen etwas vergießen
shed no tears over sth
I shall shed no tears about that factory closing – it never made a profit.

Träne • keine Träne wert sein
sbd / sth isn't worth crying over (coll)
That factory we're closing isn't worth crying over – it never made a profit.

Tränendrüse • auf die Tränendrüse drücken
to be a real tear-jerker (coll), four-kleenex (coll)
The film "Love Story" is a real tear-jerker.

Traum • Das hätte ich mir in meinen kühnsten Träumen nicht einfallen lassen.
I wouldn't have thought it possible in my wildest dreams.

traurig • traurig aber wahr
it's sad but true

Traute • keine Traute haben
to have no guts (coll)
The main reason why you can't rely upon Fantasian soldiers is that they have no guts.

Treppe • die Treppe hinauffallen
to be kicked upstairs (coll)
He was kicked upstairs into a position of no influence but with a fine-sounding title.

treu • treu und brav
as good as gold; als Adverb: like a good girl (boy), dutifully
I thought we might be going to have some trouble with the youngsters, but they were all as good as gold and went to bed when we told them to.

Treue • in alter Treue
for old time's sake
I had a wander round my old school for old time's sake.

Treue • auf Treu und Glauben
in good faith
A purchaser who buys in good faith for value and without notice of any defect in the seller's title obtains a good title himself. (juristisch)

Trick • den Trick raus haben
to have got the knack of doing sth (coll)
I had to practise billiards for years before I got the knack.

Tritt • jmd einen Tritt geben / entlassen
to kick sbd out (coll)
Although he had been a loyal servant of the company for many years they kicked him out at the age of fifty.

Tropfen • ein Tropfen auf einen heißen Stein
a drop in the ocean
People tell us that all the aid that is sent from Europe and America to Africa is little more than a drop in the ocean.

Trotzkopf • einen (seinen) Trotzkopf haben
to be contrary, to be in a mood (coll)
I asked my daughter to play the piano for us, but she was determined to be contrary and said she wouldn't.

trübe • im Trüben fischen
to fish in troubled waters
After the economic collapse many politicians were able to fish for supporters in troubled waters.

Trübsal • Trübsal blasen
to be downcast, to be down in the mouth (coll), to be down in the dumps (coll)
I was very down in the dumps all the time my girlfriend was away on holiday – I didn't go out once.

Trumpf • noch einen Trumpf in der Hand haben
to have an ace / a trick up one's sleeve (coll)
We do still have an ace up our sleeve. The enemy don't know about it, and it may cost them the game.

Trumpf • alle Trümpfe in der Hand halten
to hold all the trumps (coll)
We hold all the trumps – they haven't got a chance.

Tube • auf die Tube drücken
<u>Auto:</u> to step on it (coll)
I asked the driver to step on it because I was in a hurry.

Tuch • wie ein rotes Tuch wirken
sth makes sbd see red (coll), to be like a red rag to a bull (coll)
He is so hopelessly narrow-minded that to suggest to him that other points of view even exist is like a red rag to a bull. He loses his temper at once.

tun • Da kriegst du es mit mir zu tun!
Then you will be up against me./Then you will have me to deal with.

Tüpfelchen • das Tüpfelchen auf dem i
the icing on the cake (coll)
The new colour scheme for the Scottish branches is really just the icing on the cake.

Tür • offene Türen einrennen
to push at an open door
If you are trying to persuade me to invest some more money in that scheme, you are pushing at an open door. I've already decided to support it.

Tür • mit der Tür ins Haus fallen
to blurt out
He suddenly blurted out his opinion that the whole project was a waste of time. He may have been right, but he should never have said so.

Tür • jmd zwischen Tür und Angel sprechen
to mention sth in passing, to exchange a fleeting word with sbd
I have exchanged some fleeting words with him about it, but we haven't discussed it properly.

Türke • einen Türken bauen / etwas türken
to fiddle the figures (coll)
He fiddled the figures in his tax return.

Tüte • Das kommt nicht in die Tüte!
No way!

Tuten • von Tuten und Blasen keine Ahnung haben
not to know the first thing about it (coll), not to have a clue (coll)
He doesn't know the first thing about it – you will have to explain the whole thing to him from the very beginning.

Typ • Dein Typ ist hier nicht gefragt.
You are not wanted round here.

U

Übel • ein notwendiges Übel sein
to be a necessary evil
Prisons are a necessary evil.

übel • jmd übel mitspielen
to play a mean / dirty (coll) trick on sbd, to do sbd a bad turn, to do the dirty on sbd (coll)
They did the dirty on us by telling our rivals what we were planning to do.

überhören • Das möchte ich überhört haben!
I didn't hear that! / I don't think I heard that! / I'll pretend I didn't hear that.

überleben • Ich werd's überleben.
It won't kill me.
finanziell: *It won't break the bank.*

überleben • Das überleb ich nicht!
It'll be the death of me!

Überlegung • nach reiflicher Überlegung
on second thoughts (coll)
At first I agreed, but on second thoughts I decided I was against the scheme.

übrig • etwas für jmd / eine Sache übrig haben
to have a liking for sbd / sth, to have a soft spot (in one's heart) for sbd / sth (coll)
I have had a soft spot for him all my life. I simply find him a very pleasant person.

Übung • Übung macht den Meister. (prov)
Practice makes perfect. (prov)

Uhl • Des einen Uhl ist des anderen Nachtigall. (prov)
One man's loss is another man's gain. (prov)

Uhr • rund um die Uhr
round the clock
Our offices are open round the clock.

Uhr • seine Uhr ist abgelaufen
The sands of time have run out for him. / His number's up (coll). / He's had it (coll). / His days are numbered.

Uhr • Nach ihr kann man die Uhr stellen.
to set one's watch by sbd
Kant's habits were so regular you could set your watch by him.

umbringen • sich fast umbringen (vor Freundlichkeit)
to fall over oneself being polite (coll), to lean over backwards (coll)
He was convulsed with courtesy, and almost fell over himself being polite.

umgarnen
to catch sbd in one's net / web
She caught him in her net almost as soon as the party started. They disappeared together and were nowhere to be found for hours.

Umnachtung • in geistiger Umnachtung
to be out of one's senses, to be out of one's brain (coll)
You must have been out of your senses when you bought that car!

umsatteln
to change (swop) horses
One shouldn't change horses in mid-stream. (prov)

Umschweife • etwas ohne Umscheife sagen ▷ Berg: nicht hinterm Berg halten

umspringen • So laß ich nicht mit mir umspringen!
You can't treat me like that. / I won't stand for that.

Umstandskrämer • ein Umstandskrämer sein
to be a fusspot (coll)
He is a dreadful fusspot – he worries about the widths of the margins in his business letters.

uneins • mit sich selbst uneins sein
to be unable to make up one's mind
I simply can't make up my mind where I want to go for my holiday – Cyprus or Greece.

ungebunden • frei und ungebunden sein
to be foot-loose and fancy free (coll)
He has got no family or girlfriend and is completely footloose and fancy free.

Ungeschick • Ungeschick läßt grüßen!
<u>andere Person:</u> *Butter-fingers!*
<u>selbst:</u> *I'm all fingers and thumbs (today)!*

ungeschoren • ungeschoren davonkommen
to save one's bacon (coll)
I had a very disagreeable interview with the boss, but I managed to save my bacon by making nice remarks about the photographs of his children.

ungesund • Allzuviel ist ungesund.
Enough is as good as a feast.

Unglück • Ein Unglück kommt selten allein. (prov)
When sorrows come, they come not single spies,/But in battalions. (Shakespeare: Hamlet)
It never rains but it pours./Accidents happen in three.

Unglück • Unglück im Spiel, Glück in der Liebe. (prov)
Unlucky at cards, lucky in love.

Unglückszahl • unlucky number
Thirteen is an unlucky number.

ungut • Nichts für ungut!
No offence meant!

Unkenntnis • Unkenntnis schützt vor Strafe nicht. (prov)
Ignorance is no excuse.

Unmensch • Ich bin ja kein Unmensch. ▷ Gnade: Gnade vor Recht ergehen lassen

Unrecht • Besser Unrecht leiden als Unrecht tun. (prov)
Turn the other cheek. (bibl)

unrein • etwas ins unreine sprechen
to say sth off the record
The politician spoke to the journalists off the record, and so could not be quoted.
etwas ins unreine schreiben: to write sth out in rough
He wrote the whole essay out in rough before copying it into his exercise book.

Unschuld • wie die Unschuld vom Lande
to look as if butter wouldn't melt in one's mouth (coll), to be as pure as driven snow
That woman looks as if butter wouldn't melt in her mouth in that little girl's dress!

unsereins
the likes of us
Holidays in Bermuda are too expensive for the likes of us.

unsterblich • unsterblich verliebt sein
to be head over heels in love
He is head over heels in love with some girl from his school.

unten • Der ist unten durch bei mir.
I'm through with him. / I haven't a good word to say for him. / He's in my bad books.

unten • ganz unten sein
to be done (coll), to be at one's wit's end
I'm suffering from flu, I've just lost my job, my wife has left me … I'm just about at my wit's end.

unten • nicht mehr wissen, was unten und oben (hinten und vorne) ist
I don't know whether I'm coming or going.
I don't know wether I'm on my head or on my heels.

unterbuttern • sich nicht unterbuttern lassen
not to let o.s. be talked into / out of sth (coll)
He went to that meeting knowing exactly what he wanted and quite determined that no-one should talk him out of it.

untertauchen
to go to ground
I think he has gone to ground. He owes us money, and I doubt if we shall be seeing him again.

unverhofft • Unverhofft kommt oft. (prov)
Things always seem to happen when you least expect them.

unverfroren ▷ Stirn: die Stirn haben
to have the face / front to do sth (coll)
I don't see how you can have the face to come and tell me a thing like that.

unversucht • nichts unversucht lassen
to leave no stone unturned
We shall leave no stone unturned in our attempts to get hold of some extra money.

Ursache • Keine Ursache!
Don't mention it.

Ursache • Kleine Ursachen, große Wirkung. (prov)
Big oaks from little acorns grow. (prov)

Usus • Das ist hier so Usus.
It's the custom here.
That's the way we do things round these parts.

V

Vandalen • sich aufführen wie die Vandalen
to behave like vandals, to behave like hooligans, to go on the rampage
The football supporters behaved like vandals and smashed-up the shopping centre.

Vater • Wie der Vater, so der Sohn. (prov)
Like father like son. (prov)

Veilchen • ein Veilchen haben
to have a black eye
You have got a splendid black eye. Have you been fighting?

verachten • Das ist nicht zu verachten!
That's not to be despised. / That's not to be scoffed at. / That's not to be sneezed at. / It's better than a kick in the teeth.

Verachtung • jmd mit Verachtung strafen
to treat sbd with contempt, to cock a snook at sbd
They treated the younger members with contempt.

verarschen
to take the piss out of sbd (vulg), to take the mickey (coll), to have sbd on (coll)
I can't believe that! Are you taking the piss (out of me)?

Verbindung • seine Verbindungen spielen lassen
to use one's connections, to pull a few strings (coll)
My boss pulled a few strings to get her brother a decent job in the Air Ministry. She's corruption incarnate!

verbitten • Das verbitt ich mir!
I won't have that! / I'm not standing for that! / I won't stand for that!

verblassen • Das läßt alles andere daneben verblassen.
Everything else pales into insignificance beside it.

verborgen • Im Verborgenen blühen
<u>Talent:</u> to be unsung, flourish in obscurity
He is an unsung genius. Without his ideas, the whole enterprise would collapse, but he never gets any credit for anything.

verboten • verboten aussehen
to look a real sight (coll)
He came to school looking a real sight – he had borrowed his sister's hat and was wearing it with a pair of goggles.

verbrieft • jmd etwas verbrieft und versiegelt geben ▷ Gift

Verdacht • etwas auf Verdacht hin tun
to do sth on spec (coll), to do sth on the off-chance
I went to the meeting on spec because I thought I would see my brother there.

verdammt • Es geht ihm verdammt gut.
He is on top of the world. / She's on cloud nine.

verdammt • verdammt hübsch
damned pretty (coll)
She is a damned pretty girl.

verdammt • Verdammt noch mal!
Damn you!

verderben • es mit jmd verderben
to fall out with sbd about/over sth
I fell out with him about/over his behaviour at the office and now we are no longer friends.

verdonnern • jmd dazu verdonnern, etwas zu tun
to order sbd to do sth as a punishment
He was ordered to sweep out the barracks as a punishment.

verduften ▷ dünn: sich dünnmachen

verfallen • jmd verfallen sein
to be under sbd's spell, to be nuts about sbd
I have been under her spell ever since I met her, and I still think her one of the most charming people I have ever met.

Vergasung • bis zur Vergasung
ad nauseam
He told us funny stories ad nauseam and we were still there at two o'clock in the morning.

Vergleich • der Vergleich hinkt
It is a bad comparison.

vergraben • sich in der Arbeit vergraben
to bury oneself in one's work
I buried myself in my work in an effort to forget an unfortunate love affair.

verhext • Das ist doch wie verhext!
It's maddening!

verknusen • Ich kann ihn nicht verknusen.
I can't stand him./I can't stick him.

verraten • verraten und verkauft
well and truly sunk (coll), well and truly done for (coll), sbd's goose is cooked, to be sold down the river
After the Liberals withdrew their support in the House of Commons the Government was sold down the river and could not survive.

Vers • sich keinen Vers auf etwas machen können
There's no rhyme or reason in it.

verschonen • Verschone mich damit!
Spare me that!

verschwinden • mal verschwinden müssen
to have to spend a penny (coll), to have to excuse oneself
One problem in Fantasian towns is that there is never anywhere to spend a penny.

Versenkung • in der Versenkung verschwinden ▷ Bildfläche

Verstand • etwas mit Verstand essen / trinken
to savour sth
I savoured the excellent Tournedos Rossini.

Versuch • es auf den Versuch ankommen lassen
It's worth trying. / It's worth a try.

Versuchsballon • einen Versuchsballon steigen lassen
to send up a trial balloon (coll), to test the water, to sound out sth
We sent up a trial balloon to find out what public opinion was.

Versuchskaninchen • ein Versuchskaninchen sein
to be the guinea-pig (coll)
The school used my class as the guineas-pigs for a new English course and none of them learned a thing.

verwechseln • zum Verwechseln ähnlich ▷ Ei: sich gleichen wie ein Ei dem anderen

Verzug • in Verzug geraten
to fall behind with sth
I have fallen badly behind with my homework, and cannot go out with you tonight.

Verzweiflung • jmd zur Verzweiflung treiben
to drive sbd to despair
The quarrels of my colleagues are enough to drive me to despair – it is quite impossible to get any work done.

vier • auf allen vieren
on all fours
The children were crawling about on all fours in some noisy game involving horses and dogs.

vier • alle viere von sich strecken
to crash out (coll)
We came home from the party so tired that we crashed out at once.

Vogel • den Vogel mit etwas abschießen ▷ Schatten: in den Schatten stellen

Vogel • einen Vogel haben ▷ Dachschaden

Vogel • Friß Vogel, oder stirb!
Take it or leave it!

Vogel • ein komischer Vogel sein
to be a queer customer (coll)/bird (coll)/fish (coll)
He is a queer customer. He asked me whether I had seen his collection of plastic models of the Eiffel Tower and then disappeared again without saying another word.

Vogel • jmd einen Vogel zeigen
to tap one's forehead
After listening to what the girl had to say the boy turned to his friends and tapped his forehead meaningfully.

Volk • ein lustiges Volk sein
to be a lively lot / bunch (coll)
The people in that youth club are a lively lot – planting trees all day, and dancing in the discotheque all night.

voll • aus dem vollen schöpfen
to make hay while the sun shines
After the government agreed to support the project the managers found themselves able to make hay while the sun shone.

vorbeugen • Vorbeugen ist besser als Heilen. (prov)
Prevention is better than cure. (prov)

Vorbild • ein leuchtendes Vorbild sein
to be a shining example
He is a shining example to the other boys in the class – he always hands his work in on time.

Vordermann • auf Vordermann bringen
jmd: to get sbd to shape up (coll), to get sbd/sth into shape
The lieutenant told the sergeant he would have to get his men to shape up if they were to be ready to go into battle by May 1st.
etwas: to get sth ship-shape and Bristol-fashion (coll)
I gave the schoolgirls twenty minutes to clear up the mess they had made and get the place shipshape and Bristol-fashion again.
Kenntnisse: to brush sth up (coll)
I wanted to brush up my Italian before I went to visit my friend in Rome.

vorkauen • jmd etwas vorkauen müssen
to have to spell sth for sbd out in words of one syllable (coll)
That class is so unintelligent you have to spell everything out for them in words of one syllable.

vormachen • sich etwas vormachen
to fool oneself (coll)
You are fooling yourself if you think you have a chance of passing the exam.

vormachen • sich nichts vormachen lassen
to be nobody's fool (coll)
He's nobody's fool and sees quite clearly what the situation is.

Vorrat • solange der Vorrat reicht ...
while stocks last ...

Vorrede • ohne lange Vorrede ...
getting down to brass tacks at once ...
I won't waste words ...

Vorsicht • Vorsicht ist die Mutter der Porzellankiste. (prov)
Better safe than sorry. (prov)

Vorspiegelung • die Vorspiegelung falscher Tatsachen
under false pretences
He got the job under false pretences, saying he was a qualified architect.

vorspielen • jmd etwas vorspielen
to pretend to sbd that ..., to put on an act, to put on a show of sth
He pretends to us that he is very confident, but in fact I think he knows that he will probably lose.

Vortritt • jmd den Vortritt lassen
to let sbd go first, to let sbd go ahead
He courteously let the lady go first.

Vorzeichen • unter schlechtem Vorzeichen stehen
to be ill-omened, to be destined to fail
I thought his scheme sounded pretty ill-omened – I didn't see how it could work under the present circumstances.

W

Waage • sich die Waage halten
to balance each other out, to complement each other
His sister is very daring and he is very prudent, so they balance each other out.

Waagschale • (seinen Einfluß) in die Waagschale werfen
to bring one's influence to bear
The chairman of the committee brought his influence to bear so that the candidate from his hometown was selected.

wacker • sich wacker schlagen
to put up a brave fight (coll)
The Finnish army put up a brave fight against the Russian invaders, but had no chance in the long run.

Waffe • die Waffen einer Frau
feminine wiles
She used plenty of feminine wiles to get to her present position.

Waffe • jmd mit seinen eigenen Waffen schlagen
to beat sbd at their own game (coll)
The new MP's first speech to parliament was so successful that a well-established parliamentary orator admitted at once that he had been beaten at his own game.

Wagen • sich (nicht) vor jmds Wagen spannen lassen
(not) to allow oneself to be used by sbd
I made it quite clear that I was not prepared to allow myself to be used by him for his dishonest business schemes.

wagen • Wer wagt, gewinnt. (prov)
Nothing ventured nothing gained. (prov) / We'd better take the bull by the horns. / Faint heart ne'er won fair lady.

wägen • Erst wägen, dann wagen. (prov)
Look before you leap. (prov)

Wahl • Wer die Wahl hat, hat die Qual. (prov)
to be spoilt for choice (coll)
One is spoilt for choice in most Indian restaurants, because there are so many dishes on the menu.

Wahn • in dem Wahn leben, daß …
to labour under the delusion that …
He labours under the delusion that he can paint, but I am afraid he has no talent at all.

Wahnsinn • des Wahnsinns fette Beute sein ▷ Dachschaden

Wahnsinn • Dieser Wahnsinn hat Methode!
There is method in his/her madness. (Shakespeare: Hamlet "If this be madness, there's method in't")

wahr • das ist nicht das Wahre
That is no great shakes./That is nothing to write home about.

wahr • so wahr ich hier stehe
as sure as eggs is eggs (coll), as sure as I am standing here
If I lend you the book you'll forget to bring it back, as sure as eggs is eggs.

währen • Was lange währt, wird gut. (prov)
Slow and steady wins the race. (prov)

Wahrheit • die nackte Wahrheit
the plain, unvarnished truth (coll)
The doctor did not try to pretend that the patient's condition was other than very serious, and told him the plain, unvarnished truth.

Wahrheit • Sie nimmt es mit der Wahrheit nicht so genau.
You have to take what she says with a pinch of salt.

Waisenknabe • Gegen ihn bin ich ein Waisenknabe.
I am no match for him.

Wald • Ich glaub, ich steh im Wald!
I must be hearing/seeing things.

Wald • Wie man in den Wald hineinruft, so schallt es zurück. (prov)
You get out what you put in. (prov)

Wald • den Wald vor lauter Bäumen nicht sehen
not to be able to see the wood for the trees (coll)
The fundamental issue is quite straightforward, but most of my colleagues are so obsessed with detail that they can't see the wood for the trees.

Wand • weiß wie eine Wand ▷ kreidebleich

Wand • in seinen eigenen vier Wänden
within one's own four walls (coll)
After many months of looking for a flat the student finally found one and could live again within his own four walls.

Wand • an die Wand gedrückt werden
to go to the wall (coll)
In the ruthless competition weaker businesses went to the wall.

Wand • die Wand hochgehen (vor Wut)
to hit the roof, to blow one's top, to go up the wall (coll)
He went right up the wall when he heard about how stupidly we had behaved.

Wand • jmd an die Wand spielen
to outdo sbd (coll), to outshine sbd, to outclass sbd (coll)
That schoolboy outdid everybody else in the class at Latin and Greek.

Wand • jmd an die Wand stellen
to put sbd before the firing squad, to put sbd up against a wall (coll)
Deserting soldiers were put before the firing squad.

Wappen • etwas im Wappen führen
to have sth as one's trademark (coll)
This journalist always begins his articles with the words "News has reached me here…". He has that as his trademark.

Ware • Gute Ware lobt sich selbst.
Quality needs no advocate.

warm • sich jmd warm halten
to keep in with sbd (coll)
I am very keen on keeping in with the boss, now that the possibility of promotion has come up.

warm • mit jmd (nicht) warm werden können
to be not sbd's type, we don't really hit it off
He has worked in the same room as me for years, but we don't really hit it off.

warm • mit etwas (nicht) warm werden können
(not) to be able to get used to sth (coll)
I can't get used to modern computer technology.

warten • Da kannst du warten, bis du schwarz wirst! ▷ schwarz

warum • das Warum und Weshalb
the whys and wherefores (coll)
I don't want to explain the whys and wherefores of the new policy now – I just want to make clear how it works.

waschen • etwas hat sich gewaschen
<u>eine Geldstrafe:</u> a really heavy fine
The judge imposed a really heavy fine for the speeding charge as it was the defendant's sixth offence in two years.
<u>eine Prüfung:</u> a real stinker (of an exam) (coll)
The Greek literature exam was a real stinker.
<u>eine Ohrfeige:</u> a really hard box on the ears
The master gave the boy a really hard box on the ears and told him to behave himself.

Wäsche • dumm aus der Wäsche gucken
to look a fool (coll), to look a lemon (coll), to look a right charlie (coll)
He looked a complete fool when it became clear how completely he had misunderstood the question.

Wäsche • seine schmutzige Wäsche in der Öffentlichkeit waschen
to wash one's dirty linen in public (coll)
The trouble with being a filmstar is that all your dirty linen is washed in public.

waschecht • ein waschechter (Preuß) sein
to be a dyed-in-the-wool Prussian (coll / die feste Überzeugung betonend), to be Prussian to the bone (coll), to be every inch a Prussian
He is not a Silesian or a Huguenot, he is a dyed-in-the-wool Prussian. His family came from near Königsberg.

Waschlappen • ein Waschlappen sein
to be a wimp (coll), to be a wet blanket (coll)
He is such a wimp he could not stand up for himself in argument at all.

Waschweib • tratschen wie ein altes Waschweib
to gossip like an old woman (coll)
I heard him in the pub gossipping like an old woman about Susan's new baby.

Wasser • Die kochen auch nur mit Wasser.
They are no different from anybody else.

Wasser • Das ist Wasser auf seine/unsere Mühle.
This is all grist to his/our mill.

Wasser • Bis dahin fließt noch viel Wasser die Spree (ersetzbar durch beliebigen Flußnamen) hinunter.
A lot of water will have flowed under the bridge by then.

Wasser • nahe ans Wasser gebaut haben
to be inclined to tears
She is no more depressed than usual. She has always been inclined to tears.

Wasser • mit allen Wassern gewaschen sein
to know all the tricks (coll)
That lawyer is extremely experienced and he knows all the tricks.

Wasser • sich über Wasser halten
<u>normalerweise Essen:</u> to keep the wolf from the door (coll)
<u>nur finanziell:</u> to keep one's head above water, to make ends meet
I've brought two packets of sandwiches and that should keep the wolf from the door until we get there.

Wasser • jmd läuft das Wasser im Munde zusammen
sbd's mouth is watering
His mouth was already watering at the thought of supper.

Wasser • jmd nicht das Wasser reichen können
to be unable to hold a candle to sbd (coll)
As an actress she can't hold a candle to her mother.

Wasser • Stille Wasser sind tief. (prov)
Still waters run deep.

Wasser• Das Wasser steht ihnen bis zum Hals. ▷ Klemme: in der Klemme sitzen

Wasser • bei Wasser und Brot ▷ Gardinen

Wässerchen • aussehen, als ob man kein Wässerchen trüben könne
▷ drei

Wasserfall • reden wie ein Wasserfall
to talk nineteen to the dozen (coll), to talk one's head off (coll)
When the two sisters met again after the summer holidays they sat in the kitchen for two hours talking nineteen to the dozen.

wäßrig • jmd den Mund wäßrig machen
to make sbd's mouth water
The thought of supper made his mouth water.

Watte • jmd in Watte packen
to be over-protective about sbd
She is absurdly over-protective about her children and won't let them play football for fear they get hurt.

Wecker • jmd auf den Wecker gehen (fallen)
to get on sbd's nerves (coll), to get on sbd's wick (coll), to drive sbd up the wall (coll)
My new secretary chews gum all the time, which really gets on my nerves.

Weg • den Weg alles Irdischen gehen
to go the way of all flesh (coll)

Our rowing club has been losing members for years, and now it has gone the way of all flesh.

Weg • neue Wege beschreiten
to break new ground
We are breaking new ground with our new microwave teapots: no-one has tried to make them before.

Weg • etwas zu Wege bringen
to get sth done (coll)
He makes various clever suggestions to others, but he never manages to get anything done himself.

Weg • den Weg des geringsten Widerstandes gehen
to follow the line of least resistance
Following the line of least resistance, we agreed with all the other side's proposals.

Weg • jmd auf halbem Wege entgegenkommen
<u>finanziell:</u> to split the difference (coll)
We could not remember if he owed five pounds or ten, so in the end we split the difference and I took seven pounds fifty.

Weg • Viele Wege führen nach Rom. (prov) ▷ Rom

Weg • jmd etwas (einen guten Rat) mit auf den Weg geben
to give sbd good advice
In Hamlet, when Laertes leaves home to go to University Polonius gives him lots of good advice.

Weg • jmd / einer Sache aus dem Weg gehen
to keep out of sbd's way (coll), to get out of the way of sth (coll), to give sbd / sth a wide berth
Once I realised how ruthlessly ambitious she was I decided that the only safe thing to do was to keep out of her way.

Weg • seinen Weg gehen / machen
to make a grade, to make one's way successfully through life, to be a success in life (coll)
He made his way successfully through life, gathering both money and friends.

Weg • seiner eigenen Wege gehen
to go one's own way, to do one's own thing
They are not yet officially divorced, but each of them has been going his own way for some time now.

Weg • Der gerade Weg ist der kürzeste.
Honesty is the best policy.

Weg • jmd aus dem Weg räumen / schaffen
to get rid of sbd (coll)
The gangsters decided to get rid of the new District Attorney, and engaged a professional gunman to shoot him.

Weg • sich selbst im Wege stehen
to be one's own worst enemy (coll)
He is perfectly intelligent, but he is his own worst enemy. He simply cannot discipline himself to give up some of his pleasures and get down to work.

Weg • jmd nicht über den Weg trauen
not to trust sbd an inch (coll), not to trust sbd as far as one can throw them (coll), not to trust sbd cross the street (coll), not to trust sbd out of one's sight (coll)
The head of my school seems pleasant enough, but I don't trust her an inch. She has tricked me too often.

Weg • Der Weg zur Hölle ist mit guten Vorsätzen gepflastert. (prov)
The road to hell is paved with good intentions. (prov)

weg • was weg haben
to be pretty good at sth (coll), to have got the hang of sth (coll)
Your son is pretty good at playing the violin, isn't he?

weh • Wo tut's denn weh?
What's your problem? / What's up (with you)? / What's the matter (with you)?

Wehe • Wehe, wenn sie losgelassen! ▷ Katze: Wenn die Katze aus dem Haus ist …

Weiberheld
ladykiller, womanizer, to be a he-man

Weiberherrschaft
government by petticoat, petticoat government
The President was so influenced by his mistress that the country endured a period of government by petticoat.

Weiberwirtschaft
a place / group in which women wear the trousers (coll)
The women wear the trousers in this family.

weich • nicht weich werden (sich nicht erweichen lassen)
not to soften, not to yield
I was determined not to soften and I continued to demand that the whole debt be paid over immediately.

Weide • noch auf die Weide müssen
sbd needs more experience
That young man needs more experience before we can promote him.

weiden • sich an etwas weiden
to gloat over
The psychopathic killer gloated over his victims once he had them at his mercy.

Weihnachten • Das ist ja wie Weihnachten!
It's like Christmas! / Is it sbd's birthday?

Weihnachtsgans • jmd ausnehmen wie eine Weihnachtsgans
to fleece sbd (coll), to take sbd to the cleaners (coll)
The greedy young girl fleeced her wealthy boyfriend for as much as she could get out of him and then left him.

Wein • jmd reinen Wein einschenken
to tell sbd the truth, to come clean with sbd (coll), to talk turkey (U.S.)
After prevaricating for few minutes he told the boss the truth – that he had lost the vital papers.

Wein • Im Wein ist Wahrheit. (prov)
In vino veritas. (prov)

Wein • heimlich Wein trinken und öffentlich Wasser predigen
not to practice what one preaches
He liked his subordinates to have tidy desks, but he did not practise what he preached and never bothered to tidy his own.

Wein • Wein, Weib und Gesang
Wine, women and song

weinen • Es ist zum Weinen.
It's enough to make you weep.

Weisheit • Behalte deine Weisheiten für dich.
Keep your pearls of wisdom to yourself.

Weisheit • der Weisheit letzter Schluß
That is the essence of all wisdom.

Weisheit • Sie tut, als ob sie die Weisheit mit Löffeln gefressen hat.
She thinks she knows it all. / She thinks she knows all the answers.

Weißbluten • bis zum Weißbluten
to be bled white
After paying the blackmailer a thousand pounds a month for two years he was bled white and could not pay any more.

Weißbluten • jmd bis zum Weißbluten schinden
to bleed sbd white
The blackmailer bled his victim white, demanding a thousand pounds a month to keep silent.

Weißglut • jmd zur Weißglut bringen
sth makes sbd see red, sth makes sbd's blood boil, sth drives / sends sbd up the wall
His constant moaning drives me up the wall.

weißwaschen • sich weißwaschen ▷ sich reinwaschen

weit • Weit gefehlt!
Far from it!

weit • Das geht zu weit
That's going too far!

weit • jmd ist nicht weit her ▷ Leuchte

weit • das Weite suchen ▷ Beine: die Beine in die Hand nehmen

weiter • und so weiter und so fort
and so on and so forth
My accountant came round and bored me with details of pension plans and endowment mortgages and so on and so forth.

Weizen • den Weizen von der Spreu trennen
to separate the wheat from the chaff (bibl)
The publishers cut two thirds of the poems from his first book of verse, separating the wheat from the chaff.

Wellen • hohe Wellen schlagen
to create a stir (coll)
He created quite a stir among the political journalists with his announcement that he intended to challenge the Prime Minister for the party leadership.

Welt • Wer / warum in aller Welt …?
Who / why on earth …? / Who / why in the world …?

Welt • Was kostet die Welt! ▷ Fuß: auf großem Fuß leben

Welt • Eine Welt brach für mich zusammen.
My whole world collapsed about my ears.

Welt • nicht die Welt kosten
not to cost the earth (coll)
You ought to buy your son a bicycle. They don't cost the earth.

Welt • in einer anderen Welt leben
to live in a different world (coll), to live on another planet (coll)
He is quite uninterested in money or friends or influence. He seems to live in a different world.

Welt • Vornehm geht die Welt zugrunde.
keeping up appearances to the bitter end...

ein Wendehals sein
to be a turncoat (coll)
The turncoats welcomed home the very king they had exiled.

wenig • Viele Wenig machen ein Viel. (prov) ▷ Kleinvieh

(na) wennschon
What of it?/So what?

wennschon • wennschon, dennschon
in for a penny, in for a pound

Werk • ein gutes Werk tun
to do sbd a good turn (coll), to do one's good deed for the day (coll)
He helped me with the washing up and that was his good deed for the day.

Wespennest • ins Wespennest stechen (greifen)
to stir up a hornets' nest
When he tried to compose the differences between his wife and his daughters he found he had stirred up a hornet's nest.

Wespentaille
wasp waist (coll) (<u>oft als Adjektiv:</u> wasp-waisted (coll))
She was a wasp-waisted girl with a liking for tight jeans which revealed the curves of her hips.

Weste • eine weiße Weste haben
to have a clean slate (coll)
He has never been in trouble with the police and has a clean slate.

Westentasche • etwas wie seine Westentasche kennen
to know sth like the back of one's hand (coll)
I know Paris like the back of my hand, having lived there for several years when I was younger.

Wichtigtuer • ein Wichtigtuer sein
to be a pompous ass (coll), to be a stuffed shirt (coll), to be big for one's boots
The Foreign Minister had a way of peeling grapes with a knife and fork which made many people dismiss him as a pompous ass.

Wickel • jmd beim Wickel haben / nehmen
to have / take sbd by the scruff of the neck (coll)
I took him by the scruff of his neck and threw him out of the room.

wickeln • schief gewickelt sein
to be very much mistaken (coll)
If you think I am going to recommend you for that job you are very much mistaken.

Wiege • von der Wiege bis zur Bahre
from the cradle to the grave
His disability handicapped him from the cradle to the grave.

wiegen • gewogen und zu leicht befunden
to have been weighed in the balance and found wanting (bibl)
After many months of hard competition between the two firms, the products of Blue Co. began to conquer the market. The rival firm's product had been weighed in the balance and found wanting.

Wiegenfest
birthday party

wiehern • Das ist ja zum Wiehern!
That's dead funny!

Wiese • auf der grünen Wiese
in the open countryside, greenfield development
Many D.I.Y. stores are greenfield developments.

Wiesel • (flink) wie ein Wiesel
quick as a flash (coll)
Quick as a flash he ran to the wicket, raised his hand and caught the ball.

Wille • Wo ein Wille ist, ist auch ein Weg. (prov)
Where thers's a will there's a way. (prov)

Wille • Der Wille kann Berge versetzen. (prov) ▷ Glaube

Wille • den guten Willen für die Tat nehmen
to take the thought for the deed
He had said he would come round, but in the event he found he had no time and could only ring me up. But I took the thought for the deed.

Wille • beim besten Willen nicht
with the best will in the world (coll)
The doctor told him that with the best will in the world he could not give him an appointment before next week.

Wimper • ohne mit der Wimper zu zucken
without turning a hair (coll), without batting an eyelid (coll)
The boss was so ruthless he could sack sixty employees without turning a hair.

Wind • ein frischer Wind
the wind of change
The wind of change is blowing through the Middle East.

Wind • Mach nicht soviel Wind!
Don't make such a fuss!

Wind • Daher weht der Wind!
So that's the way the wind is blowing!

Wind • jmd den Wind aus den Segeln nehmen
to take the wind out of sbd's sails (coll)
They took the wind out of our sails by anticipating all our best arguments.

Wind • von etwas Wind bekommen
to get wind of sth (coll)
I had got wind of the reorganization a few days before it happened, so I was not as surprised as everybody else.

Wind • Wer Wind sät, wird Sturm ernten. (prov)
He who sows the wind will reap the whirlwind. (prov)

Wind • in den Wind schlagen
guten Rat: to turn a deaf ear to sth
He turned a deaf ear to all my advice and continued industriously to make the same mistakes as before.
Vorsicht, Vernunft: to throw / cast sth to the winds (coll)
He threw caution to the winds and decided to invest all his money in a risky speculation.

Wind • sich den Wind um die Nase wehen lassen
to see a bit of the world (coll)
He had had an interesting life, and met many people and seen a bit of the world. But he always said nowhere could compare with the town where he had been born.

Wind • bei Wind und Wetter
in all weathers
Farmers and fishermen have to work in all weathers.

Wind • wissen / merken, woher der Wind weht ▷ Glocke: wissen, was die Glocke geschlagen hat

windelweich • jmd windelweich schlagen
to beat the living daylights out of sbd (coll)
The thugs beat the living daylights out of the two policemen.

Windhund • ein Windhund sein
to be a rake (dated)
After his wife left him he speedily turned into a rake. But drinking too much and spending a lot of time and money with loose women ruined his health and he died at the age of forty.

Windmühle • gegen Windmühlen ankämpfen ▷ einem Phantom nachjagen

Wink • jmd einen Wink geben
to give sbd a hint (coll), to give sbd a tip
I gave him a hint that he had no chance with the girl he was after.

Wink • ein Wink mit dem Zaunpfahl
to drop a broad hint (coll)

I dropped a broad hint that I wanted them to go, but they didn't leave until I said I was going to go to bed.

Wirbel • großen Wirbel machen
to make a great to-do (coll), to make a great commotion, to make a stir (coll), to put the cat amongst the pigeons, to make a ruckus (U.S.) (coll)
He made a great to-do about his stomach ache, but it turned out to be nothing serious.

Witwe • eine grüne Witwe sein
to be a grass widow (coll)
Her husband spends so much of his time abroad that she is practically a grass widow.

Woge • wenn sich die Wogen geglättet haben
when sth / sbd has calmed down (coll), when it's all blown over
I can't speak to him now – you can see how furious he is right now – but I'll ask him when he has calmed down.

Wohl • das Wohl und Wehe
the weal and woe (dated), the ups and downs
He told me all about the weal and woe of a dentist's life.

Wolf • Ich fühle mich wie durch den Wolf gedreht.
I feel as if I've been on the rack. (coll)

Wolf • mit den Wölfen heulen
to go with the crowd (coll), to swim with the tide
Youngsters often don't think for themselves – they simply go with the crowd.

Wolf • ein Wolf im Schafspelz sein
to be a wolf in sheep's clothing (coll)
That young lawyer looks extremely friendly, but she is really a wolf in sheep's clothing and can be absolutely merciless.

Wolke • aus allen Wolken fallen ▷ baff sein

Wolkenkuckucksheim
cloud cuckoo land (coll)
I listened to his lunatic ideas on how to set the world to rights in three months – he clearly lives in cloud cuckoo land.

Wolle • sich mit jmd in die Wolle kriegen
to fall out with sbd (coll), to have a row with sbd (coll)
I had a row with him about the new computer system he said we needed. I thought it would be a waste of money.

Wort • Das ist ein Wort!
Wonderful!

Wort • Nichts als Worte!
Nothing but words / talk!
Sounds good, but there's nothing behind it.

Wort • Hast du da noch Worte!
It leaves you speechless. / What more can I say.

Wort • geflügelte Worte
familiar quotations, well-known sayings
This book is full of familiar quotations.

Wort • jmd das Wort abschneiden
to cut sbd short
He was clearly about to begin a long explanation, but the teacher cut him short.

Wort • jmd mit leeren Worten abspeisen ▷ abspeisen

Wort • jmd das Wort aus dem Mund nehmen
to take the very words out of sbd's mouth
I was about to tell him what I thought of the matter when he took the very words out of my mouth and said exactly what I had been going to say.

Wort • ein Wort gab das andere
one thing led to another (coll)
He asked his wife when supper would be, and one thing led to another and before long they were arguing furiously about who should do the housework.

Wort • Du sprichst ein wahres Wort gelassen aus.
How true!/Too true!

Wort • sein Wort halten
to keep one's word, to be true to one's word
He had promised to call round and although he was very busy he kept his word.

Wort • jmd das Wort im Munde umdrehen
to twist sbd's words (coll)
He was very skilled in debate and twisted his opponent's words, quoting them out of context and making them sound ridiculous.

Wort • Dein Wort in Gottes Ohr!
Let us hope so!

Wort • etwas in schöne Worte kleiden
to dress something up in fancy talk (coll), to use euphemisms
They dressed it up in a lot of fancy talk, but essentially the answer is no.

Wort • Schöne Worte machen den Kohl nicht fett.
Fine words/promises butter no parsnips.

Wort • jmd beim Wort nehmen
to take sbd up on an offer (coll)
He said he would drive me home in his car and I took him up on his offer.

Wort • Da ist das letzte Wort noch nicht gesprochen.
The final decision hasn't been taken yet.
I don't think we've heard the end of it yet.

Wörtchen • Da habe ich auch noch ein Wörtchen mitzureden.
I think I have some say in that.

Wörtchen • Wenn das Wörtchen wenn nicht wär … (, wär mein Vater Millionär.)
If ifs and ands were pots and pans, there'd be no need for tinkers.

Wunde • eine alte Wunde aufreißen
to open up/re-open old wounds/scars (coll)
He met his ex-wife the other day and just seeing her opened up a lot of old wounds.

Wunde • den Finger auf die (brennende) Wunde legen
to bring up a painful subject (coll)
After a few minutes' friendly chat he brought up the painful subject of the money I owed him.

Wunde • tiefe Wunden schlagen (bei jmd)
to hurt sbd deeply
My sister's unkind remarks about my daughter hurt me deeply.

Wunder • Das grenzt an ein Wunder.
It verges on the miraculous./It's like a miracle.

wundern • Ich wundere mich über gar nichts mehr.
Nothing surprises me anymore.

Wunsch • Da ist der Wunsch der Vater des Gedanken.
That is just wishful thinking.
Shakespeare, Henry IV: "Thy wish was father to that thought."

Wunsch • einen Wunsch frei haben
to have one wish
If I had one wish, I would work for a different company.

Würfel • Die Würfel sind gefallen.
The die is cast.

Wurm • Da ist der Wurm drin!
There's something wrong somewhere.
There's something funny/odd about this.

Wurst • Jetzt geht's um die Wurst.
The moment of truth…

Wurst • Das ist mir Wurscht!
It's all the same to me!

Wurzel • Wurzeln schlagen
to put down roots (coll)
He only intended to stay in Cambridge as long as he was at the University, but he married a local girl, put down roots, and stayed there the rest of his life.

Wüste • jmd in die Wüste schicken
to send sbd into the wilderness
After a scandal involving a girl the Deputy Chairman of the party had to resign and he spent three years in the wilderness before he was given another job.

Wut • vor Wut explodieren
to explode with rage (coll)
When he heard that his orders had not been obeyed the Commander exploded with rage.

Wut • eine Wut im Bauch haben
to be seething, to be hopping mad, to be livid
I disagreed with every word that was said and sat there seething at some of the unkind remarks that were made.

X

X • jmd ein X für ein U vormachen
to fool sbd (coll), to hoodwink sbd
He fooled me with his slick talk and his convincing manner.

X-Beine • X-Beine haben
to be knock-kneed, to have knock-knees
One unfortunate boy in that class has knock-knees.

X-mal
umpteen times (coll)
I have explained it to you umpteen times!

Z

Zack • auf Zack sein ▷ Draht: auf Draht sein

zack-zack!
chop-chop!

Zacken • Da wird dir kein Zacken aus der Krone fallen.
That won't hurt you! / That won't kill you!

Zahl • rote Zahlen schreiben
to be in the red (coll)
The company has been in the red all year, but now there is some hope of its making a profit again in the near future.

zählen • auf jmd zählen
to count (rely) on sbd
I rely on my secretary to remind me of my appointments.

Zahn • die dritten Zähne
false teeth, dentures
My father has had to wear false teeth since he was forty.

Zahn • sich an etwas die Zähne ausbeißen ▷ Granit

Zahn • bis an die Zähne bewaffnet
to be armed to the teeth (coll)
The American soldiers were armed to the teeth with sub-machine guns, bazookas and flame throwers.

Zahn • der Zahn der Zeit
the ravages (passage) of time
The passage of time had left its mark upon her once beautiful face.

Zahn • einen Zahn drauf haben
to be going like the clappers (coll)
The car came down the street going like the clappers, well over the speed limit.

Zahn • jmd auf den Zahn fühlen
to grill sbd (coll), to give sbd a grilling (coll)

The professor gave his students a good grilling in the oral examination to find out exactly how much they knew.

Zahn • ein steiler Zahn sein
to be quite a girl (coll), to be a sexbomb (coll)
Your sister's quite a girl. I really like the clothes she almost doesn't wear.

Zahn • die Zähne zeigen
to show one's teeth (coll)
The police started by being quite polite, but after a couple of hours they started showing their teeth and threatening us.

Zahn • jmd den Zahn ziehen
to scotch that (coll), to put paid to that (coll), to put the (tin) lid on that (coll), to knock that on the head (coll)
My daughter really wanted to go to Spain on holiday, but I had to scotch that.

Zahn • einen Zahn zulegen
to get a move on (coll)
We have to get a move on, otherwise we'll miss the bus.

Zahn • die Zähne zusammenbeißen
to bite on the bullet, to grit one's teeth and keep going, to keep a stiff upper lip (coll), to keep one's pecker up (coll)
He was very upset when his girlfriend left him, but he kept a stiff upper lip and did not show his feelings.

Zahnfleisch • auf dem Zahnfleisch gehen
to be all in (coll), to be on one's last legs (coll), to be knackered (coll)
After sixteen hours solid work I was all in.

Zange • jmd in die Zange nehmen
to give sbd a grilling (coll), to grill sbd
He gave his daughter a grilling as to where she had been all night.

Zank • Zank und Streit
trouble and strife
We shan't get the children to accept the idea without a lot of trouble and strife.

Zankapfel
to be the bone of contention, to be the source of discord
The main bone of contention in the family is my father's will.

zartbesaitet
to be highly strung
My daughter is very highly strung. She worked too hard before the exam and then had an attack of nerves during the exam itself and couldn't write anything.

zappeln • jmd zappeln lassen
to keep sbd in suspense, to keep sbd on tenterhooks (coll)
He deliberately kept his girlfriend in suspense, waiting for his phone call.

Zauber • ein fauler Zauber
a fishy business
I thought the whole of his refinancing scheme was a fishy business, and I refused to have anything to do with it.

Zauber • der ganze Zauber
the whole lot

zaubern • Ich kann doch nicht zaubern!
I can't work miracles. / I'm not your fairy grandmother.

Zaum • sich im Zaum halten
to keep oneself in check, to control oneself, to keep a grip/hold on oneself
He was clearly furious at the news, but he kept himself in check and did not lose his temper.

Zeche • die Zeche bezahlen müssen
<u>bezahlen:</u> to foot the bill (coll)
I had to foot the bill for the repairs to my son's car.
<u>Verantwortung übernehmen:</u> to take the rap (coll), to face the music (coll), to carry the can (coll), to be left holding the baby (coll)
He had to take the rap for making a mess of the new accounting system.

Zeche • eine Zechtour machen
to go on a pub-crawl (coll)
The two brothers went on a long pub crawl, starting at the "Angel" and going by way of the "Narrow Boat" and the "York" to the "Slug and Lettuce".

Zeichen • die Zeichen der Zeit erkennen
to recognize the mood of the times, to see the writing on the wall (coll)
The government can see the writing on the wall and they realise they have to reduce taxes or be voted out of office at the next election.

Zeichen • Es geschehen noch Zeichen und Wunder!
Wonders will never cease.

zeigen • Denen werden wir's zeigen!
We'll show them!

Zeilen • zwischen den Zeilen lesen
to read between the lines (coll)
My daughter doesn't say so, but reading between the lines of her last letter from Tokyo I would say she is very lonely.

Zeit • Alles zu seiner Zeit!
All in good time.

Zeit • zu nachtschlafender Zeit
in the middle of the night
I had to get up in the middle of the night to answer the door.

Zeit • die gute alte Zeit
the good old days (coll)
Back in the good old days there were always Sunday mail deliveries.

Zeit • Das waren noch Zeiten ...
Those were the days ...

Zeit • mit der Zeit gehen
to follow the trend, to keep up with the times, to keep abreast of the times
The company followed the general trend and invested in new microelectronic equipment.

Zeit • Kommt Zeit, kommt Rat. (prov)
Time will bring better counsel.
Where there's life, there's hope.
Don't rush your fences.

Zeit • Spare in der Zeit, so hast du in der Not. (prov) ▷ sparen

Zeit • jmd die Zeit stehlen
to waste sbd's time
He wasted a lot of my time with unnecessary questions.

zeitlich • das Zeitliche segnen ▷ Weg: den Weg alles Irdischen gehen

Zelt • seine Zelte abbrechen
to retire defeated (coll)
After the TV crew had waited for better weather for six weeks it had to retire defeated, with its job not done.

Zenit • im Zenit seines Lebens
to be at one's peak, at the peak of one's career, in the prime of life, at the height of his fame
So far as his skills as an orator were concerned, Churchill was at his peak in 1940.

Zepter • das Zepter schwingen
to call the tune (coll), to rule the roost (coll), to lay down the law (coll)
The boss's son calls the tune around here – no-one else has any influence at all.

zerfleischen ▷ Fetzen

Zerreißprobe • jmds Geduld auf die Zerreißprobe stellen
to try sbd's patience
Listening to the ludicrous plans of my colleagues tried my patience to the utmost.

Zeter • Zeter und Mordio schreien
to scream blue murder (coll), to raise a hue and cry (coll), to raise Cain (coll), to scream the place down (coll), to raise merry hell (coll)
As soon as they heard about the cuts that were to be made in their de-

partment all the sociologists screamed blue murder and protested to the Treasurer of the university.

Zeug • jmd etwas am Zeug flicken wollen
to find fault with sbd, to carp at sbd, to pick holes in sbd (coll), to nag at sbd (coll)
She was constantly finding fault with her neighbours from the day she moved house.

Zeug • das Zeug zu etwas haben
to have (got) what it takes to be sth (coll), to have the makings of sth (coll), to have it in one to be sth
He has got what it takes to be a very good doctor.

Zeug • ... was das Zeug hält
like mad (coll), for all one is worth (coll), like anything (coll), like blazes (coll), hell for leather (coll), like a bat (coll), out of hell (coll)
The tennis player chased after the ball like mad, but could not reach it before it bounced.

Zeug • sich ins Zeug legen
<u>bei Arbeit:</u> to work flat out (coll), to put one's shoulder to the wheel (coll), to keep one's nose to the grindstone (coll), to put one's back into it (coll), to pull one's finger out, to work with a will
I worked flat out all night and had the documents drafted by the morning.
<u>jmd/etwas unterstützen:</u> to stand up for sbd/sth, to put in a good word for sbd/sth
When everybody wanted to sack that secretary he was the only one who stood up for her.

Zeug • dummes Zeug reden
to talk a lot of nonsense, to talk drivel (coll), to talk through the back of one's head
The Minister of Finance talked a lot of nonsense at the press conference.

Ziege • eine alte Ziege sein
to be an old hag (coll)
My grandmother is an old hag, she is always nagging at me.

Zicken • Zicken machen ▷ Faxen

ziehen • einen ziehen (fahren) lassen
to let off (vulg), to fart (vulg)
A boy in the front row let off and everyone started gasping and choking.

Zierde • eine Zierde ihres / seines Geschlechts
to be a flower of the female sex, to be a fine specimen of the male sex, to be a young Adonis
That girl is a flower of her sex – sweet sixteen and never been kissed.

Ziel • übers Ziel hinausschießen
to go too far (coll), to stretch things a bit
With his request for yet a further personal assistant, when he already had two, the top management felt he was stretching things a bit.

Zimmermann • jmd zeigen, wo der Zimmermann das Loch gelassen hat ▷ achtkantig

Zins • jmd etwas mit Zins und Zinseszins zurückgeben (-zahlen)
to return sth with interest, to pay sbd back for sth with interest
The second boy returned the blow with interest and within a few seconds both were fighting furiously.

Zittern • mit Zittern und Zagen
in fear and trepidation (bibl)
I approached the headmaster's office in fear and trepidation.

Zittern • Da hilft weder Zittern noch Zagen.
It's no use being afraid.

Zopf • ein alter Zopf
an antiquated custom
There is an antiquated custom in the Royal Navy that one does not stand for the loyal toast.

Zubrot
to earn (make) a bit on the side (coll)
He has earned a bit on the side with his articles for newspapers.

Zuckerbrot • mit Zuckerbrot und Peitsche
with the carrot and stick treatment
The only way to teach some children is with the carrot and stick treatment, they say.

zuerst • Wer zuerst kommt, mahlt zuerst. (prov)
First come, first served. (prov)

Zug • Zug um Zug
step by step, stage by stage
We built the company up step by step and were always careful not to do too much too quickly.

Zug • Das ist kein schöner Zug von ihm!
That's not one of his nicer characteristics.

Zug • in vollen Zügen
to the full
In telling me about her sister she indulged her taste for catty remarks to the full.

Zug • in den letzten Zügen liegen
<u>bald sterben:</u> to be on one's last legs (coll), to be at the end of one's days, to be approaching the end of one's days, to be at death's door, to have one foot in the grave (coll)
My dog is very old and on his last legs. I ought to have him put down.
<u>mit etwas fast fertig sein:</u> to be on the last lap (coll), to be on the home stretch (coll)
We are on the last lap of this job and will have it finished by next week.

zugeknöpft ▷ angebunden

Zügen • etwas in großen Zügen darstellen
to outline sth in general (broad) terms
He outlined his plan in broad terms and left the details to be explained by his assistants.

Zügel • die Zügel fest in der Hand halten
to have things firmly in hand (coll), to keep things firmly under control

When he first came to this department he did not seem to know what was going on, but now he has things firmly in hand.

Zügel • die Zügel locker lassen
to slacken one's hold on the reins (coll)
At this school we think it is right to slacken our hold on the reins once the boys are in the Sixth Form.

Zuschnitt • für / auf jmd / etwas zugeschnitten sein
to be geared / adjusted / trimmed to sth / sbd, to be tailored to suit / to meet sth / sbd, to be tailor-made for sbd / sth (coll)
This job is geared to his abilities and he should have no problems with it.

zukommen • etwas auf sich zukommen lassen
to wait for things to happen , to sit back and wait (coll), to just let things happen (coll)
We have done all we can and started the process. Now all we can do is wait for things to happen.

Zukunftsmusik
a dream of the future, pie in the sky
Regular flights to the moon are still a dream of the future.

Zumutung • Das ist eine Zumutung!
That's a bit too much!
<u>ironisch:</u> *That takes the biscuit!*

Zunder • brennen wie Zunder
to burn like tinder / cindling
The dry leaves and twigs in the woods burn like tinder once they have caught fire.

Zunder • jmd Zunder geben ▷ abkanzeln

Zunge • sich die Zunge abbrechen
to tie one's tongue in knots (coll), to not be able to get one's tongue round sth
I found the pronuciation of Russian turned my tongue in knots.

Zunge • Es liegt mir auf der Zunge.
It's on the tip of my tongue.

Zunge • sich eher die Zunge abbeißen, als …
I'd do anything rather than …(coll), I'd rather shoot myself than …(coll)
I'd do anything rather than tell her what has happened to her children.

Zunge • seine Zunge im Zaum halten
to keep / hold one's tongue in check, to curb one's tongue, to watch one's tongue (coll), not let one's tongue run away with one (coll)
When invited to reply to the proposal, he kept his tongue in check and simply and reasonably pointed out the weak point in the suggestion; nevertheless, inside he was seething with rage.

Zünglein • das Zünglein an der Waage sein
to tip the scales, to hold the balance of power
After the last election the extremists almost held the balance of power.

Zungenschlag • ein falscher Zungenschlag
an unfortunate turn of phrase, a slip of the tongue
He used an unfortunate turn of phrase and upset her badly, though he did not mean to.

zupaß • jmd kommt etwas zupaß
sth suits sbd down to the ground (coll) / to a T (coll), sth serves sbd's purpose well
Two days' stay in Dresden suits us down to the ground, because I would like to visit my cousin there, and you can look at the picture galleries.

zusammenläppern • Es läppert sich zusammen.
It adds up. / It multiplies.

zusammennehmen • Nimm dich zusammen!
Pull yourself together!

zuschustern
<u>jmd etwas:</u> to subsidize sth / sbd, to sub sth / sbd (coll)

I subsidized my son's holiday in America to the tune of one thousand pounds. He paid five hundred himself.

Zustand • Zustände kriegen ▷ Decke: an die Decke gehen

zustehen • es steht dir nicht zu ...
it's not for you to ... (pass judgment, etc.), it's not up to you to ... (pass judgment, etc.)

Zuwachs • Zuwachs bekommen
to have an addition to the family
They have just had an addition to the family – a baby girl.

Zwang • Tu dir keinen Zwang an!
Don't feel you have to be polite! / Don't force yourself! / Don't put yourself out!

Zweck • Der Zweck heiligt die Mittel.
The end justifies the means.

Zweifel • über jeden Zweifel erhaben sein
to be as honest as the day is long
He won't overcharge you. He is as honest as the day is long.

Zweifelsfall • im Zweifelsfall für den Angeklagten
to give sbd the benefit of the doubt
I was very suspicious of him and thought he was guilty. But in English law, you give the accused the benefit of the doubt.

Zweig • auf keinen grünen Zweig kommen
not to reach the top (coll), not to get in the dough (coll), to be not getting anywhere (with)
He worked hard for twenty years for that company, but did not reach the top.
I'm not getting anywhere with that job of mine.

zweimal • sich etwas nicht zweimal sagen lassen
not to need to be told twice (coll)

When the pupils heard that a teacher was ill and they could go home early they did not need to be told twice.

Zwerchfellmassage
an absolute scream (coll), a hoot (coll)
The new play by Alan Ayckbourn is an absolute scream.

Zwickmühle • in einer Zwickmühle sein
it's catch 22 (coll), to be damned if one does and damned if one doesn't (coll), to be in a dilemma, to be caught between two stools
There is no right thing to do. Anything we do will be wrong. – It's catch 22.

Zwist • einen alten Zwist begraben
to bury the hatchet (coll)
After quarrelling for years they finally decided to bury the hatchet.

Zwietracht • Zwietracht säen
to sow discontent, to stir up trouble (coll)
My sister-in-law was always sowing discontent in our family and did not rest until she had broken up our friendly relationship with each other.

Keith Hollingsworth/
Edward Martin

Sounds Good!

Ein unterhaltsames Aussprachetraining

In acht Units haben Sie die Möglichkeit, mit unterhaltsamen Hör- und Sprechübungen Ihre englische Aussprache zu verbessern.

Enthalten sind Tips und Regeln, wie man Ausspracheprobleme in den Griff bekommt, außerdem nützliche Wörter und Wendungen für wichtige Alltagssituationen. Ein Grundwortschatz von 2000 Wörtern wird vorausgesetzt.

Das Package besteht aus Buch und Cassette **oder** Buch und CD.

Hueber
Sprachen der Welt
Max Hueber Verlag

Jody Daniel Skinner

In Writing

Ein umfassendes Schreibtraining für Englischlernende

Sie möchten – oder müssen – in englischer Sprache einen Text verfassen: einen Brief, eine Bewerbung, einen Aufsatz. Ob beruflich oder privat, erfolgreich schreiben ist auch und vor allem das Ergebnis von Lernen und Üben.

»In Writing« bietet Ihnen das Material, das Sie dazu benötigen. Das Besondere an dem vorliegenden Buch: es kombiniert Schreibanleitung und Übungsbuch, deckt ungewöhnlich viele Schreibanlässe ab und wurde speziell für Benutzer mit deutscher Muttersprache entwickelt.

Dazu lieferbar: Teacher's Notes.

Sprachen der Welt

Max Hueber Verlag